Issues and Approaches
in Personal Construct Theory

Issues and Approaches in Personal Construct Theory

Edited by
D. Bannister

MRC External Scientific Staff
High Royds Hospital
Menston, Ilkley
West Yorkshire, England

1985

ACADEMIC PRESS

(Harcourt Brace Jovanovich, Publishers)

London   Orlando   San Diego   New York
Toronto   Montreal   Sydney   Tokyo

ACADEMIC PRESS INC. (LONDON) LTD.
24–28 Oval Road
LONDON NW1 7DX

United States Edition published by
ACADEMIC PRESS, INC.
Orlando, Florida 32887

BRITISH LIBRARY CATALOGUING IN PUBLICATION DATA

Issues and approaches in personal construct theory.
    1. Personality
    I. Bannister, Don
    155.2   BF698

Library of Congress Cataloging in Publication Data
Main entry under title:

Issues and approaches in personal construct theory.

    Includes index.
    1. Personal construct theory. 2. Psychology, Applied.
I. Bannister, D. (Donald)
BF698.I77 1984   155.2   84-14479
ISBN 0-12-077980-3 (alk. paper)

Contents

Contributors

Numbers in parentheses indicate the pages on which the authors' contributions begin.

D. BANNISTER (1, 67), MRC External Scientific Staff, High Royds Hospital, Menston, Ilkley, West Yorkshire LS29 6AQ, England

C. T. PATRICK DIAMOND (15), Department of Education, University of Queensland, St. Lucia, Queensland 4067, Australia

GAVIN DUNNETT (37), Whiteley Wood Clinic, Sheffield, South Yorkshire, England

SHEILA HARRI-AUGSTEIN (47), Centre for the Study of Human Learning, Brunel University, Uxbridge, Middlesex UB8 3PH, England

JEAN E. HUDSON (127), Department of Psychology, University of Florida, Gainsville, Florida 32611

SHARON R. JACKSON (67), MRC Project Grant, High Royds Hospital, Menston, Ilkley, West Yorkshire LS29 6AQ, England

L. M. LEITNER (83), Department of Psychology, Miami University, Oxford, Ohio 45056

HELENE B. LINDER (183), Psychology Department, Binghamton Psychiatric Center, Binghamton, New York 13901

HELEN McCONACHIE (105), Hester Adrian Research Centre, University of Manchester, Manchester M13 9PL, England

GREG J. NEIMEYER (127), Department of Psychology, University of Florida, Gainesville, Florida 32611

ROBERT A. NEIMEYER (143), Department of Psychology, Memphis State University, Memphis, Tennessee 38152

PHILLIDA SALMON (173), Institute of Education, University of London, London WC1H OAL, England

CHARLES STEFAN (183), Psychology Department, Binghamton Psychiatric Center, Binghamton, New York 13901

PETER STRINGER (210), Department of Social Psychology, University of Nijmegen, Montessorilaan 3, 6500 HE Nijmegen, The Netherlands

Contributors

LAURIE F. THOMAS (233), Centre for the Study of Human Learning, Brunel University, Uxbridge, Middlesex UB8 3PH, England

W. G. WARREN (253), Department of Education, University of Newcastle, Shortland, New South Wales 2308, Australia

Preface

This book is a child of *New Perspectives in Personal Construct Theory* (1977), a grandchild of *Perspectives in Personal Construct Theory* (1970), and kissing cousin to *Constructs of Sociality and Individuality* (1979). It was compiled on the same basis as the earlier three volumes: a variety of people with a commitment to personal construct theory were invited to write on any theme that concerned them and thereby demonstrate the degree to which the theory has inspired or confused them.

Although many of the contributors to this volume did not appear in its predecessors, the book has the same kind of feel as its ancestors in that it is diverse in topic, yet seems to dwell on certain central aspects of Kelly's 1955 theoretical argument, particularly its concern with human freedom and understanding.

One feature of this volume represents a kind of progression. In the 25 years following the publication of Kelly's *The Psychology of Personal Constructs,* most writers in the field found themselves heavily committed to teaching the theory, repeatedly explaining and expounding it, because academic psychology in no way undertook the task. University psychology departments tend to teach either the traditional or those simple and fashionable minitheories that can be compacted into handy one-concept-size capsules. Personal construct theory proved unacceptable on both counts, being radical and complex. If students and professionals were to be acquainted with construct theory, it had to be done by that travelling missionary and wandering minstrel, the written page.

However, given the passing of a quarter of a century, construct theory has made its way into the marketplace of psychology, and the sheer accumulation of texts has freed writers in the field from the need for constant exposition. We can now move further into broad-ranging comment, critical analysis, elaboration, and the free use of our individual imaginations in relation to construct theory. This is what is beginning to show more clearly in the present volume.

The evolution in our thinking about personal construct theory will demonstrate, in the next quarter of a century, that there never was a need to preserve the theory by making it sacred; it has a toughness and liveliness that will enable it to grow by, as well as in spite of, rough handling.

References

Bannister, D. (ed.) (1970) "Perspectives in Personal Construct Theory", Academic Press, London.

Bannister, D. (ed.) (1977) "New Perspectives in Personal Construct Theory", Academic Press, London.

Stringer, P., and Bannister, D. (eds.) (1979) "Constructs of Sociality and Individuality", Academic Press, London.

Kelly, G. A. (1955) "The Psychology of Personal Constructs", Vols I and II, Norton, New York.

1

The Patient's Point of View

D. Bannister

It was as recently as the early nineteenth century that the mad fell into the hands of the medical. In the seventeenth and eighteenth centuries, although constructs of mad, melancholic, and maniac were part of the social vocabulary, for practical purposes, many forms of distress and deviancy were construed together. Thus, the vagrant, the epileptic, the aged, the destitute, the prostitute, the cripple, the begging, the venereally diseased, the homeless, the alcoholic, the orphan, the rowdy and the socially incomprehensible: all those construable under the French category of *les miserables,* were grouped together as constituting essentially the same social problem and were often housed together in a variety of bridewells, poor houses, work houses, prisons, religious retreats, private madhouses and penal colonies.

At a superordinate level such people were construed as having a constellation of characteristics which in turn suggested necessary courses of action. Primarily these notions included (1) that such people should be excluded from society, certainly until they could be returned to it with some different status, (2) that they should be made to work and so make a productive contribution to the society which they were seen as being parasitic upon, (3) that a degree of guilt (inherent or acquired) existed that needed punishment to be administered, and this was connected to the idea (4) that moral reform was desirable and should be undertaken.

In the nineteenth century, the medical profession largely took over responsibility for the subcategory of this population which was thought to be "mad"; medical responsibility for psychological distress was institutionalised in what we now know as psychiatric hospitals. The effect of reconstruing psychological distress in medical terms was to produce a view of its nature and categories of response to it which were analagous to the constructs of general medicine and the range of responses of the general hospital. Doctors attempted to repeat the evolution of diagnosis that was taking place in general medicine. By a kind of introspective factor analysis (noting what went with what), sets of "signs and symptoms" were argued to be clustered, were assumed to signify a disease entity and were accordingly named. Historically, the names changed from the era of melancholia, neurasthenia and masturbatory insanity to the era of schizophrenia, anxiety state, reactive depression and so forth but the intellectual procedure remained the same.

This "noting" of grouped characteristics in psychiatry involved (and still involves) a strange mixing of physiological and psychological constructs and a parody of the "medical science" style. For example Furneaux Jordan in 1886 "notes" a battered wife syndrome thus.

> Several years ago I noticed that a very large proportion of the women who came into hospital suffering from injuries inflicted by their husbands had, as a rule, something peculiar in their personal appearance. . . . I came slowly to see that the skin of the assaulted women was often clear, delicate, perhaps rosy. Their hair-growth was never heavy nor long, and the eyebrows were sparse and refined. Their upper spinal curves were so formed as to give a somewhat convex appearance to the back and shoulders and a more or less forward pose to the head. This bodily conformation, by the way, is a favourite one with artists, one of whom states that, in a well-formed woman, a plumb-line dropped from the tip of the nose should fall in front of the toes. The friends and neighbours usually let it be known that these unfortunate women whom they brought had sharp tongues in their heads and an unfailing—unfailing by repetition—supply of irritating topics on which to exercise them.

Current constructs of "mental illness" are less quaintly assembled but have the same status in that they hang in the air, devoid of the kind of valid theoretical and experimental framework which was available for general medicine. The perceived clusters of signs and symptoms in general medicine were eventually refined, corrected, elaborated and validated by the developing sciences of physiology, anatomy and biology, in such a way that the constructive cycle was reasonably complete in many cases. Thus the clinical appearance of "tuberculosis" and its observed processes could eventually be linked to and validated by the discovery of the tubercle bacillus. Science provided the means for tightening the loose constructions of medicine. However, there exists no equivalent science of psychiatry or psychology which can provide meaning or validation for loose constructions of the "schizophrenia", "depression" kind.

The dubious nature of "psychiatric illness" constructs becomes clearer if we replace, say, schizophrenia with any equally psychological construct which has no medical pretensions, say, "indecision". Thus statements of the type "schizophrenia clearly has an organic cause" or "schizophrenia is inherited" or "we may find a specific drug treatment which will cure schizophrenia" are comparable to and are no more viable than statements of the kind "indecision has an organic cause" or "indecision is inherited" or "we may find a specific drug treatment which will cure indecision".

Indeed, when psychiatric diagnostic labels are tested in terms of agreement as to definition and use, stability and structure (Agnew and Bannister, 1973; Bannister, 1968), they are found to be more poorly formulated than are ordinary lay psychological terms. Equally, there appears to be little useful relationship between psychiatric diagnosis and treatment (Bannister, Salmon and Lieberman, 1964), and it appears that it is implicit institutional superordinate constructs (e.g., long stay versus short stay, favoured patient versus unfavoured patient, multiple previous treatments versus single previous treatment) which relate most powerfully to choice of treatment.

Additional effects of the medical construing of psychological distress may include

1. a deflecting of attention from the person: the personal meaning of the questionable behaviour and experience is bleached out by regarding it as "symptomatic" of illness; for example, a "depression" is something to be cured rather than a personal experience to be understood and learned from,

2. the inducing of passivity and irresponsibility in the patient since he or she is neither to be blamed for having contracted the "illness" nor to be expected to play any important part in its cure, this being a matter for medical expertise, and

3. the encouragement of irresponsibility in the community around the patient, since the notion of "illness" locates the problem *inside* the patient and does not recognise that the problems lie between people (belatedly this is recognised in family therapy).

Self-Diagnosis

The sociality corollary of personal construct theory states that "to the extent that one person construes the construction processes of another he or she may play a role in a social process involving the other person". Clearly, to invite, induce or force anyone into a psychiatric hospital, to supervise their daily life, and to give them treatment there, is to play a role in a social process involving that person. This raises the issues of what kind of construing of the patient's construction processes informs the playing out of that social role and of what kind of construing by the patient informs their part of the relationship. The study to be reported is an exploratory examination of this issue.

Sixty new admissions (people who had never before been patients in a psychiatric hospital) were randomly selected and interviewed within 3 days of their admission, that is, before there had been much "negotiation" of their view of their problem with the hospital's view of their problem. The interview was leisurely and informal (of the order of 1 to 3 hours) but structured so as to cover for each patient four main aspects of their self-diagnosis. These were as follows:

1. Their view of the nature of their problem/condition (e.g., What do you think your main problem is? How did your problem start in the first place? What is it about you that needs treatment? and so forth.)

2. Their view of the cause of and responsibility for their condition. (e.g., Do you think this problem was your fault in any way? Is there something about you

which causes you to have this kind of problem? Do you think other people behave in the same way when faced with your kind of problem? and so forth.)

3. Their treatment expectations (e.g., What do you think the hospital can do for you? What sort of treatment do you think really would *not* help you? What do you think is the most useful way of spending your time in hospital? and so forth.)

4. Their outcome expectations (e.g., What do you think you will be like if the hospital really helps you? Are there any problems you expect to havè to live with whatever happens? How will people behave towards you when you are better? and so forth.)

All interviews were tape-recorded and transcribed (with the patient's permission). After each patient's discharge, his or her case notes were closely examined and an abstract was made of official views (particularly those of the consultant) covering, as far as possible, the issues raised in the interview. During a period from 1 to 2 years after the interview a brief follow-up assessment was made for each patient, using social work follow-up notes and other sources.

Theories of Breakdown

A content analysis of the interview transcripts yielded a number of "counts" for this population. First, interviews were analysed for broad approach to the question of why the patient became "ill" and was admitted to the hospital. There were eight different underlying theories proposed by the patients themselves as to the causes of mental illness. Using these categories yielded the percentages shown in Table I.

In some cases, the patient's explanation of their condition strongly suggests that they have two theories of mental illness, one of which they are currently applying and the second of which is held to be equally valid but is, in a sense, in reserve in case the theory currently being held proves inadequate or untenable. Twenty-five percent of the sample held such "double theories". A wide variety of different combinations of theories were held though it was noticeable that the notion of mental illness as caused either by lack of social skills or by strain, was usually held independently with no "reserve" theory.

Other characteristics of the sample were examined and were distributed as follows:

Hospital–patient agreement as to cause of breakdown: there was broad agreement for 61% of the sample.
Personal responsibility: 50% of the patients interviewed held themselves to be, in a major way, personally responsible for their condition while the remaining 50% denied responsibility.
Congruence of treatment desired and treatment received: in 43% of the sample the treatment given was broadly that for which the patient had expressed a

TABLE 1. *Sixty Patients' Theories of Causes of Mental Illness*

Hypothesised cause of breakdown	Percentage of patients
Distressing events (e.g., bereavement, loss of job, financial distress)	12
Physical trauma (e.g., head injury, infectious disease)	12
Poor personal relationships (e.g., conflict, rejection)	26
Lack of social skills (resulting in isolation)	7
Bad childhood experiences (e.g., parental rejection or oppression)	8
Morbid thoughts (e.g., jealousy, feelings of inferiority)	3
General strain (e.g., work, bringing up children)	7
Constitutional factors (e.g., inherited nervousness)	7
Total mystery (no explicit or implicit theory evident)	18

desire. In the remaining 57% of the sample there was a clear difference between the treatment desired by the patient and the treatment given.

Outcome: for 60% of the sample, the outcome of treatment (on follow-up after 1 year or more) was reasonably good, by a combination of criteria which included return to work, no readmissions or outpatient treatment needed, satisfaction expressed by patient and relatives and satisfaction expressed by hospital medical and social worker staff. For the remaining 40%, the outcome was considered bad in terms of the same criteria.

Interrelationship between Variables

The five aspects of the patient population discussed previously (outcome, degree of agreement between the hospital and the patient as to cause of breakdown, sense of personal responsibility, congruence of treatment desired with treatment given and implied theory of mental illness held by the patient) were examined, in relation to each other, by chi square. A number of statistically significant relationships emerged.

Not surprisingly, if the hospital and the patient were agreed as to the cause of breakdown, there tended to be congruence between the treatment desired by the patient and the treatment received ($p < .05$).

Interestingly, congruence of treatment given with treatment desired was not related to good or bad outcome, while agreement between patient and hospital as to cause of breakdown was significantly related to good outcome ($p < .01$). This suggests that patient–hospital agreement as to treatment does not guarantee that the treatment will be effective; on the other hand, agreement as to cause of breakdown between hospital and patient seems to generate some harmony beneficial to outcome.

The differing theories of mental illness held by patients, when grouped, related to a number of other population characteristics. Specifically, if patients holding either of the two theories relating largely to "external" cause (i.e., distressing events and physical trauma) were grouped together and compared with those holding "internal" cause theories (i.e., poor personal relationships, lack of social skills, bad childhood experiences), then significant relationships emerged as follows. Patients proposing internal theories of mental illness (poor personal relationships, lack of social skills, bad childhood experiences) were more likely to recover (have a good outcome) than were patients attributing mental illness to external forces (distressing events and physical injury) $p < .05$. Those patients who favoured internal theories of mental illness were more likely to be in agreement with the hospital as to the cause of their breakdown than were those favouring external theories ($p < .05$). Patients favouring internal theories of mental illness were more likely to accept a degree of personal responsibility for their breakdown than were patients favouring external theories of mental illness ($p < .05$).

Cases in Point

The degree to which the hospital inquires into and appreciates the patient's "self-diagnosis" is a complex function of the particular hospital personnel concerned, the persuasiveness and clarity of the particular patient in putting forward his or her viewpoint and issues such as whether or not the hospital has the personnel and facilities to respond to the problems declared by the patient (we tend not to hear pleas that we are unable to respond to). A detailed examination of the 60 patient interviews and case notes revealed greatly varying levels of understanding and negotiation between hospital and patient as to the nature of "the problem".

At worst, the hospital seems trapped in its official pseudo-medical construing and is thereby unable to appreciate problems, as presented in lay terms, by the patient. A medical language and style of thought can prevail to the extent illustrated by a doctor's report which stated that the patient was "unkempt, ragged, and an alcoholic failure who has the paranoid idea that people are making disparaging remarks about him". Two exemplary cases in which the hospital seems to have failed almost entirely to construe the construction processes of the patient are detailed as follows:

> *Patricia* (age 33) was admitted to the hospital after revealing that she had urges to smother her baby and had made gestures to that end. In interview, she argued that her unfortunate childhood experiences and the many stresses of her life had finally pushed her into her present disturbed frame of mind. She related a long history of extreme violence towards her from her father, followed by many beatings from her first husband to the point where she eventu-

ally tried to poison him. As a result of this she lost the children of her first marriage at the time of divorce. Following the birth of her baby in her second marriage, she was upset by a rather painful womb scraping operation and began to experience urges to hurt her child. These she had to keep secret because "I couldn't tell my husband, he would have gone mad, so I just fell into myself". The official medical formulation simply compounded this life history into the summary statement that Patricia was "schizophrenic", "neurotic", "in a psychotic state", "showed obsessional features", and "is essentially depressive," and she was treated exclusively with drugs and electroconvulsive therapy. Follow-up after discharge showed that she was twice readmitted, in the second case for a period of 4 months.

Elaine (age 23) was admitted following an occasion when her landlady threatened to raise her rent substantially and to evict her unless she paid it, after which Elaine became very anxious, trembled a great deal and was unable to go to work. In interview she repeatedly described herself as "obsessional" on the grounds that all her life she had been over concerned about her appearance and since her recent marriage had been cleaning their rooms over and over again "to get rid of the tiniest fingerprints". She described herself as lacking in security, "You know like I've got a very good husband, a really good husband and I've been told if I don't keep myself looking marvellous I'd perhaps lose him you see. I get worried you know, he looks so good you know". She related how she had dieted to lose half a stone in a week so as to look good and complained that she could not enjoy sexual intercourse because she was "worrying about the cleaning and polishing". She catalogued many worries and complained that 2 years of tranquillisers from her general practitioner had never enabled her to relax. Her view as to how this had all come about was that there had been some bad events in her childhood which she'd forgotten about and that she needed psychiatric help to remember and understand them, then she would be alright.

The consultant took the view that none of Elaine's complaints were of a severity which justified them being thought of as "psychiatric" and when she asked for a note to get on the corporation housing list, on medical grounds, he came to the conclusion that this was in fact "her main reason for coming into hospital". She was discharged as he did not "think there is any need for her to be regarded as in need of psychiatric help".

This kind of case poses an interesting problem about patient "presentation". If problems are not presented in a form which makes them seem well beyond the range of everyday complaints and if they are not presented in such a way as to form a recognisable symptomatic pattern, then they may be disregarded. The complex of the patient's interaction with his or her life may be seen as nothing more than a manoeuvre for immediate situational gain.

Two equally exemplary cases in which the hospital appeared to relate its own view and response specifically to the patient's own account of his or her problems are given:

June (age 24) was admitted following repeated feelings of suffocation and a suicidal gesture. Her account of the immediate cause of her breakdown was that her husband was in jail and while in there he had constructed a model caravan which he then gave to her mother-in-law and not to her, thus showing who he loved most. This incident was part of a long history, according to June, of oppression by her mother-in-law, who spied on her, bullied her, repeatedly picked quarrels with her and told tales about her to neighbours and to her husband. Farther back in her history was an account of having to leave home at 17 because her father was violent towards her and of repeated beatings from her husband and failure on his part to support her and her children adequately so that she was now facing severe money problems.

The hospital case notes' summary followed the research interview account closely and concluded with a diagnosis of "reactive depression". Interestingly the use of the term *reactive* (as opposed to *endogenous*) is an explicit recognition that the patient has something to be depressed about which can be responded to and understood. This contrasts with the alleged mystery of endogenous depression which has to be responded to in terms of medication because it cannot be identified or defined in a way which is socially meaningful and manageable. Thus, though the patient was given medication, she was also given support and encouragement, considerable social welfare help, and assistance from her husband's probation officer to improve her financial position and to establish her status in relation to her mother-in-law.

Michael (age 34) was admitted when his wife said she would leave him unless he did something about his "obsessional habits and slowness". Michael's account of his own behaviour in interview tied with aspects of his wife's complaint, for example, "I used to have a ritual of going round and round checking all the plugs, locking up and drawing curtains every night before I used to go to bed and the time it had taken me to lock up meant that my wife had probably been in bed half an hour or so. This of course affected our sex life as well because by the time I went to bed my wife was either past it, was annoyed or just was no longer interested". He blamed the obsessionality on his childhood upbringing, claiming that his mother had trained him to attach enormous importance to exactly where ornaments were to be placed and so forth. He believed that his obsessionality's becoming a "serious problem" was linked to his marriage, arguing that although his obsessionality had been lifelong, it had never seemed to matter when he lived in the parental home. Even now he felt that the problem would be solved if he was freed of his obsessions *or* if his wife became more tolerant of his behaviour.

The hospital view followed Michael's account closely, though adding to it the argument that Michael's obsessions provided him with an alternative to confronting his wife personally and sexually. He was seen as entirely unable to assert himself within the marriage, in which his wife played a dominant role. Following the general underlying argument of both patient and hospital, it was agreed that Michael should have behaviour therapy for his obsessive tidying and that he and his wife should have marital therapy.

In broad terms it can be argued that the cases where the hospital was relatively successful in negotiating and understanding the patient's point of view were those in which, for whatever reason, the hospital personnel most completely abandoned the "medical" approach and framework and worked in terms of lay or social work or "life problem" styles of construing.

The patients' need to converse in terms of their own constructs is reflected in the importance many of them attach to talking with nurses and fellow patients. Frequently this is seen as a source of support and counsel of greater value than the specific treatment aspects of the hospital, such as medication and occupational therapy.

Tragical, Pastoral, Comical, Historical

Although the people interviewed in this study were first time admissions to a psychiatric hospital, many of them had a history of referral to school psychology services, outpatient clinic contact, medical examinations because they had been in trouble with the law and general hospital admissions. The constructs of such intitutions had become threaded into the patient's own construing and interacted with it in a complex way. This is not clearly manifest in the rather straightforward cases previously cited to illustrate high levels of hospital–patient communication or non-communication. As an illustration of the interweave of personal and institutional construing, consider the following case:

Glen (age 20) was admitted to psychiatric hospital following car theft, drunkenness and a violent outburst in which he broke up furniture in his mother's house. The case notes gave a history of early maltreatment by his father and 2 years in children's home from the age of 12 to 14. He began regular drinking when he was 14 and at 18 served 6 months in a detention centre. His history was marked with violent drunkenness, clashes with the police and suicide attempts. A few months prior to his admission he became very stiff, developed a tremor and excessive salivation, and complained of feeling desperately ill. He was admitted to a general hospital where encephalitis was suspected but it was later decided that the entire condition was hysterical.

In his account of his condition, Glen stresses how depressed and nervous he gets but blames this entirely on the "encephalitis". His anger and violence he sees as justified by the way in which he has been treated. For example, he and a girl had been living together some distance away from her parents, who disliked him. Her parents then promised they would welcome him if he came to live in their home, so the two of them joined the parents. A short while later he was thrown out of the home and the girl stayed with her parents. Again he became violently angry when, in his view, he was unjustly sacked from a park gardening job to make way for a relative of the head gardener. He spoke of such incidents and the general tenor of his life as follows:

> Well I lived with my mother until I met a girlfriend, then we started having problems with her parents and she decided to come with me you know and we moved out and we lived in Harrogate. And then the parents decided to accept me, so I thought for her sake we'll move back to Leeds. So we moved back to Leeds and her parents went straight off again. You know they hated me again and she'd had enough trouble and that and she decided to stick with them you know. I still don't know why she ended it all.

Much of his experience he finds difficult to interpret.

> It's like I'm trapped inside myself you know. It's just getting me down and down and down. The doctors they say it'll wear off gradually but it doesn't. . . . It's just been like a dream. I mean it's just like being in one complete dream all the time. As if all my life's been a dream. There's no awareness there you know. . . . I mean I felt like doing myself in but I don't want to you know. I know for a fact that I don't want to. I don't really want to but I can't see no other way out. I don't really want to live yet I don't want to die. I'm stuck in the middle.

Diagnostically Glen was listed as "psychopathic personality with depression" but the interesting conclusion of the mixture of languages and constructions which had been applied to Glen was the consultant psychiatrist's final comment as Glen left the hospital to go to court: "In my opinion this youth is not suffering from any psychiatric illness which would in any way affect his judgment as regards to stealing. When he was last seen he was perfectly clear in his mind and well aware of the consequence of his acts". Earlier the same doctor had referred to him as "a very immature young man with very little or no sign of discipline".

Thus, while Glen takes into his own construct repertoire the idea of encephalitis and uses it to explain his conduct, the psychiatrist uses a mixture of psychiatric terms (psychopathic personality with depression) to describe him, while ruling that his behaviour (the theft) is not to be accounted for psychiatrically but to be construed morally ("no sign of discipline") and therefore to be dealt with legally.

The Medical Model as an Epidemic Ailment

However an individual person presents to a psychiatric hospital, he or she is most likely to be construed medically in that they are entering an institution which was designed architecturally, legally, socially, and professionally as a "hospital" with *mores* that closely parallel those of the traditional general hospital. The primary professional group, psychiatrists, are initially and lengthily trained as doctors and often have only a veneer of psychology added as overlay to the well-learned concretisms of physical medicine. Other involved professions (e.g., psychiatric nurses, occupational therapists, clinical psychologists) have training systems which take many of their themes and preoccupations from the medical model. Thus, the group who are most intimately concerned with helping the psychologically distressed have defined themselves and have been defined as "nurses" and they see themselves as the equivalent of nurses in general hospitals. This "nursing" image and form of organisation persists in spite of the fact that it creates enormous problems. In general medicine there is a workable (if questionable) distinction made between treatment (which is the province of the doctor) and that kind of general care and support work which is the province of the nurse, that is, "nursing". In psychiatry, such a distinction comes close to being a nonsense. Everything that happens to psychologically distressed persons in psychiatric hospitals is *treatment* in the sense that it tends either to help them or hinder them, to make them better or worse. The idea that their central and essential progress relates specifically to treatment while it is some other, less central aspect of them that is being nursed, is bizarre. Yet psychiatric nurses become involved in a whole series of paradoxes and internal conflicts about this distinction between treatment and nursing. On the one hand, they rightly feel that what they do to and with the patient is as central and significant as a doctor's treatment; on the other hand, if they are offered the opportunity to accept direct responsibility (as group therapists), they often retreat into the notion that they are only nurses and should not be held responsible for treatment.

Occupational therapists have struggled for decades to elaborate their work out of the raffia lampshade era to which it was restricted by the view that treatment is administered by doctors and that occupational therapists are there pleasantly and usefully to occupy the patient's time, while he or she is waiting for the treatment to work. The extension of occupational therapy to cover a much wider range of activities only partially enables its practitioners to confront the essential personal problems of patients.

Clinical psychology, up to the middle 1960s, was a profession which came close to boring itself to death because it tried to find a raison d'être within the limited space allowed to it after the claims of medicine had been met. Initially, clinical psychology was forced into *psychometrics* (assessment and diagnostic testing) because the central preoccupation with medicine created a clinical psychology roughly on the model of the pathology laboratory. Just as the doctor might send along a blood sample to be analysed and use the resulting information from the pathology lab as incidental information contributing to his or her treatment decisions, so he or she might send the patient's "intelligence" along to be assessed and analysed as part of a general review. Recent decades have seen an increasing involvment of clinical psychologists in directly helping patients. This is in contention with what is construed by psychiatrists as their "responsibility" but which can be alternatively construed as their political power.

The Pervasiveness of Medical Construing

Medical patterns of thought and action pervade every aspect of psychiatric institutions, and the following issues are chosen merely as examples.

It has been argued that the wearing of uniforms alienates patients from staff in psychiatric hospitals. Uniforms are a kind of officious formality which set the nurses apart from patients and symbolises their control over them. It is perhaps significant that experimental units such as psychotherapeutic communities, which seek to create a warmer peer relationship between patients and staff, almost invariably abandon the wearing of uniforms as a first step. However, the issue is not that the wearing of uniforms is bad but that the wearing of uniforms was never an option. Uniforms could never be freely chosen or rejected in psychiatric hospitals, because they copied the pattern of medical institutions generally and thereby accepted nurse uniforms automatically.

Every psychiatric patient has—again in line with patients in general hospitals—a set of case notes. These case notes are filled with the remarks and decisions of the staff and they are entirely and specifically secret from the patient. Again it is arguable that this has harmful effects, inducing in many patients a more or less justifiable paranoia about what is being said and thought about them. It can be argued that psychologically distressed people might benefit from a very different form of "case notes", for example, a kind of diary which the patients kept and to which they might request the addition of comments and notes by others. This might form part of the patient's own growing insight into his or her condition and problems. Again, the idea of no case notes or of alternative forms of case notes has not been developed or explored in psychiatric institutions, because their patterns of construing are so dominated by the traditions of general medicine.

A psychiatric hospital is essentially a collection of wards—the general hospital ward is the architectural and social model for the psychiatric institution. Yet there are many models for ways in which the psychologically distressed might live together: models such as the hotel, the commune, the boarding school, the summer camp, the village, and so forth but rarely have these models been at all effectively explored.

Equally, other aspects of psychiatric institutions closely mimic practices in general medicine. Admission routes largely exclude self-referral; political structures are steeply hierarchical and authoritarian; and, most important, the language of psychiatric institutions of all kinds is largely medical, with inevitable effects on the construing within these institutions. Thus communication between professionals and to a fair extent in negotiation with patients is carried out in terms of constructs such as doctor, patient, nurse, diagnosis, prognosis, treatment, cure, medication, ward round, admission, discharge, case, clinical presentation, symptom, remission, relapse, chronic, acute, and so on and so forth.

Case conference and demonstrations are carried out in psychiatric institutions exactly on the model of similar ceremonies in general medicine, in spite of the fact that what is on display and being exhibited is the *person,* not an ailment. Nothing more vividly illustrates the blinkering effect of medical construing than a gathering of psychiatrists unable to see the difference between having one's varicose veins publicly discussed and examined and being *as a person* publicly discussed and examined. Such a gathering can remain blind to the embarrassment, confusion, and pain of the person being turned into a public display because they are unaware that the vigorous exercise of group expertise by doctors can be wildly inappropriate in such psychological contexts.

Conclusions

Psychiatric hospitals construe the patient's complaint in very mixed terms, ranging from classical diagnostic categories to discussions in a lay language very similar to that of the patient. This mixing seems to be partly due to a cultural shift whereby the strict medical viewpoint is weakening professionally and patients themselves seem to acquiesce less readily to the pathologising of their problems within an "illness" model. Some professional groups—particularly social workers—habitually use a "life problem" rather than an "illness" form of construing. Additionally, prolonged conversation with a patient (e.g., a nurse–patient exchange) inevitably tends to resolve itself into non-medical terms since illness labels are difficult to elaborate over time. For the same reason, the small number of patients who are given any form of psychotherapy tend to find themselves engaged in a more personal and less medical interchange.

Nevertheless, as already argued, the forms of superordinate medical construing endemic in psychiatric institutions still induce a degree of passivity in the patient who may well accept the official role of the sickly ignoramus requiring authoritative treatment from expert professionals. Equally, the notion of illness has a tendency to blind the patient to the significance of his or her personal experience and reflection. Initially, when people become anxious, they may seek to understand why they are anxious. They may try to relate their feelings of anxiety to the kind of life they have been leading, to their experience of failure and rejection, to the content and significance of what they have done and what has been done to them. However, when the experience is psychiatrically transmuted into "an anxiety state" or "neurotic anxiety", their understanding of their condition in relation to their history is seen as less relevant. More and more see themselves as "suffering from" an extraneous attack, an illness which can only be understood and dealt with by professionals in professional terms. "I was walking along one day and I caught 'anxiety' ".

The discrepancy between the patient's construing of their own problems and the official, medical subsuming of patients' complaints by psychiatric hospital staff seriously limits both groups in their capacity to react imaginatively and effectively to psychological distress. Insofar as the patient's formulation is seen as itself symptomatic of illness, it is not listened to seriously, nor is it interrogated in a way which would help the patient to reflect and elaborate.

After nearly two centuries of dedication to the task of construing psychological distress in medical terms, our conclusion may be that we had best begin again.

References

Agnew, J. and Bannister, D. (1973). Psychiatric diagnosis as a pseudo-specialist language. *British Journal of Medical Psychology,* **46,** 69–73.

Bannister, D. (1968). The logical requirements of research into schizophrenia. *British Journal of Psychiatry,* **114,** 181–188.

Bannister, D., Salmon, P., and Lieberman, D. (1964). Diagnosis-Treatment relationships in psychiatry: A statistical analysis. *British Journal of Psychiatry,* **110,** 726–732.

2

Becoming a Teacher: An Altering Eye

C. T. Patrick Diamond

"The eye altering alters all."
(William Blake, 1805)

Introduction

Ray Bradbury (1961) sees human beings as filling

> ourselves with sounds, sights, smells, tastes and textures of people, animals, landscapes, events, large and small. We stuff ourselves with those impressions and experiences and our reaction to them. Into our subconscious goes not only factual data but reactive data, our movement toward or away from the sensed events. . . . [This is] a fantastic storehouse, our complete being. . . . All that is original lies waiting for us to summon it forth. . . . (p. 9)

People are often depicted as having invisible knapsacks on their backs from birth. Everything goes into the sack which is carried everywhere, indiscriminately added to all during life while providing material whenever wanted. In contrast, Kelly (1955) emphasizes the way that people interact with their world and actively process rather than passively store their experiences. He describes people as developing sets of hypotheses or construct systems in which their present abstractions are tentatively placed on past experiences and then later are projected upon future events in order to cope with those events. These hypotheses are individually constructed from experience and through them each person sees and interprets the world. The system is more like a pair of spectacles than a filing cabinet or knapsack since not only does the person get information through it but it even conditions what and how he or she experiences. The construct system busily seeks verification and does not wait.

If people can understand their own construct systems, as well as those of others, they can not only understand their past but they can also make predictions about their likely behaviour in a given situation, such as the classroom, because they know something about what that series of events is likely to mean to themselves and others. Kelly invented the repertory grid to help people exhibit

ISSUES AND APPROACHES
IN PERSONAL CONSTRUCT THEORY

15

their construct systems. If grids are elicited over a salient period of time and then reflected upon, the processes of change, growth, and decay in each person's system may be interpreted variously as massive or neglegible, ordered or chaotic, sudden or gradual, desirable or not. The aim of the present study was to encourage teachers during their year of professional preparation first to see into and then out of themselves.

Like other professionals in training, student teachers come to grips with the specific domain of expertise by plotting their observations (or elements) against their dimensions of appraisal (or constructs) and by testing their constructs against their observations. Since the repertory grid expresses the finite systems of cross references between the personal observations that are made and the personal constructs that are devised, it acts as a kind of psychological equivalent of the first rough ground plane mirror (Thomas, 1978, p. 51) of their developing conceptual networks. The present study seeks to show that

> the direct experience of discovering emerging patterns of personal meanings within oneself, by oneself, or in close conversation with another, [may] enable an individual to set out on a voyage of exploration, within the private space of his/her own phenomenal world. No one returns from such a voyage unchanged. Focused grids are one major step towards making this process of change available.
>
> (Thomas, 1976, p. 3.)

Method

PARTICIPANTS

Seventeen students who were reading for the Diploma in Education with a core of educational studies and a variety of curriculum subjects as offered in secondary schools volunteered to participate in the present study. They completed repertory grids at the beginning, midway through, and at the end of the year-long course: that is, after teaching once in primary schools and twice in secondary.

Procedure

The researcher explained that the purpose of the study was to explore the student teachers' views of teaching and of people over the course of the academic year. The first step was to identify the elements or items extending over the range of convenience—in this instance, the people to be compared. A common set of 16 elements (see Table 1) was derived from studies by Adams-Webber and Mirc (1976) and Pope (1978). Diamond (1981) studied what 73 former Diploma students considered to be the major human elements of teaching. The grids were elicited in groups of six to eight by offering the student teachers a randomly derived list of triads (Bannister and Mair, 1968) and asking how two of the three were alike in some important way that distinguished them from the third. The students were asked to write a word or short phrase description under

TABLE 1. *Role Title List*

Figure number	Figure description
1	*Self*
2	*Past self*
3	*Ideal self*
4	*Teacher I am*
5	*Teacher I fear to be*
6	*Teacher I would like to be*
7	*Mother*
8	*Father*
9	*Siblings*
10	*Spouse/Steady*
11	*Friends*
12	*Pupils*
13	*Principal and Deputy*
14	*Subject master*
15	*Supervising teacher*
16	*University tutor*

"construct" indicating similarity and the opposite of the characteristic under "contrast". Each element was finally rated on the scales defined by the pairs of poles from 1 to 5 (that is, from *most* to *least* on each of the emergent poles) and their allotted values were recorded. This process continued for about an hour and a half, using different triads, until 12 constructs were identified.

On each of the three occasions, only the original elements were preserved so that comparative analyses of change between successive grids could be made. Since one of the usually avowed aims of teacher education is the development of fresh and even radical perspectives, this provided opportunity for any new constructs to emerge. Care was taken to ensure that the statistical calculations did not distract the students from the focusing procedure and the major purpose of the study: that is, the revelation and exploration of personal and shared patterns of meaning as they evolved over the year. To further promote feelings of ownership and self-invention the teachers were encouraged to keep a learning log or teaching journal. Devising a fable or dialogue was one of the activities suggested to aid the process of making personal sense out of the course experiences.

Analysis

Thomas's (1979) FOCUS computer program analysed each teacher's three grids. This program provided a two-way cluster analysis in each case in order to re-order the rows of constructs and the columns of elements so as to produce a FOCUSed grid in which there was the least variation between adjacent constructs and adjacent elements. This analysis was done with respect to the way the elements were ordered by the constructs. The relationships were visualised as tree diagrams for the constructs and the elements which showed the highest similarities in the clusters.

The SOCIOGRIDS program (Thomas, 1979) helped on the same three occasions to explore the similarity and differences in construing between the teachers. This technique is based on Kelly's commonality assumption that there are areas of shared meaning among individuals. The program analysed each set of repertory grids elicited from the group and based similarity in terms of the ordering of the element set. Three mode grids were thus extracted from the group, and in each case the number of modal constructs was comparable to the number of constructs in the separate individual grids. Thomas, McKnight, and Shaw (1976) originally suggested considering every occasion where two constructs from different grids are adjacent and weighting the occurrence with the level of match in which it occurs. Using this stable but sensitive measure, each of the mode grids was made up of those constructs which clustered adjacently at a high level of match. The constructs chosen as representatives of group construing were firmly based in the ways in which the elements had been construed similarly by the majority of the group.

SOCIOGRIDS produced three sequences of sociometric diagrams designated *socionets* from the matrix of similarity measures between pairs of individual teachers' grids. The highest related pair on each occasion was featured as a subgroup where commonality of construing occurred, followed by the subgroups defined by the rank ordering of all the similarity measures. As the pattern of links or nets developed, both modal and more isolated construers were located. While the socionets revealed the structural properties of the group, the actual content of the shared construing was exhibited in each of the mode grids.

Findings

Figure 1 shows that at the beginning of the Diploma course, after the primary and before the first secondary practice, the 17 intending teachers formed one superordinate construct at the 75% level. In terms of their verbal labels, this large cluster consisted of RESPONSIBLE/INEXPERIENCED, RESPECTED EXPERTISE/INEXPERIENCED, SECURE TEACHING IDEAS/OTHER IDEAS, WORK FULFILLMENT/FRUSTRATION, OTHER CONCERNED/DIFFERENT, PATIENT/MOODY, SIMILAR/DIFFERENT LIFE ATTITUDES, and AMIABLE/AUTHORITARIAN. A subcluster consisted of MAINTAINS CONCENTRATION/UNABLE, CAPABLE OF/LACKS APPLICATION, and UNDERSTANDING/TOO EMOTIONALLY INVOLVED. The superordinate seems to express an overarching concern for professional and personal qualities.

One very wide element set was formed tightly at the 80% level, together with *siblings* and *pupils* paired at the 83% level. The *teacher I am* was described

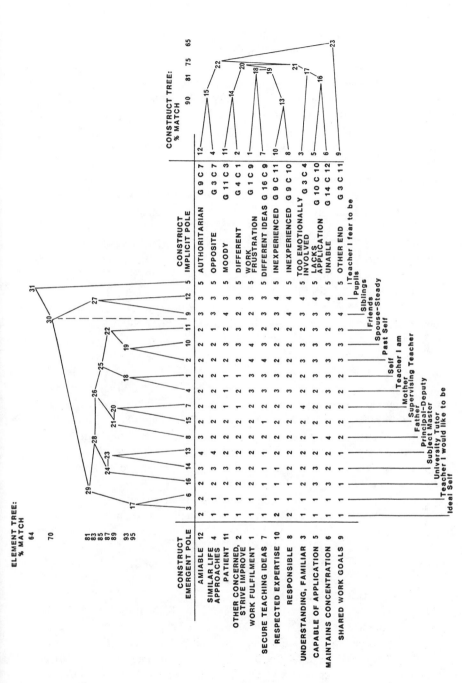

Figure 1. Intending teachers (N = 17) FOCUSed early mode grid.

as very patient, amiable, similar in life approaches, other concerned and striving to improve, understanding and familiar, and capable of application and sharing work goals. The group was undecided about themselves on 5 of the 12 dimensions. Pupils were similarly not clearly perceived on 6 scales but they were seen negatively on the remaining ones; that is, as very inexperienced, too emotionally involved, lacking application, unable to concentrate, and not at all sharing teachers' work goals. While the 68% level of match between the *teacher I am* and *pupils* seems to indicate a degree of initial good will, the acceptance may have been conditional.

After the first secondary practicum midway through the course, the group formed two superordinates marginally more tightly at the 78% level (see Figure 2). The wider cluster grouped EMOTIONALLY STRONG/WEAK, SELF-CONFIDENT/NOT, FUTURE CONCERNED/NOT, ADULT/CHILDLIKE, CARING/NOT, EFFICIENT/INEFFICIENT, CONCERNED WITH STUDENT NEEDS/NOT, MATURE/IMMATURE, and LEADERS/FOLLOWERS. Many of these constructs seem quite categorical, while INDEPENDENT/DEPENDENT and FRIENDLY/INTIMIDATING, which were paired, are less so. In addition to some tightness in formation, the construct labels suggest greater emphasis on pupils and a movement towards more instrumental concerns relating to motivation, discipline, and managerial effectiveness.

A more inclusive element set was formed than before, leaving only the *teacher I fear to be* as an isolate. However, *pupils* were one of the last elements to be related to the other significant people. They were associated at an even lower level than previously with the *teacher I am* (64%) and delineated clearly and negatively on seven dimensions as very immature and childlike, followers, not having teachers' goals, dependent, not confident, and not future oriented. A more preemptive view of *pupils* seems to be emerging. The *teacher I am*, in contrast, was seen more decisively and positively as mature in knowledge, caring, emotionally strong, adult, and friendly.

At the conclusion of the course the intending teachers construed people and teaching somewhat abstractly in terms of two equally broad and more closely knit superordinates. The tightest of these (84% level of association) consisted of MATURE, KNOWING OWN MIND, ADVISING and ASSURING, EMOTIONALLY and MORALLY SECURE, KNOWLEDGEABLE OF OTHERS' LIVES, and RESPONSIBLE. The second cluster was made up of SENSITIVE TO OTHERS' FEELINGS, CARING FOR INDIVIDUALS, CRITICAL and ANALYTICAL, WELL ROUNDED and ORGANISED, and CONCERNED. Despite this literal concern for clients, the elements were split into three exclusive groups. The largest cluster consisted of *self*, the *teacher I am, spouse, university tutor, subject master, past self, siblings, friends*, and *supervising teacher*. The second group paired *ideal self* and the *teacher I would like to be* at the 100% level, while the third was made up of *pupils* and the *teacher I fear to be*

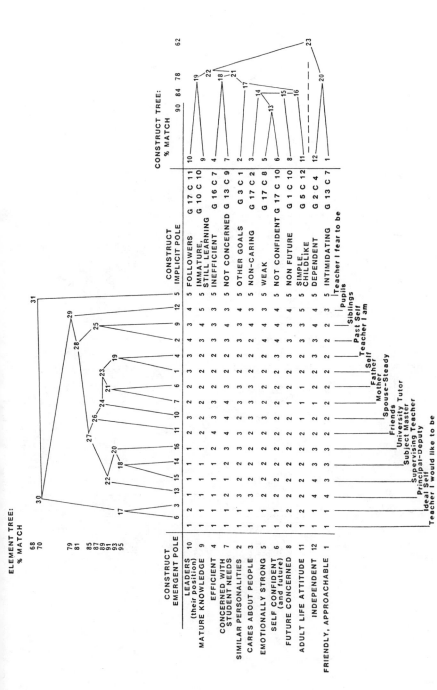

Figure 2. Intending teachers ($N = 17$) FOCUSed mid-mode grid.

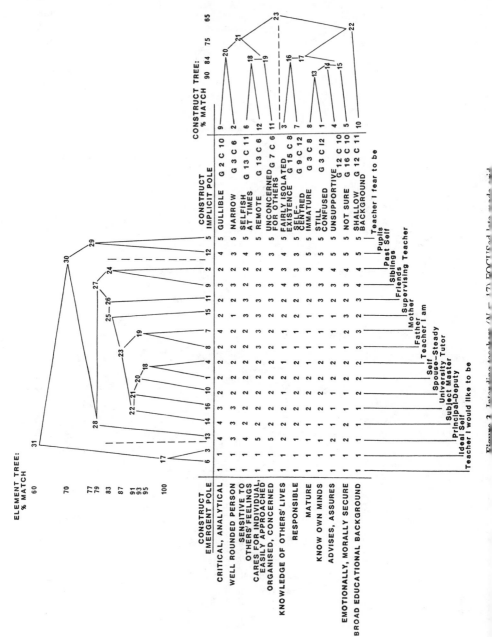

Figure 2. Interacting teachers (N = 17). FOCUSed late-made grid

TABLE 2. *Meaningfulness Index (The Amount of
Undecided Responses)*[a]

Grid	Element	
	Teacher I am	*Pupils*
Early	5	6
Middle	4	5
Late	0	3
	9	14

[a]$N = 12$ on each occasion.

(77%). The intending teachers' element boundaries were firmly defined by personal and pedagogic ideals on one hand, and by pupils and undesirable teacher on the other (Figure 3).

The teachers were now sure on 9 dimensions how *pupils* should be described; that is, they were extremely immature, confused, unsupportive, unsure emotionally and morally, and with a very shallow educational background. In contrast, the *teacher I am* was definitely and positively seen on all 12 dimensions. As shown in Table 2, fewer undecided responses (ratings of 3) were made to the *teacher I am* and *pupils* in the mode grid as the year progressed. These two key elements were increasingly perceived in more meaningful ways.

In order to analyse the changing relationship between the pedagogical self and the client elements, the degree of association between the *teacher I am* and *self, the teacher I would like to be,* the *teacher I fear to be,* and *pupils* is shown during the early, middle, and late components of the course in Table 3. These matching scores are drawn from the matrix of element matching scores for each of the 17 teachers and the group as a whole.

The group began with a very high degree of role identification which was maintained and even intensified (95%) over the year. Teacher 4 (Anne) wrote,

> I have wanted to be a teacher for as long as I can remember and by the end of the second prac. I knew it was still the right decision. . . . Though it's hard, I really love working with kids.

While the group as a whole initially experienced only a moderate degree of compatibility (64%) between the teachers they were and the teachers they wanted to be, this level of congruence steadily increased to reach almost 80%. Their process of accommodating reality and ideal was dramatised by teacher 18 (Sonya) in a short dialogue between two facets of her teaching self, the *teacher I am* (TA) and the *teacher I would like to be* (TB):

> TA When I'm teaching I always think about you and how I don't measure up to you and worst of all that I never will.

TABLE 3. *Percentage of Association with Teacher I Am during the Three Components of the Course*

Teacher number	Early				Middle				Late			
	Self	Teacher I would like to be	Teacher I fear to be	Pupils	Self	Teacher I would like to be	Teacher I fear to be	Pupils	Self	Teacher I would like to be	Teacher I fear to be	Pupils
Mode	93	64	35	68	93	68	33	64	95	79	20	43
1	83	56	52	68	85	81	41	70	95	85	35	70
2	79	64	45	64	68	56	62	66	81	50	62	81
3	93	81	25	62	93	81	25	62	91	87	16	37
4	87	75	31	75	86	72	26	60	95	85	14	52
6	89	77	33	45	81	68	43	41	72	79	20	25
7	85	77	25	64	91	70	43	70	89	89	16	52
8	93	68	29	68	79	58	68	70	87	60	50	79
9	83	66	39	37	56	87	12	25	79	66	39	52
10	87	56	62	66	87	66	55	73	91	68	45	75
11	62	56	54	68	77	59	48	65	79	72	37	72
12	87	77	37	72	87	81	27	70	83	64	39	60
13	91	58	45	66	85	47	54	58	83	85	12	50
14	81	62	41	62	87	68	33	75	87	75	29	72
15	77	56	60	50	76	60	55	60	60	39	75	64
16	87	77	27	54	81	75	31	58	79	83	20	54
17	93	85	14	68	93	81	20	70	83	75	25	54
18	95	72	64	72	97	64	45	85	91	68	45	75

TB Look, it's not a problem. Think of me as something you can work towards. Just
    don't let it get you down. Your trouble is that you want to achieve as quickly as
    possible. Instead you should let time work on you. Experience is the best teacher
    you know.

The teachers also continued to escape from the *teacher I fear to be*. However
the gap that opened up between them and pupils threatened to yawn into an abyss
by the end of the year with 43% replacing the previously higher levels of match.
Not surprisingly, pupils proved to be a major construing problem for these
intending teachers.

The socionets revealed how closely on each of the three occasions each teacher's perceptions of the similarities and differences between the elements re-
sembled each other teacher's. The summary in Table 4 shows that teachers 3
(Paula) and 10 (Helen) were consistently most like the group in their construing,
while teacher 9 (Sam) was most unlike in his. These three construers were
selected on this basis and studied in detail so that changes might be related to
more particular personal influences.

Teacher 3

Paula was preparing to teach English and Social Science. She associated her
self with the *teacher I would like to be,* the *teacher I fear to be,* and *pupils* almost
exactly as the group did during the year (see Table 3). Paula wrote in one of her
last journal entries:

> Mostly what I want is to be successful at teaching—to be sure of myself and confident in
> what I do as a teacher.

Fuller (1969, p. 268) also found that most beginning teachers really want to
succeed, and they relate personal and pedagogical elements highly.

Like most of the group Paula reported some final estrangement from *pupils*.
Her degree of association with them first remained at 62% but then ebbed
dramatically to 37% by the end of the year. Though she was practising at a
difficult government school, she wrote:

> I don't fear them so much as feel uncertain about them. The aspect of having to control
> and discipline pupils is one of the major causes of the ambiguity of feeling towards them.
> Lack of experience in handling discipline promotes feelings of uncertainty about one's
> ability to cope.

Paula felt similar uncertainty and hostility towards her own younger *siblings*.

Aesop's Fable of "The Man and the Ass" summed up the experience of
becoming a teacher for Paula:

> No-one can please everyone all the time. . . . Truly, it is very confusing and frustrating
> to find that when you please either superiors, teachers, parents, pupils or yourself more
> often than not you displease someone else. . . . We are like the donkey, pushed and

TABLE 4. *Kinds of Construers*

Grid	Modal	Isolated
Early	3, 10, 16, 17	9, 15, 13
Middle	1, 3, 10, 14, 18	2, 4, 7, 9, 16
Late	3, 6, 7, 10, 13	1, 4, 9, 12

pulled from one side to the other. It is difficult to fulfil successfully the dual role of university student and intending teacher.

Teacher 10

Helen intended teaching English as a second language and social science. She felt the content of her superordinate constructs changed greatly: INEXPERIENCE and LACK OF CONFIDENCE were finally replaced by being QUESTIONING, ANALYTICAL, and CRITICAL. Helen's increased confidence was reflected in her teaching self moving progressively closer to her ideal and to her pupils, but away from her feared teacher. Unlike the group as a whole, Helen's degree of empathy with pupils increased from 66 to 73 to 75%. She wrote: "I've got to adore my kids this semester. They're lovely!" Helen attributed this "altering eye" to a change in practising schools. She ended the year in a small, fee-paying girls' school where she was supported and encouraged and thus able to relax and innovate in her teaching. Helen represented her own delayed self-recognition by drawing upon Eliot's "Four Quartets":

> We shall not cease from exploration
> And the end of all our exploring
> Will be to arrive where we started
> And know the place for the first time. (1944, p. 43)

Teacher 9

Though Sam had enrolled to teach chemistry and general science, the Army Reserve was his main declared interest. Sam's association of *self* and teacher dropped significantly from 83 to 56% by midyear. Though this score improved to 79%, his level of commitment seemed well below that of the group (95%). Sam also began being more alienated from students though this gap lessened.

Sam wrote that his previous and continuing role as an instructor in the Reserve stood him in better stead than the Diploma as a form of teacher preparation. Early in the year he explained:

> I'm disappointed in the course. I expected to be taught definite ways of teaching. . . . I fear my commitments to the Reserve are going to suffer. I'd better read only what is necessary and no more.

Midway through the year Sam found that it was easy to "get by":

> During prac. even preparation the night before is not really required. I find myself looking forward to my Army courses. The Army takes me away from the uni. environment where I feel enclosed, chained to the ivory tower. Hopefully I'll last it out to the end. My mind has been totally oriented toward the Army.

During the last practice session Sam admitted:

> I'm not even as interested as I was last time. I don't think I have been as receptive through the course as I should have been.

Perhaps Jarrell's sleeping bats objectify Sam's reluctant induction into teaching as it was presented in the course:

> [The little brown bat said:] "The next time you wake up in the daytime, just keep your eyes open for a while and don't go back to sleep."
>
> The other bats were sure they wouldn't like that. "We wish we didn't wake up at all," they said. "When you wake up in the daytime the light hurts your eyes—the thing to do is to close them and go right back to sleep. Day's to sleep in; as soon as it's night we'll open our eyes."
>
> "But won't you even try it?" the little brown bat said. "Just for once, try it?" The bats all said: "No." "But why not?" asked the little brown bat. The bats said: "We don't know. We just don't want to."

> (Jarrell, 1964, pp. 3–4)

Teacher 14

As a representative construer in the middle of the year, Carole is included as one of the "little brown bats" by way of contrast. Carole was practising to teach English and social science and felt that her growing commitment to her pupils (62, 75, 72%) resulted from "*self* butting in on the *teacher I am* and establishing a more humane relationship with them". If she did not get to know the students as individuals, she felt she would be just an actor performing in front of a blank class.

Carole's construct matching scores show an interesting progression in her teaching perspective. In her first grid the greatest match was with FLEXIBILITY, IMAGINATION, TRYING NEW THINGS, and BEING ENERGETIC. In the second it was with STRIVES TO ACHIEVE, SHY/QUIET, BORED WITH REPETITION, and ZEST FOR LIFE. In the third, it was CARES FOR CHILDREN and SENSITIVE TO OTHERS' FEELINGS. Carole was increasingly focusing on pupils and her responses to them.

Carole's personal approach to teaching was evidenced by the way in which she construed the *pupils* over the year. In the first grid she described them in positive terms (imaginative, innovative, in constant change, fairly energetic, flexible). In the second grid she was also optimistic (zest for life, feeling out new ground, bored with repetition, needing specific knowledge) but her view was tempered by some of the realities that had been discovered in the first prac. period. The third grid was also enthusiastic (casual, sense of humour, confident) with the exception of fairly selfish which rated a 2. Despite this criticism, her grids showed an overall higher match between the *teacher I am* and *students* (62, 75 and 72%) than did those of the mode (68, 64 and 43%).

It is interesting to note that while *teacher I am* and *pupils* were associated comparatively highly, *self* and *pupils* gained an even higher percentage match of 77, 66, 81% respectively. This establishes an important distinction for Carole between *self* and the *teacher I am*. Perhaps this can be explained in terms of the novel, authoritarian position that a beginning teacher inevitably has to adopt:

> Since I am not by nature an authoritative person, I felt a greater rapport with students as *self*. I often felt the presence of this conflict while I was on prac., and found it difficult at times to reconcile dealing with the pupils on a personal basis, yet still maintaining my authority.
>
> (Carole)

Sam was tougher minded and ready to declare his position. He wrote:

> You just have to let the kids know who's boss.
> You can't be their friend. That's all.

In the main, the intending teachers found the practice periods extremely threatening. As Sonya commented:

> It's eight weeks of living in a pressure cooker!

Teacher 15 felt beseiged by a headmaster described as "Mr. Law", by name as well as deed. The style of a beginning teacher's haircut was of crucial importance in his school. Teacher 16 experienced conflict with an authority figure closer to home, her father, who had refused to allow her to apply for a government scholarship, alleging she should not become a teacher since "she didn't even know that cows could swim!"

Discussion

The socialisation of these 17 beginning professionals into their occupational roles was able to be indexed at least in part by their developing a common frame of reference. Their homogeneity in outlook was revealed in the three successive mode grids which were able to be extracted. As well, the socionets showed there were subgroups which differed not only in their subject specialisation but also in their perception and acceptance of pupils. In general, however, there were increasing levels of role identification and of reconciliation with teaching ideals. Finally, there was a marked shift in meaningful "seeing" as more definite rather than undecided responses were made to the centrally important elements of the *teacher I am* and *pupils*.

In general, the mode constructs changed from expressing personal and professional qualities to categorical, instrumental concerns which then merged either into discipline or pupil-centred ideas. Another feature of the three mode grids was the tendency for the large construct clusters also to become progressively tighter over the year (75, 78, 84%) in their association. While Adams-Webber and Mirc (1976) reported increased levels of integration in student teachers' construct systems after practice teaching, this present pattern may mean that the teachers' construct systems were becoming increasingly less permeable; that is, rather than broadening their outlook and construing teaching in different ways, they were seeing it in a tight, rigid way, from an increasingly fixed point of view. However, the same pattern could indicate instead that the group became more firm or confident in their construing. As constructs gradually take shape, they are then more tightly formulated and prepared for an eventual rigorous test for either confirmation or disconfirmation. It seems that neither tight nor loose construing is good in itself and that instead ''development is a word for movement between the two'' (Bannister and Fransella, 1980, p. 96).

Uncertainty about initial teaching ideas was lessened by real life experience. Carole, for example, explained that she had first imagined the worst and had to grope desperately for more secure ideas. In her fable, teacher 11 (Christine) describes the shifts from recent graduate to student teacher and finally to qualified teacher:

> In Dip.Ed., as in any fairy tale, just when you think you're out of the woods, there is suddenly more to them than you ever imagined. Just when you think you have escaped to an open quiet place it turns out you're still in them. Even later the woods you're wandering in turn out to be yourself.

According to Carole, the group's construct matching scores revealed a progression in content from RESPECTED EXPERTISE/RESPONSIBILITY as an important construct in the first grid to EMOTIONALLY STRONG and SELF-CONFIDENT in the second grid. This could indicate a change from the idealistic pre-prac. climate to that of the post-prac. where many of the student teachers found that their ideals had to be abandoned in order to maintain order and to please supervising teachers. The constructs of the third grid, MATURE, KNOWS OWN MIND, ADVISES, ASSURES, and EMOTIONALLY, MORALLY SECURE, perhaps indicate that the student teachers were coming to confront the discipline problem and were looking to their own maturity and were taking on an advisory role. It is possible only to hypothesize about these results, however, because the constructs changed in so many different ways.

What is clear is that the group had a narrow, pessimistic view of the pupils at the end of the year. This empathetic gap is discussed by Fuller (1969) who found it less characteristic of more experienced teachers who focused on gaining satisfaction from pupils rather than on controlling them. The group's negative, apprehensive view of pupils may have been conditioned by the need to control them. This is revealed in how pupils were characterised as lacking background, application, and concentration, and as being immature, childlike, and unsupportive. Many of the teachers expressed a fear of losing control, of not being able "to get on top" in the classroom.

When the modal and more isolated construers were studied, Anne was found with only a few others to have finished the year with positive constructs of pupils. Yet even her development was highly personal since it represents something of a "comeback". Anne agreed that her most interesting figures related to *pupils* (see Table 3).

> In the first prac. I saw 75 per cent similarity between *pupils* and the *teacher I am*, while in second prac. there was a dramatic 30 per cent drop to 45 per cent. I was quite apprehensive towards students at first; however, there were no discipline problems at primary prac. As a result I didn't feel threatened by them—nor I would imagine them by me. I hardly felt like a teacher at all, just like a large version of a student pretending to be a teacher. I therefore saw the students as allies, more so than the teachers. This accounts for the 75 per cent match.

> In the second prac. at high school (in the first weeks especially) frustration best describes my reaction to students. I didn't feel I could communicate with them at all and being in an all boys' school didn't help. Although I enjoyed planning lessons, I often felt so nervous I didn't think I could give them. I felt extremely threatened and intimidated by students, more so out of the classroom than in it. By the end of the prac. I felt more relaxed and began to take more to the role of teacher than student. However, this anxiety about students accounts for the drop in similarity to 45 per cent.

> The figure for third prac. shows a change again from the former prac. session. Students have levelled out to a 52 per cent match with the *teacher I am*. My explanation for this is that I now have a clearer idea of how I view students whereas I didn't before. In the previous two pracs. my opinion of them went from one extreme to the other. In the third prac. I enjoyed interaction with students and I felt they liked me. This feeling of acceptance played a big part in returning my relaxation and confidence around them. I left third prac. feeling enthusiastic about further teaching and clearly identifying with my role as a teacher.

Anne is much more self-assured and less threatened. During her earlier secondary practicum she had written:

> I'm terrified I'm going to make a fool of myself. I don't quite know what to make of the students. They just stare at me. Like the little boy sitting in front of me today when I was marking some work. He turned round and looked at me all the while as if I were the most fascinating thing he had ever seen. I decided to ignore him.

Bannister (1981, p. 259) comments on this kind of limbo state that, though qualifying as teachers, many students feel they are still psychologically students playing the role of teacher. Teacher 1 (Mitzi) also experienced this kind of initial dissociation of self from teacher self:

First high school lesson: Me playing a double role. One is the make believe teacher at the front and me going beyond myself to where I was the other watching the person out front, giggling and gazing in disbelief: "That surely can't be you out there!" How do you become a "real" teacher and not just an authority figure?

The only opportunity for a fuller transition from playing to becoming a teacher would be in the two remaining practical periods. For some students it may not occur until the first year of full-time teaching.

Mitzi changed from being a modal construer in the middle of the year to an isolate. She wrote:

Pupils remained with me as teacher at the same 70 per cent, so much higher than the mode. I interpret this as me being more perceptive of and responsive to the needs of students.

In contrast, teacher 6 (Peter) was salient in being consistently dissociated from pupils over the year (see Table 3). Peter explained his beliefs:

Most of the teachers I felt were successful during my school days were those who had a good deal of distance but respect from their pupils. I chose to follow this "formula for success". Those teachers who tried to be less formal and more familiar were generally abused and "stirred" to the maximum. I don't mind being high on a kid's "Death List". It's actually a mark of respect.

Sam left the course convinced of the fact that corporal punishment was essential. He insisted that school discipline would collapse without the occasional belting with the cane. Unlike Carole, Anne, and Mitzi, both Peter and Sam were training to teach science and seemed to reflect only two of the concerns of beginning teachers as found by Fuller (1969); that is, they focused on "My Performance" and "Discipline" but not on "Pupil Centred". While it may be easier to look into self than to see how self is looked out of, the subject specialisation of the first degree may also affect these kinds of capacities.

During training, the group's teacher element moved further away from its feared, negative counterpart (35, 33, 20%). In contrast, Mitzi reported a very high match (52%) between these elements after the first prac.:

I found myself doing things which seemed too unnatural and out of character for me. My supervising teacher was often quite severe with some students for what seemed really trivial matters. Yet I felt obliged at times (through lack of experience I guess) to imitate her when faced with the unknown—but I felt bad about it.

A higher than group match was noted by Grant (teacher 8) during his second practice period. He too was tempted to deny his own *self:*

I swung like a pendulum. My thoughts, attitudes and feelings reacted violently to reality. I changed quickly to my supervising teacher's form. I did not like it but it was successful in dealing with the volatile situation of school. Anyway he would be assessing me. I still don't like the shift away from myself though.

This conflict remained unresolved at the end of the year for Paula:

> I felt conflict about being liked by the students and at the same time being a disci-
> plinarian. This concern about being able to handle discipline and control situations is at
> the forefront of my worries. Most teachers seem to feel control is the real test of a
> teacher.

Though Paula felt almost coerced, Peter's analogy of "The Sorcerer's Apprentice" contains elements of willing collaboration:

> I am the greenhorn apprentice and the wizards are my supervising teachers. They
> demonstrate to me the "magic" of transforming uncooperative students into willing
> learners. Maybe the kids are even cleverer and allow the teachers to give them what they
> need for the exams.

Headmaster and *deputy*, apart from *pupils*, were most consistently and closely
linked to the *teacher I fear to be*. For Mitzi administrators were

> so far removed from the real life situation of classes that they only present negative
> images of teaching. For me they are rigid, out of touch with youth, egocentric and judge
> people, especially students, too hard.

Most of the group, however, described them as knowledgeable of others, very
responsible and mature. They knew their own minds and were sure of their
advice to others.

Implications

What in teacher preparation, apart from further professional experience, might
make a difference and close even these gaps has yet to be studied. In a personal
communication, Bannister (1980) has recommended "loosening activities" or
licensing student teachers to loosen their constructs of people and teaching. Such
procedures might include role playing what it feels like to be a pupil in school or
teaching each other and then reversing roles. By participating even in fantasy in
the perspectives of pupils and in glimpsing their world, teachers may come to
grasp more readily their future clients' points of view. Radley (1976, p. 62)
describes such experiences as encouraging "the engagement of minds". This
kind of program is further supported by Rosenhan's (1969) study of the origins of
concern for others; this study stresses the importance of voluntary rehearsal
through training, as well as on-the-job interactions, in helping the attitudes of
prospective professionals to evolve more altruistically.

The prospective teachers' final superordinate constructs could help form the
basis of a program of first year induction. Grant and Zeichner (1981, p. 100)
report that carefully structured induction programs are minimal or non-existent.
Grids may better orient probationary or beginning teachers since they permit
them to indicate their views of, for example, themselves, pupils, and administrators. This would allow for support to be personalised.

The present methods of statistical analysis are acknowledged as descriptive.
Care was taken that explicit knowledge was not gained at the expense of personal

validity. The investigator sought the collaboration of the teachers in seeking to construe their constructions, and 11 of them have been heard in their own voices. This was to prevent the guided tour becoming too pale and ghostly a replica of the original exploratory experiences (Thomas, n.d., pp. 3–4).

Members of the Centre for the Study of Human Learning at Brunel University have stressed that caution must be exercised when drawing conclusions from grid studies. The grid remains a technique for accessing psychological processes that are not easily perceived. While it helps to focus individual perceptions, attempts to generalise towards collective meanings are hazardous. The mode grid perhaps most usefully provided, as shown in Table 3, a common referent with which each individual could compare his or her grid. As Harri-Augstein (1979) advises, grids are best used as a conversational heuristic for self-development.

In the present study the comparison of successive matrices and grids helped to focus the teachers' attention on how their constructions developed or remained unchanged. By exploring the personal principles of causality affecting the changes, they came to see themselves as full participants, able to use their unique positions as interpreters of their own perceptions. Bannister (1981, p. 254) writes that this capacity to reflect is both the source of a person's commentary on self and a central part of the experience of being a "self". Developing at least some understanding of how self-awareness develops and of the factors that may influence it are particularly crucial for teachers since the way that pupils see themselves depends upon the way they believe other people, and especially teachers, see them. Teachers need to reflect on the importance of their professional role in shaping the lives of pupils. By so doing they will monitor their own socialisation and development as well as that of children. The repertory grid is one way that teachers can focus their changing or static views of their role.

In teacher education where students are exposed to new ideas and to difficult, even traumatic situations, self-awareness is not simply important but vital. As Sonya concluded,

> I still feel so unready for next year. I feel so immature. Everyone else seems so much older or more experienced. I still feel like a learner rather than a teacher. I have a lot more learning to do. I want to make a firm commitment to teaching but it's such a responsibility. At least I've learned to take a good look at myself.

In contrast, Sam, the most consistently different construer, realised that he had not been receptive to the course or committed to it. He decided to teach in secondary school only until he could take up a full time position as an Army instructor. Not all trainees expect to make teaching a lifetime career.

Conclusion

Though not claiming to have defined a universal pattern in intending teachers' construing, overall trends have been usefully revealed, such as the final separation from pupils. The findings also endorse Salmon's (1976, pp. 38–39) com-

ments that the individuality corollary expresses the notion of individual uniqueness on construction systems and that just as content differs from one person to
another, so too do the directions of the detailed changes. It is precisely this
realisation that led many of the intending teachers to report greater clarity in
seeing themselves as altering, "mental travellers" (see Blake, 1805). This
awareness of the personal processes of construction enabled them to experiment
with and to change, in self-chosen ways, their own views of teaching. As
Bannister (1981, p. 261) writes, self-change needs to be based on self-know-
ledge:

> The stranger the country we are entering the more threatening the prospect becomes; the
> more we realise that some degree of self-change may be involved, the more we must rely
> upon our understanding of our own character and potential.

In order to choose, beginning teachers need as much support and insight as
possible. Pope (1978) found also that helping them to reflect on these developments is of great benefit to them. It may be that change can take place, and then
be accepted or rejected, only when individuals have a sharper picture of what
their own ideal looks like. As Sonya showed, by knowing what they are, they
can form an idea of what they would like to be, and by knowing that, they can
work towards it. In her last communication Mitzi wrote:

> Everyone was looking for something different and went about adjusting to their particu-
> lar perceived environments in different ways. However, the grid seemed to help most of
> us. To compare the three "snapshots" of my year in Dip.Ed. has been a much appreci-
> ated reflective experience for me. I came to terms with how as a person I felt about the
> prospect of teaching as a chosen career, what fears and anxieties I had in relation to
> teaching, as well as my perceptions of students. I came to see both what and how I saw.

If teachers can be helped to "open their eyes", they can see how to choose and
fashion their own version of reality. By repacking their past for whatever needs
arise, they can travel ahead in their own devices for observing and appraising.

References

Adams-Webber, J. and Mirc, E. (1976). Assessing the development of student teachers'
    role conceptions, *British Journal of Educational Psychology*, **46**, 338–380.
Bannister, D. (1981). Knowledge of Self. *In* "Psychology for Teachers" (D. Fontana,
    ed.), British Psychological Society, London.
Bannister, D. and Fransella, F. (1980). "Inquiring Man: The Psychology of Personal
    Constructs", Penguin, Harmondsworth.
Bannister, D. and Mair, J. M. M. (1968). "The Evaluation of Personal Constructs",
    Academic Press, London.
Blake, W. (1971). The Mental Traveller. *In* "The Poems of William Blake" (W. H.
    Stevenson, ed.), Longman, London, 1805, pp. 578–581.
Bradbury, R. (1961, July). How to keep and feed a muse, *The Writer*.

Diamond, C. T. P. (1981). "Beginning Teachers' Impressions of Their Initial Practicum", Unpublished paper, University of Queensland, Brisbane.

Eliot, T. S. (1944). "Four Quartets", Faber, London.

Fuller, F. F. (1969). Concerns of teachers: A developmental Conceptualisation, *American Educational Research Journal*, **6**, 2, 207–226.

Grant, C. A. and Zeichner, K. M. (1981). Inservice support for first year teachers, *Journal of Research and Development in Education*, **14**, 2, 99–111.

Harri-Augstein, E. S. (1979). "The Change Grid: A Conversational Heuristic for Self Development", Paper presented at the Third International Congress on Personal Construct Psychology, Utrecht.

Jarrell, R. (1964). "The Bat Poet", Collier, New York.

Kelly, G. A. (1955). "The Psychology of Personal Constructs", Vols. I and II, Norton, New York.

Pope, M. (1978). Monitoring and Reflecting in Teacher Training. *In* "Personal Construct Psychology 1977" (F. Fransella, ed.), Academic Press, London.

Radley, A. (1976). A practical approach to personal learning, *Psychology Teaching*, **4**, 1, 57–62.

Rosenhan, D. (1969). Some Origins of Concerns for Others. *In* "Trends and Issues in Developmental Psychology" (P. Mussen, J. Langer, and M. Covington, eds.), Holt, New York.

Salmon, P. (1976). Grid Measures with Child Subjects. *In* "Explorations of Intrapersonal Space" (P. Slater, ed.), Wiley, London.

Thomas, L. F. (1978). Learning and Meaning. *In* "Personal Construct Psychology 1977" (F. Fransella, ed.), Academic Press, London.

Thomas, L. F. (1979). Construct, Reflect, Converse. *In* "Constructs of Sociality and Individuality. (P. Stringer and D. Bannister, eds.), Academic Press, London.

Thomas, L. F. (n.d.). "Exploring Learning with the Grid", Centre for the Study of Human Learning, Brunel University, Uxbridge, Middlesex.

Thomas, L. F. (1976) "Focusing: Exhibiting the Meanings in a Grid", Centre for the Study of Human Learning, Brunel University, Uxbridge, Middlesex.

Thomas, L. F., McKnight, G., and Shaw, M. C. G. (1976). "Grids and Group Structure", Centre for the Study of Human Learning, Brunel University, Uxbridge, Middlesex.

3

Construing Control in
Theory and Therapy

Gavin Dunnett

Control is a word that conjures up immediate associations in most people's minds. It is one pole of a construct which can be contrasted with a wide variety of alternatives: "control versus disorganisation"; "control versus freedom"; "control versus emotion"; and so forth. To most people, I suspect, control gives the impression of order rather than chaos, of governability rather than anarchy, of a concentration of power rather than a dissipation of effort. Sometimes it may go further and invest these notions with implications of rigidity and restriction. Our language enhances these ideas by enshrining the word in key phrases—as in "being in control of oneself", "in control of one's destiny/fate", "having a controlling interest in a project or enterprise", "being at the controls of a car, aeroplane, or whatever", and so forth. In each situation the possession of this quality "control" enables something to happen. Without it disorder reigns, power dissolves, and the ability to achieve desired ends vanishes. In literature too, the word takes on a symbolic significance. The Control in the Le Carré "Smiley" novels is the apparent hub of activity, the source point of all decisions and actions. In Orwell's *1984,* although the notion of control is not explicitly defined, the negative aspects of an all-powerful state unresponsive to personal whim and fancy clearly outline the view of the effects of control.

It is perhaps this ambivalence of emotion associated with control that seems to have made it, and the psychological processes associated with it, one of the least written about areas of personal construct psychology. For if the essence of Kelly's theory is that individuals predict and experiment with their worlds in order to make sense of events around them, then the process by which they choose which prediction to make and which experiment to enact must be fundamental. The theme that we are not "victims of our biography", that we can *choose* which direction we take in our lives places great emphasis on this process of choice and the way we make our decisions. Indeed the great cry of the "free" society is that choice is available; and not only is it available, but more importantly, it is enactable. Kelly underlines this importance by his introduction of a choice corollary into the primary structure of his theory. He defines *choice* thus: "A person chooses for himself that alternative in a dichotomised construct

ISSUES AND APPROACHES
IN PERSONAL CONSTRUCT THEORY

37

through which he anticipates the greater possibility for extension and definition of his system'' (p. 561). This question of choice is of vital significance in the theory, but although a variety of alternatives may exist, it is only the possibility of putting them to the test that makes them ''real'' for that individual person.

Personal construct theory is based upon the philosophy of constructive alternativism (that is, the possibility of making sense out of any given situation in a whole variety of alternative ways). Thus there is no guarantee that two people will make sense of—construe—the same event similarly. Included in the basis of this philosophical approach is both the uniqueness of the individual and an optimistic view of the possibility of change. It is, however, the belief in the existence of the ability to take control and *do* something that converts this philosophy to a psychology for living. Without any doubt, control is a key issue in personal construct psychology, and as such, merits further and fuller explanation. It can be approached from at least two angles (constructive alternativism suggests more but space is limited!): that of the theory as it is already written and expounded, and that of the problems faced by clients in therapy where issues of decision making and action are concerned. Hopefully, these diverse reflections on the same landscape will serve not to define but better to raise further issues that every individual can consider in the light of their own experience.

Control exists in personal construct theory in two forms. First, it appears as the final stage of a cycle of construing that Kelly called the (CPC) circumspection–pre-emption–control cycle; and, second, it exists as a psychological state which can be examined in its own right and with its own implications for therapy.

The *CPC cycle* is defined as ''a sequence of construction involving in succession circumspection, pre-emption and control, and leading to a choice which precipitates the person into a particular situation'' (565). Within the theory, this is the psychological process of coming to a decision. This is the mechanics of making choices, an issue which Boxer (1982) discusses in relation to the choice corollary. He makes the point that construct systems not only have two-dimensional hierarchy but also three-dimensional depth. He describes various levels of construing as part of that depth and then postulates the CPC cycle as a cycle moving in that third dimensional plane (as opposed to the creativity cycle which moves in the hierarchical plane). This approach certainly elaborates the implications of making a choice but does not seem to help much in the practical understanding of how choices are made psychologically.

Broadly, circumspection involves reviewing the alternatives available, pre-emption reduces these alternatives to two contrasting possibilities, and control involves the choice of one of these possibilities upon which to base future action. The purpose of the whole cycle is to lead to a state of control without which action is impossible. Reaching control allows the person to experiment with the pole of the pre-empted construct he has chosen, and this then validates or invalidates the underlying hypothesis. It must be emphasised that control does not lead inexorably to action. In Kelly's terms, it ''precipitates the person into a particular situation'' (p. 565). A controlled decision to travel to America by aeroplance does not demand that the person immediately lift off. Various other decisions have to be made before that event occurs. But a ''particular situation'' has been reached; the person now knows that tickets must be bought, luggage weighed, and so forth. It might be worth mentioning here that one theoretical problem which may occur is that the person, having reached control on some major issue, may then proceed to act with no regard to the other, but also important, factors involved. This would be like deciding to fly to America one minute and setting off for the airport the next (leaving job, wife, cat, and a cake in the oven . . .). Such people might be described as ''blinkered'', perpetually wondering why decisions made apparently quite sensibly fail abysmally in practice. This kind of activity is part of the group of disorders, called impulsivity, of the CPC cycle as a whole; it is, however, the only form of impulsivity to be caused by faulty use of the control phase of the cycle.

Control therefore is the stage needing to be reached to enable action—behaviour–experiment to occur. It terminates the decision-making process but does not, of itself, demand action: it may instead demand that further CPC cycles occur before action takes place. Action, however, depends on control and as Kelly writes,'' All behaviour may be seen as controlled'' (p. 927). He goes further than this, though, by arguing that all behaviour is based ultimately on construing and construct systems, and therefore ''in a sense . . . all disorders of construction are disorders which involve faulty control'' (p. 927). But if this is so, it is important to look at the relationship of a person's construct system to control in its own right. What sort of state is control; what is implied by being there; and what problems may arise?

Kelly describes control both as the final state of the CPC cycle and as one pole of a professional construct in its own right. The contrast pole is either less available for application to events or has been excluded by continued revision of his construing (that is, submerged or suspended), and seems occasionally to change in emphasis. Nonetheless he makes some definite statements about control, which need to be examined. At one point he defines it as ''an aspect of the relationship between a superordinate construct and the subordinate constructs which constitute its context'' (p. 926). This seems to mean that given a controlled pole of a pre-empted construct, the kinds of experiments and the psychological significance attached to it will depend not only on that construct, but also upon the superordinate which subsumes it. To return to the travel analogy, although a decision to fly to America may have been reached (assuming that other operational decisions are not causing problems), it may not simply be enough to approach the first airline office in the street and purchase a ticket. Other, more superordinate constructs may be involved. For example, the traveller may be determined to ''buy British versus foreign''; he or she may feel charter flights are ''less well maintained versus reliable'' then scheduled ones; and further, the traveller may not wish to fly with an airline that is backed by some abhorred political regime. Although the second of these constructs has a direct and obvious bearing on our traveller's safety (is this always an important superordinate, though?), the others are clearly superordinate constructs related to much wider aspects of life than travel plans.

Although the CPC cycle may start by viewing a range of constructs propositionally, and may successfully pre-empt one of them, it is only at the control stage of the cycle that the pre-empted construct's position within the whole system is assessed and taken into consideration. I discuss later the problems that occur when faulty use of superordinate implications occur, especially when these are brought into the cycle before the control phase. My point here is that it is at the control stage that they can be successfully incorporated into the decision-making process. Once control is reached, although a decision is made, and a course of action planned, the operation of this course of action has to be looked at in the context of the position of the construct in relation to its superordinates. Conversely it seems reasonable to postulate the reverse position; that is, when deciding amongst more superordinate constructs, the subordinates will have to be considered at the point of control. In the process of deciding always to "buy British", a person has to examine what this will mean for him in practical terms—what kind of person, for him, is one who always buys British. To act upon a controlled construct without consideration of its context, be it superordinate or subordinate, is a little bit like crossing a road without looking left or right; an accident will almost certainly ensue. Control is thus the point of interaction between a chosen line of action and its superordinate and subordinate implications, as well as the different "levels" of construing described by Boxer (1982).

Given the interactive nature of control, different kinds of action may be theoretically predicted from different types of (and indeed absence of) superordinate constructs. When a person is described by others as having controlled behaviour, what is usually meant is that his or her day-to-day actions are clearly governed by long-term ideas; in order to achieve a desired goal, all minor matters are considered subordinately to it. Thus a person who has an ambition to be a professor of clinical psychology might see all other activities in his or her life as subordinated to this overriding goal; work, relationships, leisure, and so forth would all be geared towards this ambition. Such a course of action would be highly controlled. By contrast, a person with a more hedonistic structure, or even minimal or no superordinate structure at all[1] would be more inclined to act out

---

[1]As with all examples based upon extreme positions, there is some element of conjecture. It is difficult, if not impossible, to imagine someone with "no superordinate structure" at all. Indeed if you take the view that any construct that is superordinate to its subordinate is "superordinate structure", then it is hard to imagine a person with only a single level of constructs and no superordinate of any kind. Clinically, however, there are clients whose system, while having some hierarchy, is restricted to concrete practical objectives. The pattern is restricted and exclusive and the problems that occur in reflection occur less or not at all. It is therefore more correct to say "absence of abstract superordinates" rather than a literal one-dimensional construct system as a whole.

the control phase immediately and with no apparent long-term theme evident. This might well be described as impulsive behaviour although it should not be confused with impulsivity (this being the foreshortening of the CPC cycle as a whole). This impulsive behaviour has some of the characteristics of playfulness about it; pick up a construct and run—where and why do not matter. Behaviour here seems uncontrolled and possibly irrational (depending upon the viewer's own system). It is an interesting digression to consider how in different sub-cultures of our society, different kinds of construing are more or less valued; the view of class, for example, seems in many ways to reflect different usages of control as well as differing superordinates themselves. In some jobs, long-term goals are encouraged, while in others short-term gain is the order of the day. Indeed our industrial management–worker problems might well be rooted in different forms of using control, and a lack of construing of each others' resulting behaviour. However, this is a detour, albeit interesting, which serves as an additional example of the importance of understanding control.

However, not only is control affected by the content of superordinate construing, it is also significantly affected by the quality of those superordinates. Provided a blind dash across a busy road is ruled out, then it will make a difference if the superordinates are loose or tight, permeable or impermeable, and so forth. Of the variables, the relative permeability seems to be one of the most important. Increased permeability in a construct enables it to absorb new elements which the construct has not previously been used for. Where superordinate constructs are concerned, permeability is an essential quality which enables a person to deal with the ever-changing events in his daily life. If the person's superordinate structure has to be altered every time something "new" occurs, then the process of adapting to new events would be slow and painful. Indeed in some people this is precisely the case, but for most of us, our superordinates are permeable enough to deal with new elements as they arise. A further aspect of permeability and control is contained in the modulation corollary: "The variation in a person's construct system is limited by the permeability of the constructs within whose range of convenience the variants lie". Clearly if permeability is limited, the variation in the system is also limited, and further, if this is true at a superordinate level, the variation in possible actions resulting from control will also be limited. Thus, through control, the modulation corollary applies directly to behaviour, and the issue of superordinate permeability becomes critical in therapeutic encounters. A client with highly permeable superordinate structures will both be able to circumspect amongst a wider range of possible constructs than his or her impermeable counterpart, and the client will also be able to maintain a long-term course of action more easily. The highly controlled long-cycle experimenter is likely to have permeable superordinates; whilst the impulsive short-cycle person, given the existence of any adequate superordinate structure at all, is likely to have impermeable superordinates. In clinical practice, this variation between long- and short-term experimenters is not often so marked, and it is important when laddering important constructs to make some attempts to assess the permeability of the abstract superordinates. Facility for change in therapy depends on some permeability as the therapeutic encounter itself is a new element requiring incorporation into the client's system.

The second important variant in superordinate quality is looseness–tightness. It is worth mentioning here that the CPC cycle bears some resemblance to the creativity cycle (a cycle which starts with loosened construction and ends with tightened and validated construction.) To validate tight construing, control must be reached, but the similarity is superficial. One may circumspect, pre-empt, and indeed take control with either loose or tight constructs, and the process of taking control is not equivalent to tightening. Control is important in relation to creativity in that the purpose of the creativity cycle is to provide new constructs with which to construe new events, and such construction is ultimately dependent upon an ability to enact experiments. It is said that tight construers are "doers" but this is only true if the CPC cycle works efficiently; if a tight construer cannot achieve control, the value of the creativity cycle may well be lost. With respect to the superordinate structure, however, a tight but permeable system allows the maximum use of the CPC cycle and therefore leads to greater ease of control; a loose but permeable system might well lead to ease of control but uncertainty would soon happen as the context seemed to change; the most difficult combination with which to work would be a loose and impermeable superordinate structure leading to both rejection of, and confusion in face of, new elements.

One further relationship needs mentioning: that of constriction and control. So far the only route to control has been via the CPC cycle—the process of choice. In some cases this choice may seem impossible and yet some action appears necessary. Here a process of constriction may take the place of both the circumspection and pre-emption phases of the cycle. A constricted construct remains, with one pole suspended, and this can then be used to take control. Such situations may occur in severely fragmented systems where the alternatives have no common superordinate structure within which a choice is meaningful. This is the position of "if I do this, x will happen; while if I do that, y will" where neither x nor y seem a desirable outcome. Here the tendency may be to constrict the system until only one possible choice remains, and then to take control from that. This approach has several disadvantages but effectively avoids major reconstruction of superordinate structure. The sight of someone clearly constricting their system in order to facilitate action should immediately alert the therapist to the possibility of mutually incompatible superordinates warring amongst themselves.

One final point needs to be made in the theoretical consideration of control; this is that control is but one pole of a professional construct. It may also therefore be defined to some extent by its *contrast pole*. So some view of what the contrast pole might be should be useful. Kelly himself considers the construct of "control versus spontaneity" but dismisses this by saying that both a controlled person and a spontaneous person are psychologically doing the same things, and since control is per se a psychological construct it encompasses both viewpoints. The most obvious remaining possibility is that of "control versus lack of control". In this case, what would a person who showed lack of control be like? If lack of control were total, he would be dead: no action or behaviour of any kind would be possible. But if it were less than absolute, then there might be some marked diminution in the ability to make decisions, and most activity would stop. The two states that seem to go some way towards exemplifying this in clinical psychiatry might be a severe retarded depression and a catatonic schizophrenia. Indeed a client with the symptoms of this last diagnosis shows almost no control at all and is, for long periods, almost totally malleable by the environment.

So far we have viewed control from a theoretical aspect: construing it in relation to Kelly's writings and anticipating certain possible problems if it is not achieved. The alternative is to look at a few common problems from the clinical standpoint and consider where faulty control may be important. It is my contention (prediction) that an understanding of control is essential for a therapist, and this understanding in turn enables him or her to subsume the client's system. For the sake of argument and brevity I have chosen three hypothetical problems/ issues. A person is unable to make a decision; a person makes repeated immediate or apparently thoughtless decisions; and the interesting question of habit arises.

We have all experienced times in our lives when we have said "I can't decide". For some people such a state is endemic—they are classified as indecisive and are usually scorned for it. Decisiveness seems to be valued in our society. What might be happening when someone says they cannot decide about an issue, or worse, they cannot make decisions at all? From our theoretical discussion, we predict that a state of control is not being reached, at least not satisfactorily. This may be due either to faulty application of the CPC cycle or to problems arising at the point of control. Our client may be stuck in circumspection, endlessly revolving around a treadmill of alternatives unable to pre-empt a major issue to resolve the crisis. Alternatively he or she may have reached pre-emption only to be denied the final stage by the apparent incompatibility of the choices they have presented themselves with. The point in the CPC cycle at which superordinate/subordinate contexts are considered in relation to the element under question seems to be the critical issue. Control itself is defined, as we have seen, as a relationship between the superordinate and subordinate constructs which define its contexts. It is at the point of control that these limiting implications should be considered. In other words, the superordinate structure associated with all the propositional constructs in circumspection, and with pre-emption, are irrelevant to the issue. Presented with a problem, all possibilities should be considered and the process adhered to. Once a final choice is made, *then* the limitations placed upon it by the superordinate can be considered. To return again to our intrepid traveller: it is only once he or she has chosen to fly that the political/moral questions come into consideration. To have introduced them at the circumspection phase introduces the propositional nature that "I could fly" but it might be with an airline I don't approve of. It is too early in the process to deal effectively with such implications. Further, matters may become worse once pre-emption takes place because the contrasting poles of the pre-empted construct may themselves be mutually incompatible. Flying might involve a terrible airline, while not flying might involve being late. Both superordinate systems may be important but unconnected. Only by allowing the process to advance as far as control can our traveller be prepared to deal with the wider more fundamental issues of his decision. Once having decided to fly, he must attempt to reconcile that decision with this superordinate context. And this is not forgetting that the final choice made will be the one most likely to elaborate and extend the system (choice corollary). Even though the final decision to fly may bring about a confrontation with a phobia about flying, this could lead to treatment being sought for it and so to a successful elaboration. Earlier consideration of such a superordinate would have blocked control, maintained the status quo, and elaborated nothing! Clearly therefore the review of superordinate context before control is reached is likely to inhibit action and behaviour. Not only are all alternatives weighed up, but so are all possible consequences. Almost inevitably, even in the best organised most integrated systems, conflicts arise which themselves require control to solve. In this state it behoves the therapist to act as simplifier, encouraging the client to disregard implications of his choices until he has reached control. Many clients with work problems have this kind of difficulty; often there is a strong superordinate related to continuing work or being successful and so forth. They become inhibited about considering the problem as it presents. One client, repeatedly depressed about a thankless and exhausting job simply refused to give it up because it was a "helping" job and being a "helping" person was a superordinate core role construct. Eventually she allowed herself to decide that she wanted to give up her job (take control of the issue) and then embarked on consideration of the operational issues involved—income, filling her time . . . and how to continue to be "helping". The important point about control is that it is the basis *from which* to act; it is not action itself. In order to discover how to do something, you have first to reach the point of knowing what it is that you want to do. Frequent consideration of the superordinate context during circumspection and pre-emption of the CPC cycle prevents that knowing.

The second clinical problem mentioned was that of immediate decisions.

Kelly discusses the question of impulsivity in some detail, as the foreshortening of the CPC cycle, but it is not impulsivity as such that is here the issue. Take a client, Andrew—for him, the most important fact about himself is that he was an illegitimate child. Everything is viewed, reacted to, and related to with this powerful superordinate in mind. Everyone is judged on an "illegitimate versus legitimate" construct, and its wide frame of subordinate constructs. Not only people, however, are caught in this mesh: events, objects and activities—all are subsumed in some way under this (what now becomes evident) highly permeable superordinate. For Andrew, therefore, decisions are surprisingly simple. He has only to take control and the context of action is always defined. Whole series of acts and behaviours in his life are carried out solely on the basis of this one viewpoint. In one sense for Andrew there is never any choice: he always does what this one theme of his life demands. Other clients do this in different ways— an all-encompassing religious view and being an adopted child are two recent client issues that come to mind as having similar consequences. This is not to say that such superordinates are wrong; what it does mean, however, is that *all* control is set in one context, and one theme alone defines all living. Here, a lesser degree of permeability of the construct, and a wider range of superordinates with which to work, may allow more variable responses and a wider range of action following control. In the case of Andrew, he eventually succeeded in construing himself in other ways equally important to "illegitimate versus legitimate" and so managed to restrict both the range of convenience and the permeability of the construct. Some clients are in even greater difficulty because their single all powerful superordinate is also pre-verbal (and by pre-verbal here I mean before the acquisition of language as opposed to non-verbal constructs acquired after language but with no verbal label.) Clients with a highly permeable, pre-verbal construct operating exclusively, present as demanding, manipulative, and impossible to please. It doesn't matter what you do, it is never enough. Here again the principle is the same: their control needs different contexts in which to act, and the creation of a more appropriate range of superordinates is a priority in therapy.

Third, the question of habit seems important. Clients often present asking for help in breaking a habit; or early in the course of therapy some activity is seen by them to be undesirable. Not only in therapy, however, is habit important. In daily life too it has its place. Whether you squeeze the toothpaste from the end of the tube or the middle may only be a habit, but if the apocryphal story is right, it may lead to the end of your marriage. So what is a habit? By now it will be clear that habit has to relate to control in some way, but since a person may have (will have) many different habits in different situations, it cannot be compared with the immediate decision-making process discussed previously. Nonetheless, in some situations, apparently repetitive behaviour is carried out almost regardless of whether or not it is appropriate. Kelly speaks of habit as an increasingly foreshortened circumspection phase with ultimately a reduced level of cognitive awareness. (A low level of cognitive awareness constructs implies that there is poor expression in socially effective symbols; that there are inaccessible alternatives; that the constructs are outside the range of convenience of the client's major constructions; and that there is possible suspension by superordinating constructs). This however suggests that the CPC cycle is still being used as a base for the action and that cognitive awareness is lost. This appears to be a rather complicated set of events for such a frequent activity, and an alternative view would be to consider the possibility that habits are formed by achieving control by constriction rather then by circumspection. Instead of viewing all possibilities and increasingly foreshortening circumspection, the person simply reduces his perceptual field drastically and acts accordingly. The antidote to bad habits therefore is not necessarily to encourage circumspection (that is, to ask the question—how else can I do this?) but to encourage dilation, that is, to broaden his perceptual field in order to reorganise it on a more comprehensive level. In other words, to ask the question—what is going on when I do this? By broadening the perceptual field, the inappropriateness of the habit may become evident and at that point new circumspection can begin. It seems that this is the process that takes place in many forms of behavioural treatment for unwanted habits such as phobias or obsessions. A client is encouraged to broaden his perceptions by actually doing things differently. Once the field has dilated somewhat, then a new cycle of circumspection, pre-emption, and ultimate control can take place. The problems of unwanted habits are most probably combinations of constriction and foreshortening of the cycle. Approaches which look at one or the other in isolation may turn out in the long run to be ineffective.

I have attempted to consider the role of control in both theory and therapy. It is not (nor could it ever be) a comprehensive review, but it may bring to the forefront of thought and discussion one area of personal construct theory that has been conspicuous by its absence from the accumulated writings around the theory. To reiterate: the issue of control is of vital importance because control is the link between thought and action; between anticipation and experiment. In practical terms, it is the lynch pin of personal construct psychology psychotherapy.

References

Boxer, P. J. (1982) The Flow of Choice: The Choice Corollary. *In* "The Construing Person" (J. C. Mancuso and J. R. Adams-Webber), Praeger, New York.

Kelly, G. A. (1955) "The Psychology of Personal Constructs" (Vols. I and II), Norton, New York.

4

Learning-to-Learn Languages: New Perspectives for the Personal Observer

Sheila Harri-Augstein

Education and Learning by Experience

To a greater or lesser degree all humans share a capacity to learn by experience. This frees us as a species more than any known other, to take greater control of the direction, quality, and content of our lives. Ultimately, through our personal destinies, we contribute to the "mindpool" (Harri-Augstein, 1978, p. 87) of our culture and so to the evolution of our societies and our species. In a society which is forced to review its deepest social attitudes and institutions, an ability to go on learning through the process of living is needed in order to participate in changes, to adapt to them, and to creatively influence them. Unless this capacity is widespread, society will inevitably re-stabilize into malfunctioning and unacceptable systems.

At a superficial level this is widely acknowledged, but, as yet, education is only fumbling towards a methodology by which it can be effectively achieved. The sandwich system, project work, and open learning offer opportunities for learning by experience but in themselves do not embody a model for learning to learn. These discovery and guided approaches offer some freedom to learn, but their products, i.e., the report, a personal essay, or even art work are nevertheless traditionally assessed by "the experts" in their own terms. Those maverick learners who have taught themselves how to learn go on to develop their capacity to learn by experience and take off in ways which enable them to create effective opportunities for learning in life. Generally, however, on the educational escalator, the flair demonstrated by the pre-school child and the self-taught learner becomes stunted. Common pathologies include a sparse range of underdeveloped skills which have consolidated into fixed habits. Partly because of the social and educational climate, mediocre skills are viewed as innate or environmentally determined and therefore unchangeable. For any improvement to take place, education must enable people to learn to get in touch with their own learning processes in ways which can free them from self-perpetuating cycles of behaviour. How can this be achieved?

The study of how humans learn raises fundamental issues, some of which are now being faced by cyberneticians and computer engineers in their approach to expert systems and knowledge engineering (Pask, 1976; Thomas 1978). Psychology is also beginning to develop a technology of its own which can help to transform the quality of human learning. Systematic methods for encouraging learners to develop awareness of how they learn and to review the success of their learning are being developed, and there is already sufficient evidence that people can significantly enhance their capacity to learn (Thomas and Harri-Augstein, 1982a,b; Harri-Augstein and Thomas 1979b). Self-organised learners who have been enabled to learn to learn can stroll around the system of public meaning or mindpool and remain free to interact and influence it in personally meaningful ways. In such transactions they value the process of learning at least as much as the content. For them learning is an enriching experience; the meanings that emerge become personally significant in some part of their lives. The viability of these meanings depends on how richly the individual incorporates them into his or her experiences.

Inarticulate Learners and Personal Myths

People of all ages, professions, and status are by and large inarticulate about their own learning processes. When invited to describe how they learn, they are either struck dumb or fumble towards some statement which systematic scrutiny can easily reveal to be wildly inaccurate. Worse even, some give very lucid accounts which have very little bearing on the ways in which they control (or do not control) the process. Many struggle to learn, being vague about their aims and purposes and believing that learning is something which happens to them, and since the assessment of learning is done by someone else (the experts), the best they can do is successfully submit to being taught.

In therapy, emotional and attitudinal illiteracy is universally acknowledged, and most forms of treatment from Freud to Kelly and Rogers offer techniques for raising the awareness of the person in process. Most therapeutic models are based on ways for psychologist and client, sometimes more the former than the latter, to develop appropriate descriptions of the self in process—descriptions which can then be recruited to free the knotted and disabled sufferer. Education assumes that, beyond the primary years, people should ''know'' how to learn, so the teaching system gets on with what it sees to be its job: instruction in the subject matter. When it becomes obvious that little learning is taking place, the individual is either discarded as an inferior robot or selected out for special treatment by the remedial tutor or educational psychologist. In the mainstream of education, only the gifted teacher cajoles the learner to develop greater awareness and so enhance the quality of learning. The premises on which psychotherapy is based can be applied to learning, as Kelly (1955) and Rogers (1969) have clearly shown. But in its obsession with the *content* of learning, education has ignored (if not eradicated) the individual's natural capacity to learn how to learn.

PERSONAL MYTHS

In an initial statement about how they learn, students volunteer such statements as

I learn the usual way
I learn by trial and error; I try over and over again
I learn in short bursts
I either can or can't learn something
I don't really know what I do
I always concentrate on the important bits
I go for the rules, there's no more to it

Such replies often reveal personal myths which deeply influence how people learn. For example, some cannot concentrate without a background of music: Bach, Ellington, Led Zeppelin can all be thought to help (or hinder) the process of learning. One student moved five times during his examination term because he had convinced himself that swotting for his exams had to take place in total silence. Most easily articulated myths are about these conditions of learning. They are concerned with sitting up, lying down, being on one's own, working with others, taking regular breaks to smoke or drink, and so forth. Following careful elicitation, deeper myths begin to emerge. Using biographical, repertory grid, or structures of meaning procedures (Harri-Augstein, 1978) learners can be aided to identify their tacit assumptions, prejudices, and understanding of their own learning processes. Often these are associated with their own innate incapacities. They feel that they have no talent for maths or dancing, for writing, manual tasks, chess, or learning foreign languages. One student who found it impossible to reproduce pronunciations of simple French words, finally remembered that in his first term at grammar school he had to stand on his desk and demonstrate to the class how *not* to say *le pupitre*. Deeper still, personal myths about intelligence, personality, and learning style emerge. Such myths operate at the level of "personal magic" and block any attempt to develop and change.

Interestingly, convictions about the process of learning tend to be either vague or fragmented and give little indication that an awareness of process is being recruited for flexibility and growth.

I have to write it down to really understand it
I learn best by listening carefully
I first skim, then scan, to learn by reading
I learn through visual images
When I learn, I throw out most of it as rubbish and decide very carefully what I
  commit to memory.

The last example was elicited from a mature student who was convinced that his memory was of a fixed capacity, and for every new item he learned, he would have to forget one already committed to memory. In real life, this myth about his own learning process coloured most of his activities as a student.

The increased capacity that results from recognising that one's mode of learning is not fixed, nor is it a genetic built-in characteristic of us all, can become a quantum leap in personal learning. All that is needed is a system whereby all the bits of information can be brought together into a coherent language to reflect upon the whole process. In our terminology, people need to invent a representative language for satisfactorily communicating about the process of learning, that is, a *meta language for learning to learn* (Harri-Augstein and Thomas, 1979b).

Many personal learning myths become a handicap to effective learning. For instance if a learner believes that learning is to do with the reception of instruction, he or she is not going to value personal experience, and no amount of exposure to enriched environments will change his or her stance. Often many of the most disabling myths are clothed as positive personal attributes, such as toughness, femininity, common sense, logic, and so forth. In themselves, any or all of these can be positive when they describe certain potential for personal learning. They become counter-productive when formulated as the absence of personal learning abilities which are derided in others and suppressed in oneself. For self-organised learners who are not caught up in their own myths, living becomes an opportunity for learning, but how it is used depends on what they bring to each event and what they make of each experience. This is true of reading a book, relating to a marriage partner, entering a new job, preparing for finals, living on one's own, attending a lecture, or participating in an encounter group.

In one sense personal myths about learning, that is, a mix of metaphor, analogy, observation, and self-validating hypothesis, do not differ from the majority of myths about the human race, nor do they differ from those of the majority of psychologists and educators. Luria, Bruner, Piaget, Rogers, Socrates, and Kelly hold myths about learning, and the controversy about the relative merits of their myths has hidden the more interesting congruence that each client (or student) constructs a viable myth of their own.

Diminishing educational resources, open learning systems, youth training schemes, and demands for retraining are challenging educators to reconsider their myths about teaching. Such schemes depend on learners who have the capacity to continue learning adaptively when formal instruction and training has ceased. Learning by experience has to be formally recognised as a core process which needs to be systematically studied and sensitively managed and encouraged (Harri-Augstein and Thomas, 1978).

Learning on the Job

"Sitting by Nellie" can be a most rewarding experience. If Nellie knows her job and the learner knows how to ask the right questions, both can learn much.

An obsessive concern with measuring the effectiveness of training coupled with a partly misplaced belief in behavioural objectives has blinded trainers to people's ability to learn for themselves, from experience. Nellie may be inspecting the quality of colour TVs, supervising a production section, developing new products, running an office, handling an advertising account, managing a buying department, directing a research team, managing a complete company, or even training trainers. At any level and in all areas of specialism, working alongside an expert is a superb opportunity.

LEARNING A MANUAL SKILL

The results of a research project sponsored by the Industrial Training Board of the hotel & catering industry illustrate the idea of "self-organised learning" (Thomas and Snapes, 1968). As a representative sample of a catering skill which appeared to be simple although reported as notoriously difficult to acquire and maintain at an adequate quality level, we selected "making an omelette". A lecturer-chef from a school of catering helped us to produce a series of film loops illustrating the process of making omelettes. These films were organised hierarchically at four levels of detail. The single film at Level 1 showed the whole process of preparing and cooking. Four loops at Level 2 illustrated preparing the materials, mixing, cooking, and serving. At Level 3 detailed skills such as whisking an egg, heating the pan, and folding an omelette required eight loops, and at Level 4 fourteen motor co-ordinations (often referred to as knacks) were spelled out, for example, cracking an egg one-handed, holding the fork for whisking.

The trainees in the experiment were a group of teenagers from a local school unacquainted with cooking and catering. They were left to learn to make omelettes on their own, being provided with the following resources: (1) a set of magazine-packed film loops, a quick loading film projector, and a simple guidebook; (2) all necessary ingredients and equipment, including a cooker; and (3) a panel of judges who evaluated each omelette. The results were interesting. The performances of these learners fell into two (statistically) distinct groups. One group learned quickly and easily, rapidly reaching criteria. The other group learned only very slowly. The first group used the film loops effectively, following up their own experience and the comments of the judge. They diagnosed their own weaknesses by selecting and studying the appropriate film illustrations. These we designated the self-organised learners. The other group used seemingly random, trial and error approaches. These we designated as disabled learners.

A matched control group were taught the same skill by an orthodox lecture-demonstration followed by supervised practicals. The lecturer–chef was highly motivated to prove his effectiveness as a trainer. The performance of this group fell squarely between that of the two experimental groupings. Thus the predetermined structures offered by the trainer seemed to impede the self-organised learners and to help the disabled ones.

The film loops can be seen as a passive Nellie-like resource that had to be interrogated and interpreted. "Learning from Nellie" involved knowing how to do this. This experiment merely spells out what many of us have experienced with apprentices, sandwich course students, and management trainees. Some make much better use of their learning opportunities than others. The terms *intelligent* and *stupid* are widely misused to describe this difference. The idealised view of the top management seminar is as much over-simplified as the assumption that all omelette makers require detailed step-by-step instruction. Training at all levels must allow for some component of self-organisation in learning. Unfortunately, training usually involves accepting the trainer's purpose, going along with his or her selection and ordering of the material, and submitting to his or her measures of success. Being instructed requires the suspension of judgment. Self-organised learners may or may not do well at school, at college, or in the training department. Indeed, they are often represented as a disruptive influence on the conveyor belt of education and training. It will depend upon the extent to which their purposes include or overlap with those of the teachers and trainers. What they can do is to learn from experience. Thus they go on learning when the others stop. They are able to define their own purposes, devise their own strategies and tactics, and assess success in their own terms.

STRUCTURES OF MEANING AND THE CREATIVE PROCESS

Applying the reflective learning technology in the form of the structures of meaning procedure (Harri-Augstein, 1978) to enhance the creative process has successfully enabled certain experts to explore the frontiers of knowledge in the domain of their speciality. A senior training advisor in the civil service, briefed to design a new national open system of learning; a training manager responsible for radically restructuring industrial training programmes within an International Company; a research director of a pharmaceutical company selecting high risk drug design projects; and a chemistry professor, eminent in the field of catalysis and surface chemistry, have each been assisted to explore the scope of their topic, to identify the nature of the problem, to generate alternative solutions, and to plan a subsequent course of action, in systematic, yet for each, refreshingly open and creative ways. Brain storming on the edge of their knowledge and experience and reflecting upon the structured representations of their own understanding, in each case, enabled them to make personally significant forward moves.

Professor X, in exploring the dimensions of the problem involved in communicating with colleagues about issues of surface chemistry, was confronted with the inadequacy of conventional methods for representing sophisticated chemical processes. The complexity of the dynamics of change could not be satisfactorily captured within existing forms.

By means of content-free procedures, descriptive items were elicited relating to this topic. Various forms of representative systems were identified and associated with the epistemological advance of chemistry. Each representation became elaborated, modifed, but eventually inadequate as questions about the subject could no longer be fully formulated, nor possible answers fully represented out of the existing symbolic components. New systems were evolved to represent the expanding domain of chemical explanation more adequately. Categories of representations were identified from verbal, symbolic, structural, and transitional states, and from time sequenced phase patterns to reality models (e.g., hooks on the surface of molecules). Explanations about their respective attributes as effective forms of representation and communication emerged. Attributes such as *kinetics, speed, valency, types of bonds, specificity, energy dimensions,* and *physical transformations* were clarified. It became clear that the history of chemistry could be traced in the development or extensions of appropriate categories of symbolic representations of the subject matter. Items spanning different aspects of the topic were generally elicited, and the elicitation process was reflected on as it shifted in intention and direction. The elicitor guided the "creative learner" to reflect upon areas of doubt, provisionality, certainty, specificity, functionality, and applicability; upon logical, evaluative, and inferential construings; and upon different aspects and levels of organisation of the topic; and to consider alternative representations as well as grey, submerged, and less-differentiated areas. The conversational encounter enabled psychologist and client to take better control of the meta-process involved in this creative problem-solving encounter. Pre-emptive, constellatory, and core issues were recognised, and gradually the client got to grips with those aspects of the problem which had hitherto eluded his conscious scrutiny. Items relating to "strategies for achieving more satisfactory representations" were then elicited and reflected upon as well as items dealing with "criteria for effectiveness" as valued by himself, colleagues and chemistry as a whole.

Insights into the relationship between representations and objective reality became a topic for discussion. In this context relativistic and functional aspects of representations were explored and evaluated. As the topic was elaborated and reflected upon, additional explanations and further inferences emerged. Was chemistry as a domain of knowledge and experience a language within its own right? Was this language essentially verbal or best expressed in more formal terms? What were the syntactic and semantic rules for formal representational structures? How do these relate to the periodic table? Was there a private language in chemistry in the same sense as the "personal signatures" of artists and composers of musical scores?

The negotiation of needs and purposes released clusters of items relating to "private" representations invented whilst struggling with specific problems of catalysis. Comparisons were made between these and conventional representations. A private language used as aids to the imagination and aids to communication, when searching for points of growth at the edge of what was known in this important area of industrial chemistry, became the focus of review and contemplation. Grey, non-expressable areas were identified, and when participant were pushed or cajoled to reflect on these, one session led to an impasse where demands of teaching and managing the department set other priorities for personal effort. In another session a process of search and reflection at a deeper level was set in motion. Was it laziness, overanxiety, insecurity about one's own creative ability which led to a blocking off of some of the real issues? When asked directly "how did the fuzzy grey areas affect his own research?", the answer was that he "tended to slip sideways" to other "important but more handleable problems"—and "there were plenty of these to keep one busy". One grey area led eventually to a discussion about new technologies: computer graphic displays capable of representing multi-causal and three-dimensional dynamic structural processes were appraised as "possibly leading to ideal solutions", and as "fantasies remote from reality" and "trendy but not necessarily useful". In counterpoint, more familiar and simpler two-dimensional representations were valued as "aids to communication" on courses and conferences when "you did not have your expensive high tech computer with you." This led to an agreement that interpretation was a personal process, since what may appear simple to an expert could be as meaningless as a Chinese hexagram to an A-level student untutored in inorganic catalysis or I Ching. *An understanding of chemistry depended on analogy, metaphor, visual imagery, and anecdotes as much as any other domain of knowledge or language with its agreed boundaries.*

Some of the core meta-issues which emerged for further reflection included (1) When can a representational system be no longer expanded to accommodate advances in knowledge? (2) What are the indicators for determining the inadequacy of a conventional system? (3) When does a representational system become redundant? (4) Should alternative forms be sought from within the old— for instance the representation of bond angles within two-dimensional structure? (5) How best to invent forms which capture dynamic processes and energy distribution? (6) Is the idea of holding alternative forms of partial representation simultaneously the precursor of a new more total system? (7) To what extent do forms of representation constrain one's ideas? (8) To what extent should one compromise for the purposes of communication? (9) Can the process of representation itself be articulated more fully so that the essence of representational systems can be identified? (10) Is it possible to discover the essential components for the design of functionally useful representations in surface chemistry? (11) Could such core components become the beginnings of the growth of alternative forms for creating more useful representations?

This process of reflection set in motion an ongoing process of review. The outcomes of this creative encounter are in the process of being negotiated and validated.

LEARNING-TO-LEARN WELSH: THE PERSONAL THESAURUS

Despite the variety of methods and approaches for teaching foreign languages, most are based on *content* rather *processes* of learning. Aspects of the subject matter, that is, the language, are organised and selected prior to learning, and this determines the nature of the learning events and the criteria for evaluating success. Even in the new trend for the "communicative curriculum" the process of self-awareness and personal knowing is not made explicit. There is a general emphasis on public knowledge, semantics, grammatical form, register, sets of functions, the products of a language rather than the processes of achieving viable meaning.

In learning-to-learn languages projects (Valero and Julien, 1980; Harri-Augstein, Thomas, and Smith, 1982; Harri-Augstein, 1983), we have found that awareness of how personal meaning is constructed in a new language is often a new experience for learners. Rather than be aware of meaning or language solely as an object of knowledge, they come to recognise and more fully experience the process of how personal meaning is sought, constructed, stored, and retrieved. Successful outcomes of this approach have included more immediate fluency, enhanced ability to apply the language to meet personal needs, a continuation of language learning when the formal course has been completed, and an enhanced capacity for learning *other* languages.

Eliza, a mature student (Harri-Augstein, 1983), was learning Welsh in an intensive one-term course at the National Language Unit of Wales. Welsh had become important for her as a junior school teacher, in a Welsh-speaking area. She was familiar with the occasional Welsh word though she had never spoken Welsh. Eliza was one of a group of 20 adults, each with rather different needs and purposes for learning Welsh.

A feasibility study was launched in which five reflective learning procedures were introduced as part of their course. One of these is briefly described here.

The *personal thesaurus technique* is designed to make explicit the ways in which personal meaning is constructed in a new language. It is based on the concept that a group of ideas of "items of meaning" become related and personally categorised according to specific functions of language. The range and clusters of items reveal a personal thesaurus or developing system of personal meaning in the new language. For Eliza as well as her peers and tutors, it was quite surprising to discover the structure of her own meanings in Welsh. This bore very little relationship to the daily conversation drills, grammar drills, printed materials, and audio tapes which formed the main part of her language learning resources.

Yet, the structure revealed significant insights into the ways in which she constructed ideas in Welsh. Clusters of words and phrases were described as "nice-sounding words", "reminders of enjoyable experiences", idiosyncratic visual associations, memories of childhood experiences, "deep bonds with father", "commands to do with the children in her class", "commands to do with home", "private language used with her Welsh-speaking husband", "to do with the need to feel Welsh" and "pride in being Welsh", and so forth (Harri-Augstein, 1983, Appendix). Eliza used her personal thesaurus as an aid to expand her vocabulary, for effective recall of new terms and phrases, for locating important functions in the language, and for reflecting upon the process of language construction itself. This deeply influenced her growing realisation that not only was she embarking on learning a new language, but that this was influencing her life style, personality, and her image of herself.

In eliciting a personal thesaurus from each member of the group, the tutor and the learners together were evolving a language for communicating about their learning processes. The target language Welsh was seen to be separate from the process of language learning. This meta language was conducted in the mother language of the learner (in this case English), whilst the target language was being learnt. In negotiating the meta-language, Welsh was only referred to, to illustrate, emphasise, or concretise the learning process itself. At first the group and the tutors found it very difficult to talk about their own learning processes. The meta-language in which these processes were described was very rudimentary. Initially, considerable resistance was engendered as their partially developed learning skills were made explicit and challenged. This was doubly disastrous since most of them were teachers. Interestingly, the greatest impact was on the course tutors, who went on to adapt their courses to integrate some of the learning-to-learn techniques into the curriculum. The use of English for the meta-language and of Welsh for the target language proved very effective in this study. As familiarity with Welsh increased, group discussions about learning processes were subsequently carried out in Welsh.

COMPUTER-AIDED LEARNING: A CAL SIMULATOR

Records of learning performance are being used to enable Royal Navy trainees to enhance their awareness of how they learn the complex task of air intercept control, and to develop their learning competence (Thomas and Harri-Augstein, 1983). Aspects of the task addressed by the machine include safe fighter control in a congested air space and intercept control relating to intercept geometry. Examples of some learning aids include the use of *backtracks* that enable learners to appreciate more readily the consequences and implications of their actions; a *stop* facility for reflection and review of tactics and strategy; *replay* to enable learners to "relive" and therefore reflect on the process of learning so that different tactics can be invented and attempted alongside the previous attempts;

varitime so that the replay can be observed either faster or slower than real time; and an *event log* of everything that has occurred during practice. These learning aids create different manifestations of feedback about the learning task.

Used experimentally within the intense training course, in which the pressure for success is very high owing to the enormous expense involved in training, this is proving very effective as a device for developing learning competence. Aptitude tests offer inadequate selection procedures and the failure rate is very high. How do trainees learn to learn the task?

Whilst learning on the simulator, each trainee constructs his personal learning task analysis (PLTA). The trainee plans the learning purposes for a given intercept type and the intended strategy, and considers possible criteria for assessing the quality of the outcome, that is, achieving a good intercept. Using the reflective learning aids, the trainee then practises a particular intercept while taking action on the machine.

Self-debriefs conducted as the learner stops, replays, or inspects the log data enables him to reflect and review his purposes, strategies, and outcomes. By comparing one replay attempt with the next, progress can be reviewed as learning progresses; by a reflection upon "what was I intending to do when I turned to port there?", "why did I decide to start the final turn there?", and "since the results showed I was too early, what must I now do to correct this error?", the trainee learns to review performance. By freezing the replay using the stop facility, the learner can create space for reflection about "why the decision at that point contributed to success or failure" (Thomas and Harri-Augstein, 1983, p. 95). This also gives an opportunity to consult peers, an instructor, or one's own notes for guidance. The trainee can also consult a teaching aid built into the machine, namely computer solutions to the particular problem. In using self-generated knowledge of results to arrive at future learning needs, and in using the learning devices for reflection and contemplation, and in referring to other sources for guidance, the learner is enabled to take more control of the direction and quality of the learning. The trainee learns to personalise the rules taught on the course in the context of the dynamics of the individual learning process.

This learning-to-learn experience enables the trainee to assess learning skills as the individual learns to perform the task. In continuing with the personal learning task analysis, the trainee goes on to use the experience of learning to compare prospective and retrospective performance on the task. How well did the individual achieve the intended purposes? How effective was the strategy? How good was the outcome? What must the learner do next? An example illustration of the PLTA flow chart is shown in Figure 1.

In one debrief session after a poor intercept, one trainee chose to reflect upon what was meant by "coming in too early" and "coming in too late" and so revise the next course of action (Thomas and Harri-Augstein, p. 96). The personally generated causal explanations that emerged were very different from the

The Personal Learning Task Analysis (PLTA)

Opening up the conversation–getting started:

How do I (we) see the task as a whole?   What are my needs and purposes?

What are my thoughts, feelings, attitudes about the task?

What do I know already?   What skills do I already have?

How familiar am I with the resources?

| What purposes and skills relate to the sub-tasks? | How shall I organise my time? How shall I schedule my work? | How shall I divide the task into manageable parts? |

My summary of progress so far:

Process perspectives	What shall I (we) do now?	Temporal perspective
Behaviour	What action(s) shall I take?	L_p–Learner perspective
(P) Purpose	Why am I going to do this?	Personal plans for learning: A provisional explanation of the task or learning event
(S) Strategy	How shall I do this?	
(O) Outcome	How shall I judge how well I will have done, – how meaningful will the consequences of my actions be to me?	
(R) Criteria review		
Behaviour	Take action	L_o–Ongoing learning
Self-monitoring of the process as a whole (PSOR)	Thoughts, feelings, decisions, and actions	The pursuit of one course of action
	Observe the process of learning as well as the content of the task to be learnt	
	Interpret	
Records of:		
Behaviour	Reflection	L_r–Learner retrospective
(P) Purpose	What action(s) did I take?	Reflection and review of learning
(S) Strategy	Why did I do these?	
(O) Outcome	How did I achieve these?	
(R) Review		
Behaviour	Review	
	Compare your descriptions of your actions with your personal plans	
(P) Purpose	Review your actions	
(S) Strategy	Review your needs and purposes	
(O) Outcome	Review the ways you achieved the actions	
(R) Review	Review your criteria for assessing the quality of your outcomes	
(R) Review the whole processes and learn to learn	Review your task as a whole	
	Review your learning skill requirements	
	What shall I do next? Why? How?	Personal plans for learning

Figure 1. The Personal Learning Task Analysis (PLTA) flow chart.

logical intercept geometry concepts taught in the course. Each learner has to construct a personal model of the task and a model of how he learns this for an effective operational control of the aircraft. For instance, in assessing "heading", "angle of turn", "separation of the fighter from the target", and "relative speed of fighter and target", eyeball judgements, as crucial points of decision and control, had to be developed to a very precise degree of accuracy. All this has to be reflected upon in the context of safety rules relating to other aircraft. Using replay to reflect upon the "pathway through the sky" as shown by the backtracks, the trainee learns to make better judgements about the effectiveness of the control of a single intercept and of the overall sortie. A self-debrief of the event log data gives a second-by-second performance history, thus enabling the learner to grasp the commonalities between specific intercept types. An awareness of how the learner achieves this understanding then enables the individual to tackle increasingly difficult intercepts more successfully with fewer trials and less error. The trainee learns what is involved in working out the rules of "the radius of turn", "the reciprocal", and the "relative angle of bearing" between fighter and target.

One learner using all the learning aids progressed from eight unsuccessful attempts before achieving an intercept on the simplest intercept type, that is, 180° turn, to five on an intermediate, that is, 90° turn, to three for a very complex intercept type, that is, 150° turn with the target at variable speed. Another learner who did not use the learning aids got increasingly worse and failed to complete the practice sortie. Moreover, the individual was unable to handle debriefing adequately and had to rely on the instructor to do this. The former, went on to explore other aspects of the task such as the appropriateness of particular intercept types given the context of wind direction, position of the sun, fuel level of aircraft, and so on. This longer term modelling of the task takes the trainee closer to the real on the job situation with real aircraft and real pilots.

In observing their own learning on the CAL simulator, trainees approached the task with different needs and expectations, defined their purposes differently, and invented different strategies for achieving these. By using behavioural records to reconstruct experience we have found that the "personal observer" can invent a process language for reflection upon the quality of learning. Kelly (1970) saw behaviour as a personal experiment. Is it not time for the submerged pole of humanistic psychology to arise out of its murky past as a new tool for the personal construct psychologist?

Characteristics of Awareness-Raising Tools for Learning-to-Learn

These examples, of the ways in which awareness-raising tools can be used creatively to facilitate change, highlight their necessary characteristics.

Minimally, these characteristics include

1. Some observational record or external display of one aspect of learning. Purpose–strategy–outcome–review can each be separately and integratively investigated by means of awareness-raising tools.
2. A display of the learning process which facilitates effective talk-back, so that the learning event can be re-experienced.
3. A capacity to move up and down the levels of organisation of a skill, so that the skill can be reviewed as a coherent system.
4. A facility for the development of a language in which the description of behaviour and experience can be articulated in sufficient detail with such a degree of precision that a new level of awareness is achieved.
5. The testing out of alternatives and a system of evaluation which indicates the merits and demerits of each alternative and throws up indications of the directions in which more adequate alternatives may be sought.
6. A system of support which enables an individual to intensively explore the awareness and review of process.
7. A procedure for gradually weaning away from dependency on the tools, replacing these with an enhanced perception and language through which the learner can achieve the same effect unsupported from the outside.

Provided such characteristics are met, people engaged in learning to learn are able to invent specific tools to meet their individual needs. Human beings possess a tremendous capacity for learning. Our research findings show that when used conversationally, these awareness-raising tools can enhance learning competency by several hundred percent.

The artifacts in society can be recruited as awareness-raising tools for learning. Either through creation of, or by attributing personal meaning to such artifacts, individuals may become aware of and able to review process. Contemplating a Gerard Manley Hopkins poem, writing an article, building a boat, reflecting upon a surrealistic still life by Gris or Dali can be equally powerful ways in which process can be reviewed.

The problem with using culture-bound artifacts as "mirrors of process" is that they represent highly developed and content-focused devices, and one level of purpose is embedded in their form and content. Unless the individual learner can subsume this process, he or she will remain imprisoned in content. Specialist psychic mirrors have been designed so that the learner is elevated to a description of process. But, what kind of descriptive system and display device best captures the psychological processes of learning?

Psychology has fallen into the trap of continually producing statistically based descriptions such as personality categories, IQ and creativity measures, and semantic differential scales, with which the individuals concerned feel uneasy as descriptions of "the self". Rogers' (1969) gigantic step inwards into process laid the foundation for exploring the conditions of change but he pays little attention to the modelling facility itself, the unique inner processes which initiates, sustains, and restyles the "cognitive maps" of a person. Husserl (1960) opened up a new vista of phenomenological investigation, but psychology had to wait for Kelly's (1955) personal biography and the repertory grid as tools for the personal description of meaning (Bannister and Fransella, 1980). It was through Kelly's craft that a breakthrough was achieved into a humanistic technology that allows meaning to emerge in individual terms and yet retain some systematic form.

Learning, Conversational Research, and the Personal Observer

If educational research concerns itself with learning and the researcher/teacher defines learning in this way, then the priority of scientific objectivity becomes suspect. The pursuit of objectivity normally involves the educational researcher in a detailed control of the experimental situation. But studies aimed at increasing self-organisation require that the researcher recognise that the learner has his or her own point of view and needs the freedom to explore each learning situation. As the learner begins to exercise greater and more sensitive choice, so the researcher/teacher loses the capacity to insist on a rigid pre-planned design. The teacher has the choice of becoming one among a number of pre-packaged resources or of becoming a full participant and welcoming the student (as an equal but different participant) into the learning–teaching conversation. Staff may opt for one or the other of these roles depending on the situation. What happens, disastrously on occasions, is that these roles are confused and the interaction becomes neither instruction nor learning conversation, and founders in a mess of mutual misconceptions, annoyance, and frustration. Unfortunately the educational researcher and teacher seems more successful and at home, understanding pre-planned instruction.

In studying the dynamics of learning conversations, a traditional view of objectivity would seem incompatible with the pursuit of self-organisation. The positions of researcher/teacher and learner are no longer entirely dissimilar. If it is acknowledged that each is an autonomous contributor to the joint enterprise, then many of the assumptions implicit in objective research, formal instruction, and intuitive tutoring have to be examined and negotiated afresh before the enterprise can get underway. The learner recognises that learning to learn involves him or her in a unique action research project centred upon himself or herself and his or her learning skills. The teacher sees him or herself as participant adviser or consultant to the learner in his or her project. The researcher/teacher now concerns him or herself with understanding the dynamics of this joint enterprise and in negotiating multiple criteria for exhibiting the degree and nature of the learning which is (or could be) inferred from different points of view.

Action research in schools, colleges of education, polytechnics, universities, and in industry, based on encouraging self-organisation in the ways in which learners interact with available resources, has led to the identification of criteria which offer rigour and validity to a science of learning to learn.

THE PERSONAL OBSERVER AS SCIENTIST

In the double helix of learning, involving reflection on both content and process, the learning code has to be personally invented. Figure 2 summarises this research process and the role of reflective learning devices in enabling the personal observers to achieve their aims.

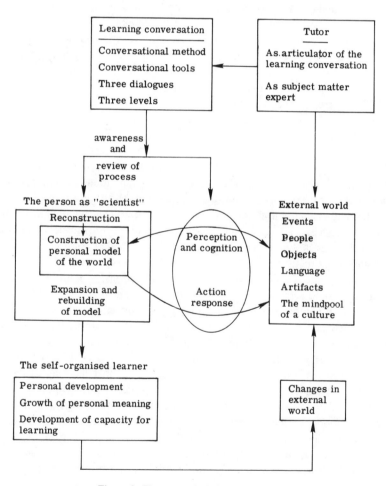

Figure 2. The personal observer as scientist.

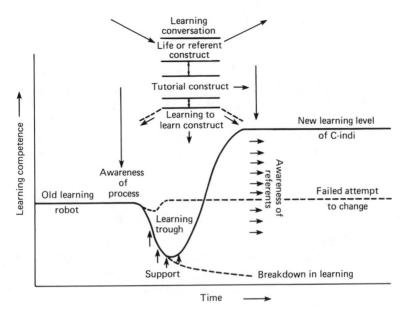

Figure 3. Learning-to-learn.

CHALLENGING THE ROBOT

Achieving new levels in learning performance usually involves serious personal change. It involves the disruption and breaking of existing skills and the establishment of new attitudes and personally strange ways of thinking, feeling, and behaving. Many of the techniques used have been specially recruited and developed for such controlled interventions. But however carefully negotiated the process, learning to learn will always involve a ''learning trough'' into which the person is pushed by anxiety and feelings of inadequacy (see Figure 3).

It is useful to talk of each learner as having a set of personal learning robots: the learning-by-reading robot, the learning-by-discussion robot, the learning-by-doing robot, the learning-by-listening robot, and so forth. Each of us has been so habituated in our own ways that we are completely unaware that each of these modes of learning is itself a learned skill. Each learning skill has become so automatic that it is no longer under conscious control. These learning robots obviously relate to the personal myths described earlier, which deeply influence how we learn. Special techniques are required to challenge the robot, bringing the skill back into awareness and thus available for revision and development of existing myths. But the disruption of existing skills produces a drop in effective performance. The learner feels that he is getting nowhere and becomes frustrated and anxious. Part of every learning conversation is concerned with offering the learner support through this learning trough.

THE LANGUAGES OF LEARNING TO LEARN

In one sense, reflection on processes of learning is conducted in one language: the accustomed language of the learner. But whilst acknowledging all the dangers (real and imagined) of offering new systems of jargon, one outstanding feature of learning to learn is that there appears to be a real need to negotiate a system of referent language with each learner. One reason for this is that much of what gets talked about is completely new. Most people find it almost impossible to talk about their own learning processes, purposes, and methods in anything but the most general and inexact terms. This is because they have only very rudimentary and bizarre models of the learning process and almost no language in which to describe their experience to themselves. This variation of the Whorf hypothesis (Whorf, 1956) continually arises in each new learning-to-learn encounter. It poses various problems:

1. There is a very difficult question raised by the non-verbal nature of many of the communications which facilitate learning to learn. Learners may develop a non-verbal language which is both more immediately relevant and productive than the more explicit verbal language. Such non-verbal languages tend to be very personal and difficult to share.

2. If there is no shared view (or theory) of the processes, purposes, and methods of learning, each term must be differentiated and mapped onto shared experience if effective communication is to occur.

3. If one dominant participant, that is, the tutor brings a pre-conceived language and theory into the situation, it is very difficult for the other to create a personal understanding out of it, unless the process of language–experience–meaning negotiation is made explicit.

4. As with any intense specialist group, the effectiveness of learning to learn seems to develop hand in hand with the emergence of a private technical language in providing a more exact and parsimonious vehicle for the articulation and exchange of experience. New levels of previously inconceivable competence can be achieved.

5. Each tool or aid to learning to learn requires its own technical terms. The explicitness of these tools seems to facilitate recognition of the need for these languages, but how each person picks it up and uses it is a question of personal style, needs, and purposes. More importantly, and with more associated difficulties, there is a need for a language in which to talk about learning, and to talk about it in ways that break long existing habits, create greater flexibility and operationalise the processes of change.

The criteria we have identified as characteristic of a meta-language has been developed out of a fair amount of varied experience which has always been fairly intensively reviewed. Other systems of language have been raided and cannibalised, as no one seemed sufficient. We find it convenient to consider the meta-language at three levels of organisation.

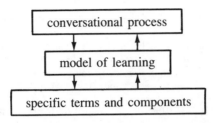

One of the most significant attributes of a learning-to-learn language is that it itself embodies a capacity for process which is capable of generating varieties of process languages to meet the needs of individual learners. Pask (1976), Kelly (1955), Bannister & Fransella (1980), Lorenz (1977), Piaget (1950), Bruner (1964), Rogers (1969), Skinner (1971), Shah (1966), Mair (1979), and Freire (1974) offer alternative but not mutually exclusive forms. All contribute to the language of the personal observer.

In offering opportunities for personal learning in our educational system, a dynamic curriculum centred on the personal observer must be evolved. A psycho-reflective technology for learning to learn provides the tools for this challenging enterprise. Learners, teachers, and researchers can learn to define their responsibilities and construct conversational networks of learning in this exciting enterprise.

The highest form of such an enterprise has been described as *joy* (Nietsche), *creative encounter* (Rogers), *peak experience* (Maslow), *faculty X—the Freedom Experience* (C. Wilson), *creative self* (Adler), *self-actualisation* (Jung), and *nirvana*. Joyce's *epiphanies* capture it. Conversational encounters using the reflective learning technology have occasionally resulted in peak experience as individuals have reflected upon their personal learning. Can we recruit this technology systematically into the curriculum to achieve meta-control of learning? This challenge may well force us to redefine our educational institutions in order to prevent the learning-to-learn encounter from evaporating and as with liquid nitrogen when exposed to air, totally disappearing, leaving no trace.

References

Bannister, D. and Fransella, F. (1980). "Inquiring Man" (2nd ed.), Penguin Books, Harmondsworth.

Bruner, J. (1964). The course of cognitive growth. *American Psychologist* **19** (1).

Freire, P. (1974). "Education for Critical Consciousness", Sheed and Ward, London.

Harri-Augstein, E. S. (1978). Reflecting on Structures of Meaning. A processes of Learning-to-Learn. In "Personal Construct Psychology 1977" (Fay Fransella, ed.), Academic Press, London.

Harri-Augstein, E. S. and Thomas, L. F. (1978). Learning-to-Learn. The Personal Construction and Exchange of Meaning. *In* "Research in Adult Learning" (M. Howe, ed.), Wiley, Chichester.

Harri-Augstein, E. S. and Thomas, L. F. (1979a). Learning Conversations: A person-centred approach to self-organised learning. *British Journal of Guidance & Counselling,* **7**(1).

Harri-Augstein, E. S. and Thomas, L. F. (1979b). The Self-Organised Learner and the Relativity of Knowing. *In* "Constructs of Sociality and Individuality" (D. Bannister and P. Stringer, eds.), Academic Press, London.

Harri-Augstein, E. S., Thomas, L. F., and Smith, M. (1982). "Reading-to-Learn", Methuen, London.

Harri-Augstein, E. S. (1983). "Learning-to-learn Welsh" (Final Report, National Language Unit of Wales Project), Centre for the Study of Human Learning, Brunel University, Uxbridge, Middlesex.

Husserl, E. (1960). "Cartesian Meditations: An Introduction to Phenomenology", (D. Cairns, trans.), The Hague, Nijhoff.

Kelly, G. A. (1955). "The Psychology of Personal Constructs", Vols. I and II, Norton, New York.

Kelly, G. A. (1970). Behaviour Is an Experiment. *In* "Perspectives in Personal Construct Theory" (D. Bannister, ed.), Academic Press, London.

Lorenz, K. (1977). "Behind the Mirror", Methuen, London.

Mair, M. (1979). The Personal Venture. *In* "Constructs of Sociality and Individuality" (P. Stringer and D. Bannister, eds.), Academic Press, London.

Pask, G. (1976). Conversational techniques in the study and practice of education. *British Journal of Educational Psychology,* **46**, 12–25.

Piaget, J. (1950). "The Psychology of Intelligence" (J. Piercy and E. Berlyne, trans.), Routledge and Kegan Paul, London.

Rogers, C. (1969). "Freedom to Learn", Merrill, Columbus, Ohio.

Shah I. (1966). "The Exploits of the Incomparable Mulla Nasrudin", Pan Books, London.

Skinner, B. F. (1971). "Beyond Freedom and Dignity", A. Knopf, New York.

Thomas, L. F. and Snapes, A. W. (1968). "Research into Training for Skills in the Hotel and Catering Industry" (Third Progress Report, Hotel and Catering Industry Training Board), Centre for the Study of Human Learning, Brunel University, Uxbridge, Middlesex.

Thomas, L. F. (1978). A Personal Construct Approach to Learning, Education and Therapy. *In* Personal Construct Psychology 1977 (Fay Fransella, ed.), Academic Press, London.

Thomas, L. F. and E. S. Harri-Augstein. (1982a). Centre for the Study of Human Learning Publication List. (Technical Papers 1–100) Brunel University, Uxbridge, Middx.

Thomas, L. F. and E. S. Harri-Augstein. (1982b). The Centre for the Study of Human Learning Reflective Learning Software, Brunel University, Uxbridge, Middx.

Thomas, L. F., and Harri-Augstein, E. S. (1983). "The Evaluation of an Intelligent Learning System, Learning-to-Learn and the CAL—Skills Trainer" (Final report, Centre for the Study of Human Learning/Applied Psychology Unit of Admiralty Marine Technology Establishment Project), Centre for the Study of Human Learning, Brunel University, Uxbridge, Middx.

Valero, V. and Julien, M. (1982). "A Learning-to-Learn Approach for Science Undergraduates Learning English (Unpublished report, Centre for the Study of Human Learning project with Universidad Autónoma Metropolitana, Mexico), Centre for the Study of Human Learning, Brunel University, Uxbridge, Middx.

Whorf, B. J. (1956). "Language, Thought and Reality", MIT Press, Cambridge, Massachusetts.

5

Growing into Self

Sharon R. Jackson and D. Bannister

If "self" is, as Kelly (1955) put it, a "proper construct", like any other, then self-construing must elaborate as does our construing of the world at large. Thus we would expect to find a developing and unfolding quality in the self-construing of children as they grow older. Kelly also argued that we may only understand ourselves to the degree that we can understand others since our understanding of both self and others is an integral part of our personal psychological theorising. Thus we would expect to find a child's construing of self to be as developed as his or her construing of others, both being characteristic of the child's quality as a "psychologist". So, just as the infant sorts *soft* from *hard* and *liquid* from *solid* by elaborating expectations which are confirmed or negated, so he or she will sort out *friend* from *foe, gentle* from *harsh,* and so forth, in people and thereby move from informative collision to more elaborated experience.

This evolutionary quality in children's psychological construing is explored and argued in work by Brierly (1967), Salmon (1970, 1976), Applebee (1976), Hayden, Nasby, and Davids (1977), Honess (1979), and others, in personal construct theory terms. The studies reported here are an attempt to elaborate the thesis with particular reference to the issue of what is problematic in self-construing.

Growing into Self

In an earlier study (Bannister and Agnew 1977), the basic developmental thesis was tested out in terms of the differential ability of younger and older children to recognise their own statements. After a 4-month gap, children were asked to identify their own statements from those made at the same time by other children, to give reasons for their choice and to say why certain statements could not have been made by them. The study showed that older children (in a range from 5 to 9 years) were more able to identify their own statements and it indicated changes, with age, in their strategies for so doing. Thus, the 5-year-olds had virtually no overt strategy other than a reliance on (what often turned out to be unreliable) memory. Children at age 7 years used a relatively simple behavioural psychology, for example, "That child says he plays football and I play football so I must have said that". The 9-year-olds elaborated into psychological inference of the kind "That child said he wanted to be a soldier and I could never kill anybody so I wouldn't have said that.'' In parallel, the children's articulation of a general basis for individual differences elaborated with age. Thus, faced with a question, ''How do we become different'', the 5-year-olds' answers ranged through ''I haven't a clue'' to ''Because you can't get all the same people''; the 7-year-olds produced arguments relating to the disastrous consequences that would ensue if we were all the same and hints at genetic sources of differences; the 9-year-olds seem to be working towards the idea that it is the cumulative effects of different experiences which create individual differences. In total this experiment added to what can be said directly about the developmental process but left open the issue of what might hinder or distort the process of development.

If, as Kelly argued, the development of construing is a function of varying validational experiences, then when a child is subjected to confusing experience (such as inconsistent or rejecting parental behaviour, social isolation, or rapid changes of subculture) the child may become a mystified and mystifying psychologist. Such a child may become problematic because he or she has been unable to develop reliable internalised guidelines for his or her own behaviour or strategies for relating to (by effectively interpreting) the behaviour of others.

Jackson (1980) piloted a self-characterisation (Kelly, 1955) and grid (Fransella and Bannister, 1977) designed to investigate the issue of ''problematic'' self-construing. A sample of younger (9- to 10-year-olds) and older (11- to 13-year-olds) were subdivided into problematic children (i.e., attending the children's unit of a psychiatric hospital or showing other signs of disturbance such as being referred to a child guidance clinic or being designated by their school as needing remedial teaching, being disruptive, being isolated and so forth) and into non-problematic children. All children were given two tasks. They were asked to write a self-characterisation, a description of themselves as if by a sympathetic friend, saying ''what sort of boy or girl you are''. They were asked to complete a grid in which the elements were ''me'' and seven children they knew, ranking the children from first to last on constructs such as *good-tempered, lazy, like I'd like to be,* and so forth.

An analysis of the degree of psychological sophistication shown in the self-characterisation and of structural articulation in the grid confirmed that self-construing elaborates with age. It showed that, as children grow older, they increasingly take into account the views which others hold of them; they make more references to their past and their predicted future so as to develop a picture of themselves over a time line; they make greater use of psychological constructs, particularly of assertions of a psychological cause and effect kind. As their construing of self becomes more complex, children achieve a greater degree of concordance as to the meaning of various psychological constructs. Also the construct of self becomes more stable over time as children see repeated themes in their history and develop superordinate ways of viewing their past and anticipating their future. Significantly, the children designated as problematic performed at a level younger than their age-showing on many of the grid and self-characterisation measures, a less-elaborated capacity to construe self.

However, from a personal construct theory point of view, it seems simple-minded to define *problematic* as merely a matter of being below age norms on some hypothetical developmental scale. Construct theory insists that we also consider construct systems in terms of their *internal* validity and thereby explore (rather than simply accept) what is meant by others when they apply the label *problematic*. Thus I may find you a "problem" but that does not necessarily mean you find yourself a problem; I may find you confusing but that does not necessarily mean that you are confused. This is not to gainsay that there will be an interaction between the child's or adult's construction of others' construing of them and of their self-construing. Kelly (1955) in his sociality corollary argues that "to the extent that a person can construe the construction processes of another he or she may play a social role in relation to that person" (p. 951). Thus, if I find you confusing, I may find it difficult to develop a social role in relation to you and, thereby, we are less likely to elaborate ourselves through each other.

Theses

The experiment to be reported in detail was designed to confirm and elaborate three of the central themes of the studies already mentioned and to add to them a fourth proposition.

1. Construing of self and others is integral and develops in harness.
2. Construing of self develops with age.
3. Many children who are labelled problematic (regardless of whether they are so labelled from a psychiatric, educational, legal or peer point of view) are so called because their elaboration of self-construing is hindered and distorted.
4. There are children within the group labelled problematic who are so labelled because they are confusing to others but who are not themselves confused. They have an elaborated view of self through which they can guide their actions and are perhaps better regarded as "rebel" or "unorthodox" or "original".

SAMPLE

The experimental sample consisted of 48 children from comprehensive schools: 24 younger (9-year-olds) and 24 older (12–13-year-olds) children. Within their age range, the children were divided into groups of eight who were familiar to each other and the groups were chosen so as to include four boys and four girls, with two boys and two girls selected by their teachers as being problematic and two boys and two girls judged by the teachers to be not problematic.

Self-Characterisation

Each child was asked to provide a self-characterisation, a personality description of themselves. The description was to be written *as if* by a sympathetic friend so that it was in the third person and began "Susie Smith is. . .''. The task was presented as a request to write roughly a page, saying what they were like, "what sort of boy or girl you are". For the purposes of the study, the children were given a choice of either writing their own self-characterisation or dictating it in order to overcome any inhibitions due to spelling or writing difficulties. (All opted for dictation.) Interjudge agreement between the two authors (independently scoring each protocol) was checked for each of the six measures derived from the self-characterisation. For the measures (listed subsequently) the score alloted to the child was the mean of the two judges.

1. *Views of others' score:* a count of the number of times the child refers to the view taken of him or her by other people, for example, "Parents would say he's a little bugger", "Her mates think she is a showoff". (Interjudge agreement $r = .80$).

2. *Personal history and future score:* a count of the number of times the child refers to his or her past or possible future in psychological terms, for example, "When Susan was little she was shy and would hide. She just says 'Hi' to people now". Non-psychological past/future references were not counted, for example, "I used to live in Barnsley". (Interjudge agreement $r = .72$).

3. *Psychological cause and effect score:* a count of the number of times a child makes an assertion of a cause and effect kind in psychological terms. Explicit psychological cause and effect statements were scored 3, implicit statements were scored 1, for example, an explicit statement was "If my sister is provoked she gets nastier", an implicit statement was "She wants to be a writer or a lawyer—likes writing stories and likes to help people". (Interjudge agreement $r = .87$).

4. *Psychological statements score:* a count of the number of psychological statements of any kind made by each child, for example, "He is a mod but his sister is a rocker". Note: if the child listed a series of likes or dislikes in the same sentence which were all on the same topic, for example, school subjects, sports, foods, clothes, then the total list was given as a score of 1. (Interjudge agreement $r = .92$).

5. *Contradictions score:* a count of the number of pairs of themes or general assertions which were contradictory in some way. Marked contradiction between two assertions was scored 3, a mild degree of contradiction between two assertions was scored 1, for example, marked contradiction: score 3, "Most people

don't like her because they think she is devious but she has got a lot of friends'';
mild contradiction: score 1, "His parents would say he is sometimes lazy. He
does as he is told". (Interjudge agreement $r = .50$).

6. *Insight score:* a count of the number of statements reflecting the child's
awareness of his or her own shortcomings and resulting problems, for example,
"He is horrible at school", "Being Neil is rubbish". It excludes references to
problems the child sees as not his or her fault but caused by others. (Interjudge
agreement $r = .74$).

Below are two examples of self-characterisations, both from older children in
the sample. Jean (judged non-problematic by teachers, scored well (i.e., a
"good psychologist") and Betty (judged problematic) scored poorly.

JEAN

Jean is temperamental at times. She likes her own way and usually gets it. When she
meets people she is rather shy and timid. She is quite good in lessons. When she's sad
she likes to cry on somebody's shoulder who will listen to her problems. She hates
listening to anyone else's sob stories. She likes meeting people if they've got the same
interests. She likes reading books. She'd like to be a lawyer when she leaves school. She
thinks she bores people about that. Her friend thinks it's a daft idea. But she's got as
good a chance as any and may as well try. She criticises people a lot, behind their backs.
Her sister thinks she is very argumentative and she thinks the same about her. Jean like
animals—has a dog and would like a horse. She likes reading and is a member of the
squash club. She is different because she is a different personality every time she meets
somebody depending on which it is. Most people don't like her because they think she is
devious but she has got a lot of friends.

BETTY

Betty is thirteen years old. She does not like school. She likes going to the school
youth club of a night. She does not get on with her brother. Sometimes she just gets her
own way with her Mum. Teachers say she is all right. She does not like some of the
teachers or some of the lessons. Her friends say she is cocky sometimes. She likes
playing about on the street with her friends. She has been to Caistor for a holiday. She
gets on all right with the boys she goes out with. She used to get on with her boyfriend's
Dad alright, but does not now.

Grid

The supplied verbal labels for the constructs of the grid were (1) *good tempered*, (2) *clever*, (3) *like I'd like to be as a person*, (4) *easily frightened*, (5) *like
I am as a person*, (6) *hard to understand*, (7) *lazy*, (8) *like I used to be as a
person*. Each child rank ordered himself or herself and the other seven children in
the group on the eight constructs of the grid.

After each child had completed the grid, he or she was presented with a sheet on which the constructs (other than the self-constructs) were laid out as an 8-inch line, for example, *clever* to *not clever* and so forth. The child was asked to predict where they (the subject child) would have been placed by each of the other seven children, by marking a cross on the line. Thus at the top of the page was the name of one of the children in the group then five lines with each end marked with the two poles of the five constructs. The child was asked to predict where the child whose name was at the top of the page had placed him or her on each construct in turn.

Finally, each child was asked to rank the other seven children in the group in order of friendship, that is, beginning first with best friend and so on down. Besides the six measures mentioned previously, a broad educational attainment measure was obtained for each child (measure 7).

The following points can be made in relation to the general design of the grid used in this study. It has been argued that it is better to elicit constructs than provide them (Adams-Webber, 1969) because this is more "natural". However, here we have accepted the counter argument (Bannister and Mair, 1968) that in a basic sense constructs cannot be "provided". All we can provide is *verbal labels* to which subjects attach *their own* constructs. The construct is not the verbal label but the actual discrimination made by the person between the elements. Obviously the verbal labels provided should be familiar to and usable by the subject: they should be part of the subject's subcultural language system. Given this, the use of supplied verbal labels is natural and allows direct comparison between one grid and another, in terms of the found relationships between constructs. Additionally, work by Ravenette (1975) indicates that if constructs are elicited from younger children, they tend to offer those which are very "element specific" and not (in Kelly's terms) superordinate enough for the kind of exploration we are undertaking here. The number of elements was restricted to eight because work by both Ravenette (1975) and by Bannister and Mair (1968) indicates that asking a subject to make rank discriminations very much above this number may result in confusion and relatively random ordering. Constructs were chosen so as to refer directly to self or to refer to what many children might see as major psychological characteristics of themselves and others and they were constructs which we had often heard children use conversationally.

All the grid scores detailed subsequently are derived from one basic form of analysis of the grid, that is, the inter-relationship between constructs. For each child, rank-order correlations were computed between each of the eight constructs and every other one. That is to say that the order in which the child ranked his or her peers on say the construct *good tempered* was correlated with the order in which he or she had ranked his or her peers on say the construct *clever*, yielding a Spearman rho. Rho was calculated for every possible pair of constructs, yielding a matrix of correlations. The Spearman rho's were squared and multiplied by 100 (thus representing variance in common) to give them a linear form. This score is always refered to as the construct relationship score and is the basis of the derived scores which are now listed.

MEASURES DERIVED FROM THE GRID

8. *Self as construct/self as element score:* this is the discrepancy between the child's allotment of himself or herself as an element on each construct and the relationship of *like I am* to these same constructs. The relationship scores were equated to ranks on the following basis: rank 1 = +75 to +100, rank 2 = +50 to +74, rank 3 = +25 to +49, rank 4 = 0 to +24, rank 5 = −1 to −25, rank 6 = −26 to −50, rank 7 = −51 to −75, rank 8 = −76 to −100. Thus the child's allotment of "self" on, say, construct 1 (*good tempered*) was compared with the relationship score between construct 5 (*like I am*) and construct 1 (*good tempered*) as converted to a rank score and the discrepancy between the two was noted. All discrepancies were added together to constitute a total descrepancy score which represented the difference between "self" ranked as an element and "self" used as a construct. A marked discrepancy is taken to indicate that the child has difficulty in aligning the individual judgments that he or she makes of himself or herself on particular constructs with a superordinate view of their own personality.

9. *Hard to understand by others score:* each child's rank positions on the construct *hard to understand* as allotted by the other seven children in the group were totalled, and this total represents the degree to which the child is considered *hard to understand* by other children.

10. *Hard to understand self-rating score:* this is the rank position the child has given himself or herself on the construct *hard to undersand*.

11. *Predictive accuracy (empathy) score*: this score is derived by totalling the discrepancy between the child's prediction of his or her position on each construct for another child and that other child's *actual* ranking of him or her. Discrepancies for all seven in the group are totalled for the five non-self-constructs (constructs other than *like I am, like I used to be, like I'd like to be*). It is a measure of how accurately the child can guess how he or she is seen by others.

12. *Popularity score:* the sum of the rank orders for each child in turn on the friendship sheet of the other seven children in the group.

13. *Hard to understand mispredictions score:* this is a measure of how hard the child is to understand in terms of the degree to which other children have mispredicted his or her judgments of them. It is derived by totalling the discrepancy between the subject's ratings of other children and how the other seven children expected he or she would rate them, that is, a measure of how difficult it is for other children to guess how the subject is viewing them.

14. *Sex stereotype by grid score:* a count of the number of times on the grid

the child has three or four boys or three or four girls grouped at the top or at the bottom of the rank order in a block. Thus it is a measure of how often the child is seeing all boys as alike and different from all girls who are also, stereotypically, seen as alike.

15. *Sex stereotype by friends score:* derived from the friendship sheet and calculated by counting the number of times that three or four boys or three or four girls are placed at the top or bottom of the rank order of best friends.

16. *Agreement with views of others score:* calculated by totalling the discrepancies between the child's self-rating on non-self-constructs and the average rating of that child by the other seven children on these constructs, that is, a measure of the amount of disagreement between the way the child sees himself or herself and the way he or she is seen by others.

17. *Salience of "good tempered" score:* the rank position, in terms of variance accounted for, of the construct *good tempered,* that is, a measure of the importance of the construct *good tempered* in terms of the size of its relationship scores (positive or negative) with the other constructs in the grid.

18. *Salience of "clever" score*: the rank position, in terms of variance accounted for, of the construct *clever.*

19. *"Ideal self" salience score:* the rank position, in terms of variance accounted for, of the construct like *I'd like to be.*

20. *Salience of "easily frightened"*: the rank position, in terms of variance accounted for, of the construct *easily frightened.*

21. *"Present self" salience score:* the rank position, in terms of variance accounted for, of the construct *like I am.*

22. *Salience of "hard to understand" score:* the rank position, in terms of variance accounted for, of the construct *hard-to-understand.*

23. *Salience of "lazy" score:* the rank position, in terms of variance accounted for, of the construct *lazy.*

24. *"Past self" salience score:* the rank position, in terms of variance accounted for, of the construct *like I used to be.*

25. *Social agreement score:* a table of the average construct relationship scores was prepared for all the constructs in the grid (except *like I am* and *like I used to be*) by averaging the construct relationship scores of the 48 children for each possible pair of constructs. These average relationships were then represented as plus (correlation of .30 or above), zero (a correlation between $+.29$ and $-.29$) and minus (a negative correlation greater than $-.30$). Each child's individual matrix of construct relationships was compared with this normative table and discrepancies were totalled: plus and zero or minus and zero counted as a discrepancy of 1, plus and minus counted as a discrepancy of 2. The total of these discrepancies for a child was that child's social agreement score. Thus the average matrix is a kind of social dictionary of construct relationships. This normative matrix is shown in Table I.

TABLE 1 *Average Relationships between Constructs for the Sample of 48 Children*

good tempered—clever	+
good tempered—like I'd like to be	+
good tempered—easily frightened	+
good tempered—hard to understand	−
good tempered—lazy	−
clever—like I'd like to be	+
clever—easily frightened	0
clever—hard to understand	−
clever—lazy	−
like I'd like to be—easily frightened	0
like I'd like to be—hard to understand	−
like I'd like to be—lazy	−
easily frightened—hard to understand	0
easily frightened—lazy	−
hard to understand—lazy	+

26. *Total salience of self score:* the sum of the rank positions, in terms of variance accounted for, of the three self-constructs (*like I used to be, like I am,* and *like I'd like to be*). This constitutes the total salience of self-score indicating how important self-constructs are with a child's grid.

27. *Component articulation score:* each child's grid was cluster analysed. A cluster was defined as two or more constructs related at the 5% level of significance or greater. This score is simply a count of the number of separate clusters excluding single constructs unrelated to any other construct (i.e., residual constructs).

28. *Bridging articulation score:* a bridging construct is defined as a construct which, at the 5% level of significance or greater, links constructs within two separate clusters. This score is a count of the number of such bridging constructs.

29. *Total articulation score:* calculated by multiplying the number of clusters by the number of bridging constructs. Thus it is an estimate of the total number of inferences that could be made within the construct system as sampled.

30. *Residual constructs score:* a count of the number of single residual constructs left over when the clusters had been worked out for the grid.

31. *Construing of self-change score:* calculated by summing the relationship scores between the three self-constructs (*like I used to be, like I am, like I'd like to be*) taking sign into account. Thus the score ranges from high minus which would indicate considerable construction of change (that is seeing a great difference between *like I used to be, like I am,* and *like I'd like to be*) through zero up to a high plus score which would indicate that there had been very little change in the past (as perceived by the subject) and that very little change was envisaged for the future.

32. *Ideal-present construing of change score:* the relationship score between the constructs *like I'd like to be* and *like I am.*

33. *Ideal-past construing of change score:* the relationship score between the constructs *like I'd like to be* and *like I used to be.*

34. *Present-past construing of change score:* the relationship score between the constructs *like I am* and *like I used to be.*

Both self-characterisation and grid measures are designed to explore the elaboration of the child's general psychological construing and construing of self, his or her construing of change over time and the degree to which they understand and are understood by their peers. Additionally, aspects of construing which may affect such understanding, namely sex stereotyping and idiosyncratic use of constructs, are examined.

Hypotheses and Results

The general thesis that construing of "self" and "others" is integral and develops "in harness" would lead us to expect that children scoring well on "elaboration of self" measures would be "good psychologists": they would score well on general measures of construing articulation, they would make sense of their peers, and (mostly) their peers would make sense of them. A study of the intercorrelations between measures generally supports this thesis.

There is a significant positive relationship between the various self-characterisation measures, that is, taking account of views of others relates positively to high Insight, which in turn goes with a high number of Psychological cause and effect statements. Interestingly enough those self-characterisations which manifested a relatively high number of *contradictions* also scored well on "good psychologist" measures. This suggests that as children develop and elaborate their construct systems they do this at the price of an increasing amount of contradiction. Perhaps the construct system of the infant achieves internal consistency by its very simplicity. As our theories about our own and other people's nature become more complex then the possibility of our holding internally contradictory views, at any one time, increases.

Some of the self-characterisation measures relate positively to grid measures: thus, those who take account of the views of others tend (in grid terms) to place importance on self-constructs. Those children with high social agreement scores make more frequent reference to personal history and future and have a higher number of psychological statements. Those with high insight scores show more complex structure and fewer residual constructs. Also, their ideal self construct is more salient.

Not surprisingly, those seen as hard to understand by their peers are less popular, they disagree with the views of others and show low social (language) agreement. Those who see *themselves* as hard to understand, have relatively poorly articulated grids. Unpopular children have a highly salient "past self" construct, low social agreement, the construct "clever" is unimportant and they are not sex stereotyped by their friends.

A high predictive accuracy (empathy) score, that is, an ability to guess accurately how others see you, correlates significantly and positively with a whole series of measures. Specifically, children who understand well how they are seen are popular, other children can predict their responses, they agree with the views of others, and they use their constructs in the same way as other children (high social agreement). The construct of past self has low salience and they want to change.

Equally, for those children whose views are accurately predicted by their peers, self constructs seem important and they construe substantial past and future change while "clever" is clearly not a salient construct.

Finally, the correlates of the construing of self-change score (31) are of particular interest. Those children who perceive themselves both as having changed and intending to change in the future (large distances between *Like I used to be, Like I am* and *Like I'd like to be*) predict other children accurately and are accurately predicted by them; they attach little importance to the construct "lazy" and "clever" and have well articulated construct systems (in grid terms). It is significant that it is specifically a marked distance between present self and ideal which most strongly implies these other characteristics.

Thus both the general direction and the specific significance of correlations between measures supports the thesis that children who have a well developed view of themselves tend also to have a well-developed view of others.

OLDER AND YOUNGER

None of the results significantly contradicts the thesis that older children are more elaborated psychological theorisers than younger children, and results on the following measures specifically support the thesis. (Two-tailed tests throughout.)

1. Older children used more psychological cause and effect statements in their self-characterisations than younger children ($p < .001$).
2. Older children manifest more contradictions in their self-characterisations ($p < .001$). This would be expected if we accept the argument that the elaboration of construing of self makes contradiction more of a possibility than it is in the relatively simpler self-characterisations of the younger children.
3. Older children showed more insight than younger children ($p < .001$).
4. Older children showed greater predictive accuracy (empathy) than younger children ($p < .01$) and were more easily predicted by others ($p < .001$).
5. Older children have fewer residual constructs (single constructs unrelated

to any cluster) in their grids than do younger children ($p < .01$). This is in line with the general expectation that older children will have more complex and articulated structures for construing.

The findings are generally in line with Bannister and Agnew (1977) even though different investigative instruments were used in the two studies. However, the relatively modest degree of difference between younger and older children in this study (where *younger* means 9–10-year-olds and *older*, 12–13-year-olds) as compared with the Bannister and Agnew study (where the age levels were 5 to 9 years) suggests the possibility that very major developments in self and other construing take place early on and although they continue (for a lifetime in terms of Kelly's arguments), the sharpest age-linked differences in psychological construing might well be manifest well prior to adolescence.

One finding that is not easy to interpret is that older children envisage less change than do younger children ($p < .001$) particularly from *like I am* to *like I'd like to be* and from *like I am* to *like I used to be* ($p < .05$). This could be variously interpreted as indicating greater perception of repeated personal themes in older children (as they develop superordinate constructs) or greater experience of change in younger children, but it might be wiser to postpone interpretation until what younger and older children actually say about change, has been more closely attended to. Mancini (1983) in his analysis of the types of constructs used by children of different age groups comes to the conclusion that younger children are psychological "behaviourists" and older children are "social psychologists", and this may well bear on the issue. Small changes may loom large when viewed behaviourially but may be seen as insignificant in social psychology terms.

PROBLEMS FOR TEACHERS

As mentioned in the sample description, the groups of eight children were so assembled that, within each, there were four children designated by the teacher as problematic and four children designated by the teacher as non-problematic. It should be noted that the differences between the problematic and non-problematic groups are modest in that all the children are within the normal school system and have not been singled out in any way by medical, psychiatric, or legal authorities as problems. In designating children as problematic, the teacher is saying no more than that they are unruly in class or appear to lack enthusiasm or do not fit in well with the classroom community or are markedly attention seeking and so on and so forth. It is in terms of this range of behaviours that the term problematic is defined.

In no case did our findings contradict the thesis that children judged problematic by their teachers will, as a group, have less-developed construing of self and others. Findings which significantly supported the thesis were as follows:

1. Problematic children made fewer psychological statements in their self-characterisations than non-problematic children ($p < .01$).

2. Problematic children are judged *harder to understand* by their peers (*p* < .001.)
3. Problematic children show less predictive accuracy (empathy) than non-problematic children (*p* < .01).
4. Problematic children are less popular than non-problematic children (*p* < .01).

PROBLEMS FOR CHILDREN

Clearly, for a child, a serious way of being problematic is to be so in relation to other children. Again, in construct theory terms, this is likely to be accompanied by confusion about self and in construing others. To investigate this hypothesis, the four children in each group who were judged most *hard to understand* by their peers in the group were considered "peer problematic". Interestingly, there was a considerable and significant overlap between children designated problematic by their teachers and children seen as *hard to understand* by their peers. In 38 out of 48 instances teacher and children were agreed as to who was problematic (*p* < .001).

None of the findings contradicted the notion that peer problematic children are less-developed construers of self than others and these findings gave some support to the hypothesis.

1. Peer problematic children are less popular (*p* < .05).
2. Peer problematic children have poorer predictive accuracy (empathy) than non-problematic children (*p* < .05.)
3. Peer problematic children's self-constructs are less salient (*p* < .05). This is to say that constructs of self are less important in terms of the strength of their relationship with other constructs, within the grids of peer problematic children.

CONFUSING BUT NOT CONFUSED

In construct theory terms a construct system can be well structured, elaborated and valid, in the sense that it enables the person successfully to anticipate unfolding events and guide his or her actions, while that same system is not necessarily clear and comprehensible to other people. For this reason it is important not automatically to equate being problematic, in terms of the judgment of either teachers or other children, with a poorly developed system of self and other construing. Clearly, the results of this study do indicate that being problematic for teachers or other children is *associated* with difficulties in self and other construing. But there remains the possibility that there are children who are confusing but not confused, children who are problematic for their teachers and for other children (i.e., *hard to understand*), but who see themselves as *easy to understand* and who are relatively "good psychologists" in terms of the measures used in the study.

A detailed examination of each child's protocol brought to light eight children who were judged problematic by their teachers and judged problematic (*hard to understand*) by their peers but who saw *themselves* as *easy to understand*. It was decided to compare this group of eight children, on all scores, with a selected group of eight children who were also judged problematic by their teachers and judged problematic (*hard to understand*) by other children, but who judged *themselves* to be *hard to understand*. The first group can be thought of as the problematic self-confident group and the second group as the problematic unsure group. In spite of the small numbers within each group (eight and eight) a number of statistically significant differences were found between them. These differences were as follows.

1. The problematic self-confident group made more psychological statements in their self-characterisation than the problematic unsure group ($p < .05$.)
2. The problematic self-confident group made, in total, more references to the views of others, references to personal history, and future and psychological cause and effect statements in their self-characterisations than did the problematic unsure group ($p < .05$.)
3. The problematic self-confident group had better total grid articulation scores than the problematic unsure group ($p < .05$).
4. The problematic self-confident group showed more contradictions (which could be taken to indicate greater elaboration and complexity) in their self-characterisations than did the problematic unsure group ($p < .05$).

Thus, chi-square analysis of these limited size samples, strongly suggests that amongst children who are equally seen as problematic by teachers and peers, those who are relatively self-confident (in the sense of seeing themselves as *easy to understand*) are also better psychologists in terms of the central measures used in this study and are relatively elaborated construers of self and others. As suggested earlier in this essay, such children may be thought of as rebel, unorthodox or original and thereby be a problem for others but not necessarily a problem for themselves. The self-characterisation of one of the older self-confident problematic children is given below as a kind of self-explanation.

Peter is bad at times. He likes jumping over people's hedges. He likes lighting other people's bonfires. He plays football for the school and for the rangers. He is bad tempered at the teachers. He likes taking motor bikes to pieces with his brother and riding them. He tells his Mum off if she gets him mad. Parents say he is bad, fighting all the time, throwing stones and running off. He gets on all right with the man across the street 'cos he learns him about motor bikes and cars. He likes picking locks on people's huts. He broke into a school and got caught in the past and was on probation for a few months. His mates would say he is always fighting them. He likes playing tag. He flies pigeons with his Dad. He likes swinging in the toilets and kicking a football about into the sinks. He usually chases next door's cat and puts it in a cage with the dog to see who wins. He goes rabbiting. Teachers would say he was bad tempered and always chewing gum and if they tell him to take it out he argues.

EDUCATIONAL ATTAINMENT

Problem children (as teacher rated) were lower in terms of educational attainment than normal children ($p < .001$). In turn, for educational attainment, positive correlations appeared with *easy to understand* ($r = .47$, $p < .001$), with predictive accuracy (empathy) ($r = .30$, $p < .05$) and attainment correlates positively with popularity ($r = .38$, $p < .01$). This needs to be borne in mind when considering group differences on these measures.

BOYS AND GIRLS

The number of boys and girls, in each of the groups compared, was equated so that the found differences cannot be attributed to gender. However, as between boys and girls there were two significant differences. The construct *lazy* was more salient for girls (accounting for more of the variance in their grids ($p < .05$), and girls seemed to have slightly more complex structures for their grids in that boys showed more single residual constructs ($p < .005$).

Conclusion

The subheading ''Conclusion'' merely means that this essay is coming to an end, not that we have any definitive and concluding truth to offer. What can be offered is a series of questions arising.

An overview of the findings of this and other studies, suggests that the child's sense of self is pervasive. Directly, in self-characterisations and implicitly in the interlinking of grid measures, we are presented with a holistic portrait. It may be that children only grudgingly and under constant social tuition accept segmentation into variegated faculties and roles. Perhaps, while psychologists are solemnly and separately studying the child's concept of number, the child's development of language, the child's moral development, and so forth, the child is living across such boundaries. Perhaps, while adults in their own partitioned domains of law, education, medicine, and so forth fashion the child at school, the child in family, the child at play, the child lives within a superordinate self which initially subsumes such casting. Doubtless, the adult world always wins at least a partial victory in that the child eventually learns the relatively unrelated parts he or she has to play and accepts a view of self which is composed of psychological segments.

A second suggestive finding was our experience of the readiness with which the children undertook formal self-examination—a complex psychological exercise. They showed a native enthusiasm for what must have been, in many ways, an unfamiliar and strange series of tasks, and they revealed a level of self-awareness which could not have been predicted from the aspects of self they are enabled to display in standard school projects. It may be that if our educational system offered formats within which children could explicitly study and extend their ''psychology'', the response might be intense and, in developmental terms, rewarding.

References

Adams-Webber, J. R. (1969). Cognitive complexity and sociality. *British Journal of Social and Clinical Psychology,* **8,** 211–16.

Applebee, A. N. (1976). The development of children's responses to repertory grids. *British Journal of Social and Clinical Psychology,* 5, 103–107.

Bannister, D., and Agnew, J. (1977). The Child's Construing of Self. *In* "1976 Nebraska Symposium on Motivation" (A. W. Landfield, ed.), University of Nebraska Press, Lincoln.

Bannister, D. and Mair, J. M. M. (1968). "The Evaluation of Personal Constructs", Academic Press, London.

Brierly, D. W. (1967). "The Use of Personality Constructs by Children of Three Different Ages", Unpublished doctoral dissertation, London University.

Fransella, F. and Bannister, D. (1977). "A Manual for Repertory Grid Technique", Academic Press, London.

Hayden, B., Nasby, W., and Davids, A. (1977). Interpersonal conceptual structures, predictive accuracy, and social adjustment of emotionally disturbed boys. *Journal of Abnormal Psychology,* **86,** 3, 315–320.

Honess, T. (1979). Children's implicit theories of their peers: A developmental analysis. *British Journal of Psychology,* **70,** 419–425.

Jackson, S. R. (1980). "The Development of Self Construing in Children", Unpublished D.A.C.P. dissertation, University of Stirling, Scotland.

Kelly, G. A. (1955). "The Psychology of Personal Constructs", Vols. I and II, Norton, New York.

Mancini, F. (1983). Personal Communication.

Ravenette, A. T. (1975). Grid techniques for children. *Journal of Child Psychology and Psychiatry,* **16,** 79–83.

Salmon, P. (1970). A Psychology of Personal Growth. *In* "Perspectives of Personal Construct Theory" (D. Bannister, ed.), Academic Press, London.

Salmon, P. (1976). Grid Measures with Child Subjects. *In* "Explorations of Interpersonal Space", Vol 1, (P. Slater, ed.), Wiley, London.

6

The Terrors of Cognition: On the Experiential Validity of Personal Construct Theory

L. M. Leitner

Personal construct theory (Kelly, 1955) was written as a comprehensive, scientifically testable theory of personality (Landfield and Leitner, 1980). In attempting to be comprehensive, Kelly presented the theory in an abstract manner. However, when a theory is presented abstractly, it may be difficult to see its concrete, day-to-day experiential implications. The "too cognitive" criticism of personal construct theory (Bruner, 1956; Rogers, 1956) can be seen as an understandable reaction to Kelly's abstract presentation. Although personal construct theorists have repeatedly protested this criticism (e.g., Bannister, 1977; McCoy, 1977), it has persisted to the present day, as any survey of introductory personality texts will show. Further, the too cognitive criticism will, in all likelihood, continue until people can see some implications of personal construct theory for the experiences of everyday life. Therefore, this chapter attempts to demonstrate the usefulness of one personal construct approach to understanding the "flesh and blood" emotional experiences of people. We attempt this by first reviewing relevant aspects of Kelly's theory. We then show one elaboration of the theory into the ecstasies and terrors of our experiential world.

Personal Construct Theory: A Selected Review

Personal construct theory begins with a fundamental assumption that the person is striving to create an understanding of the world. The person then "tests" this understanding by predicting future events. If these events are consistent with prediction, the construct is said to be validated. If the events are inconsistent with prediction, the construct is invalidated and the person experiences pressure to change the system. Kelly is thus assuming that the person interacts with the world in a manner similar to a scientist, hence the "person as scientist" metaphor.

It would seem that Kelly minimizes the importance of interpersonal relationships in his theory. However, interpersonal relating is introduced in a most profound way in Kelly's sociality corollary: "To the extent that one person construes the construction process of another, he may play a role in a social process involving the other person'' (Kelly, 1955, p. 95). This corollary defines a role in terms of interpersonal acting based upon the *understanding* of other people, not a socially prescribed course of action. Landfield and Leitner (1980) point out that "this corollary is so important that Kelly almost entitled his theory 'role theory' " (p. 10). Stringer and Bannister (1979) make a similar point when they state, "But for Kelly, the person, which is all that his psychology deals with, was only constituted in relations with others; constructs were chiefly available through interaction with others and obtained their meaning in the context of that interaction'' (p. xiv).

Further emphasizing the importance of interpersonal understanding in personal construct theory, Kelly calls our most important constructs core role constructs: "One's deepest understanding of being maintained as a social being is his concept of his core role'' (1955, p. 502). He elaborates this by stating, "Our constructions of our relations to the thinking and expectancies of certain other people reach down deeply into our vital processes. Through our construction of our roles we sustain even the most autonomic life functions. These are indeed *core role structures*'' (1955, p. 909, emphasis in original).

Thus, Kelly argues that our most defining experiences involve role constructs. We should therefore consider more carefully some of the implications of Kelly's definition of role. To avoid confusion, Kelly's definition will be termed "ROLE" while the traditional definition will be referred to as "role."

The Nature of ROLEs

Because ROLEs are so central for Kelly, let us look at some concrete implications of what it means to engage in such relationships. In so doing, we are not saying that these are the only implications of the sociality corollary. Rather, they are a set of implications that seem interesting and useful in understanding the human condition. In this discussion, it is assumed that you either establish an extensive ROLE relationship with me or you do not establish any form of ROLE relationship with me. All middle levels of ROLE relating will be ignored. Hopefully, this deliberate error will simplify without distorting the major points of the discussion. This discussion revolves around Kelly's two characteristics of ROLEs: understanding the other person's inner world and interpersonal actions based upon that understanding.

UNDERSTANDING THE OTHER PERSON

Kelly's (1955, p. 95) definition of ROLE emphasizes understanding the other person ("to the extent that one person construes the construction process of another"). This implies that people can vary in their ability to play ROLEs with others ("to the extent"). Some people may not be able to construe my construction process as extensively as others. Those people who construe my organization of my experiences in more depth will establish a more extensive ROLE relationship with me than those who construe me in less fundamental ways.

Further, in attempting to establish ROLE relationships, we do not construe static individuals. Since Kelly viewed the person as in motion, we attempt to understand a person who is changing, evolving, and growing. Thus, in establishing a ROLE relationship with me, rather than just construing my constructs, you attempt to construe my "construction process" (Kelly, 1955, p. 95). This implies several things. First, you have to see me as a person who is a process when you attempt a ROLE relationship with me. Because I can evolve and grow, you have to be willing to change your construing of me. In this context, one of the earliest empirical findings based upon personal construct theory is that change can be threatening (Landfield, 1954, 1955). If I change, you have to be willing to risk the threat of change also.

But even more fundamental is that in a ROLE relationship, you construe the *process* of my construing more than the *content* of my personal construct system (construing the construction process of another). Now, because process cannot be understood independent of content, what content is related to my construing process? In this regard, Kelly explicitly states that my core ROLE constructs— the most central aspects of my experience—are the governors of my process of construing: "*Core constructs are those which govern a person's maintenance processes*—that is, *those by which he maintains his identity and existence*" (Kelly, 1955, p. 482, emphasis in original). Kelly goes on to detail how a person's mental processes follow the lines laid down by these core structures. Thus, to establish a ROLE relationship with me, you must understand my core ROLE constructs, the most central aspects of my being. In other words, in a ROLE relationship, you come to know me intimately.

Now, my ROLE constructs, which you are coming to understand, are the same constructs that govern *my* forming ROLE relationships. This implies that, as you try to construe my construing process, I am trying to construe your construing process. True intimacy can be defined, then, as a reciprocity of extensive ROLE relationships. This reciprocity probably occurs in most, although certainly not all, deep ROLE relationships. (In psychotherapy, for example, the therapist may establish a much more extensive ROLE relationship with the client than vice versa.) Because my core ROLE is so central for me, "affecting even the most autonomic life functions" (Kelly, 1955, p. 909), I will tend not to allow you deep access to it unless I know the sort of human being you are. Thus, in most ROLE relationships, you must let me come to know you as you come to know me.

In this context, it should be pointed out that one does not establish a deep ROLE relationship with just anyone. Kelly's individuality corollary suggests that, because people differ from one another in their constructions of events, some individuals will have core ROLE constructs that are fundamentally incompatible with mine. Further, many of the day-to-day affairs of the world can be accomplished by establishing role, not ROLE, relationships. Intimate knowledge of one's pharmacist, for example, is not necessary in order to get a prescription filled.

Further, no matter how intimate one becomes in construing the construing process of another, Kelly's definition of ROLE makes it quite clear that it is still *two* people involved in a ROLE relationship. You cannot assume that others are just like you and claim to have ROLE relationships. Thus, in addition to closeness, ROLE relationships also involve respecting the integrity and separateness of the other person. In other words, ROLE relationships involve a simultaneous experience of both closeness and distance.

INTERPERSONAL ACTIONS

ROLE relationships involve more than understanding others; they involve acting on that understanding. Kelly (1955, p. 97) states explicitly that a ROLE is "an ongoing pattern of behavior." In this context, Kelly has elsewhere described behavior as the "independent variable" in psychology (1969a, p. 34). With our actions, in other words, we test our construing process. This implies that, by acting, we open our personal construct system to potential validation or invalidation. Because ROLE relationships are so deep and so personal, we, through ROLE actions, may experience the invalidation or the validation of the very core of our existence. In either case, this is not done within the private confines of our heads; it is performed in the public arena of interpersonal actions.

Further, ROLE relationships involve more than occasional actions; they also involve commitment ("an *ongoing* pattern of behavior"). Thus, in a ROLE relationship, one invests a great deal of oneself for a relatively long period of time. One does not occasionally experience the potential joys and disappointments of intimacy. Rather, in a sustained commitment, these potential experiences are always lurking in the relationship.

In summary, then, ROLE relationships sound very similar to Buber's (1970) "I–Thou" relationships. In a ROLE relationship we not only risk invalidation by placing central aspects of ourselves on the line. We also must be open to the results of this experimentation. Further, if these results work out badly, we have the *responsibility* of dealing with the situation. We cannot blame God, society, mother, father, husband, wife, friend, lover, gene, spleen, dopamine, or anyone or anything else.

> Jesus suggested that if you do something bad you should not run from the scene of the crime screaming, "I've sinned. I've sinned. I'll make up for it! I'll never do it again." He suggests instead that you stop, turn around and look at what you have done, acknowledge that it was you rather than the Devil, society, or your ulcers, examine the mistake, and reconstrue the situation so that the possibilities of making a similar mistake in the future are minimized. (Kelly, 1969b, p. 186)

Although ROLE relationships may be deeply satisfying, not many individuals develop ROLE relating as extensively as discussed previously. One reason for this may be the potential dangers inherent in ROLE relationships. Let us turn to some of the negative emotional implications of ROLE relating.

Anxiety, Fear, Threat, Hostility, and Guilt

McCoy (1977) offers a comprehensive overview of the nature of emotions within personal construct theory. Essentially, emotions can arise from the invalidation or the validation of constructs. Kelly (1955) has defined several emotions (anxiety, fear, threat, hostility, and guilt) which can be related to the validational fortunes of core ROLE constructs. We begin by discussing the emotional experiences associated with the invalidation of ROLE constructs.

INVALIDATION, ROLES, AND EMOTIONS

Anxiety (the awareness of events that lie outside the range of application of one's constructs) occurs when the events of the world invalidate our construing of them. The experience of anxiety is always inherent in ROLE relationships. Kelly (1955, p. 95) acknowledges this possibility in the first three words of the sociality corollary ("to the extent"). Thus, ultimately, the other person is a mystery (Mair, 1977) that cannot be known totally. This implies that, as you try to construe my construing process, aspects of my experience will not fit neatly into your personal construct system. Because you cannot know me totally, there is the likelihood of the invalidation of core constructs in a ROLE relationship and the subsequent experience of anxiety.

With invalidation comes pressure to change the personal construct system. However, as you anticipate changing core constructs, fear and threat enter the picture. These constructs are, after all, the central components of your organization of experiences. To modify or discard them could shake your experiential world to its foundation. If the modifications are major and comprehensive, you will experience threat. If less major changes are involved in your core ROLE constructs, you will experience fear. Obviously, then, there is the potential for threat and fear in any ROLE relationship.

If the changes called for in ROLE relationships are too threatening, the person may become hostile. Hostility (the unwillingness to change a construct even though it has been invalidated) can be seen as an attempt to preserve the integrity of a system which is being invalidated. Instead of changing the personal construct system to fit one's experience, one tries to change the environment to fit one's personal construct system. Because deep ROLE relationships carry the potential for disrupting the foundations of the personality, hostility may be an understandable consequence of intimacy.

Guilt, or the awareness that one is acting against ROLE constructs, may be linked to hostility. Kelly (1955, p. 512) has elaborated on how hostility is a way to avoid facing the "dark empty void of guilt" (not a bad metaphor, by the way, for a "cognitive" theorist). In other words, by refusing to reconstrue the ROLE relationship when invalidated, a person does not face the agony of acknowledging actions which go against his or her most central values. However, since these most central constructs are ROLE constructs, the hostile *limiting* of ROLE relationships may, in itself, be an act against these core values, resulting in the experience of guilt.

VALIDATION, ROLES, AND EMOTIONS

McCoy (1977) defines emotions such as love and happiness in terms of the *validation* of core constructs. If I risk my core ROLE and you validate these constructs, I will experience deep, positive emotions. These positive experiences may be what makes us risk the invalidation associated with ROLE relationships. On the other hand, it should be noted that the *validation* of constructs by another person *may be* most upsetting. If you validate my construing, I may be tempted to experiment with new and larger possibilities. This may leave me vulnerable to even greater invalidation in the future.

In summary, then, ROLE relationships are fundamental for Kelly, yet the very nature of ROLEs evoke emotions like anxiety, threat, fear, hostility, and guilt. For purposes of simplicity, we will call this conglomeration of emotions "terror." We now turn to some of the clinical implications of this position and discuss the experience of psychopathology and psychotherapy from this perspective.

ROLE Relationships and Psychopathology

If the terror of ROLE relationships appears overwhelming to the person (i.e., the ROLE relationship would potentially invalidate major aspects of the core of the personal construct system), one may attempt to avoid deep ROLE relationships. If this avoidance is global and all encompassing (e.g., the person cannot tolerate extensive ROLE relationships), the person will be left without an important aspect of the human condition—deep interpersonal relating. Thus, major, global avoidings of ROLE relationships can be termed pathological in that they result in experiences that seriously limit the potential of the person. Let us discuss some of the ways individuals limit ROLE relationships.

Before beginning, it seems important to emphasize several points. First, the person limits ROLE relatings when it seems that the alternative, engaging in ROLEs, will be devastating. The price the individual pays by avoiding ROLEs may be much preferred to the alternative. Further, there are many times when engaging in ROLEs is not necessary. In this section, the discussion focuses on the *global retreat* from ROLEs. For these purposes, ROLEs have been defined in an all-or-none fashion, ignoring all intermediate levels of ROLE relating.

ROLES AND ROLES

One way of avoiding ROLE relationships is to form relationships based only on social roles. In this form of relating, the individual may say and do all the "right things" but does not come to know the experience of other persons. The person may be married and have a family yet is existing in a house full of strangers rather than living in a home filled with friends since there are no ROLE relationships. The advantage of this type of existence is that the person does not have to face the terrors of ROLE relating. On the other hand, the total retreat into roles may leave the person experiencing, at some level of awareness, Kelly's (1955, p. 512) "dark empty void." In other words, if one globally retreats from the terrors of ROLEs by adopting social roles, one can pay the price in loneliness, emptiness, meaninglessness, and guilt.

To take a clinical example, Landfield (1980b) describes the psychotherapy of an individual who spent many hours discussing the things he had accomplished in life:

> He had been a collegiate golf champion, president of a fraternity, an excellent student, and a naval officer. His credentials were quite impressive. He further stated that he had traveled worldwide with his parents who had introduced him to famous people. In this context of protesting too much, I asked him what all of these events meant for him personally. A long period of silence followed this question. . . . This session marked a transition in therapy. Sam began to actively explore with the question of meaning. (p. 133)

As another example, Ed was a "good" husband, father, and employee in the sense that he always did what was expected of a husband, father, and employee. However, there was nothing in the way of ROLE relationships with his wife, daughter, or boss. He did not understand anything about their fundamental ways of experiencing the world; they did not understand central aspects of his experience. The therapy turned when, after a death in the family, Ed stated, "If I died today, the only thing that would be said is, 'Who pitches in the softball game on Saturday?'" This clearly shows the experience of emptiness and meaninglessness associated with the massive retreat from ROLEs.

CONTROL AND ROLES

Individuals who are extremely controlling may also be avoiding deep ROLE relationships. Others are conceptualized in terms of whether they enable you to get control, threaten your control, allow you to control them, or attempt to control you. This person may attempt to climb the ladder of success so that more control can be achieved. Others are not experienced as unique, evolving, feeling beings; rather they are seen as pawns in games of power and control.

For example, Susan is a highly successful business woman referred to therapy for depression. She always maintained a professional front since anything else was a "sign of weakness" and resulted in somebody "getting you." This meant, however, that she could not get involved with any man because, if he got past the professional front, he would control her. She would become dependent on him, he would be the powerful one, and she would wind up submissive, passive, and helpless. Thus, whenever a man expressed an interest in her, she would quite naturally withdraw in hostility. The emptiness in her life can be seen by her statement that, although this worked well Monday through Friday, "on Saturday nights my life consists of three quilts and a mystery novel." In the context of her massive retreat from ROLEs, Susan's depression is understandable. As a matter of fact, one can look at the experience of depression as a healthy sign because it showed that Susan realized the emptiness of her life situation. Thus, rather than a symptom to be removed, the depression was a valid reflection of Susan's life.

HOSTILITY AND ROLES

In addition to being a consequence of ROLEs, hostility can also be a way of avoiding the terrors of ROLEs. In a ROLE relationship, the personal construct system should change when invalidated. If one initially construes the person in a given manner and does not change one's construction, the relationship remains static. This is vastly different from the ROLE experience of one construing, evolving person coming to understand another construing, evolving person. In other words, hostility freezes the relationship in an early phase and does not allow the continued growth and change necessary for continued ROLE relating. In this context, Kelly states, "In order to play a constructive ROLE in relation to another person one must not only, in some measure, see eye to eye with him but must, in some measure, have an acceptance of him and his way of seeing things" (1955, p. 95). Thus hostility can be used to massively retreat from ROLE relationships.

Leitner (1980) describes an interaction in therapy where the client expresses quite directly the usefulness of hostility in avoiding the terrors of ROLE relationships. The client, Sue, would not reconstrue the therapist as "trustworthy." Rather, he was "more subtle" in his untrustworthiness:

Larry: What would it be like if I were more subtle?
Sue: I might trust you.
Larry: And if you trusted me?
Sue: You might get me . . . Better than any of them. (p. 113)

MANIPULATIVENESS AND ROLES

One way of avoiding the terrors associated with the invalidation of core constructs is to manipulate others instead of relating to them. This is obviously related to hostility in the sense that one is "rigging the deck" to have things come out his or her way. The manipulator says what she or he thinks other people want to hear so they will form the "right" impressions and do the "right" things. This relating is vastly different from the ROLE experience of central aspects of one person coming to know central aspects of another person. Sometimes the manipulations result in experiencing the emptiness of a life filled with non-ROLE relationships.

Betty was a 30-year-old woman referred to therapy for "depression." She had, after a promiscuous adolescence, decided that she was going to be "prim and proper" in order to "catch" a man. Thus, on dates she always acted in such a way that the man would never think of sex. This acting generalized to the point that she spent most of her life creating just the right impression for people to see. She married, had two children, and continued her "sugary sweet" manipulations until her thirtieth birthday. At this point, she began to realize that she had lived almost one-half her life and was without anyone who knew her as a person. Her depression, like Susan's, can be seen as a valid reflection of her life situation— not a disease to be treated.

RELIGION AND ROLES

Beliefs about God go to the core of our personal construct system. In spite of that, certain fundamentalistic, authoritarian religions (Fromm, 1950) can be used in a way that allows for the global retreat from ROLE relationships. Within these groups, God is responsible for anything and everything about your life. In contrast to the choice corollary of personal construct theory, the *person* makes no choices in life; God makes all of the decisions. Further, anyone who does not see the world in the same way is a "sinner" in need of "saving." Thus, the authoritarian insists that you become one also. You cannot be your own unique, separate person. Rather, you are "prayed for" if you try to be different. In reaction to such hostility, the other person usually withdraws—leaving the authoritarian with little in the way of deep ROLE relationships.

George was referred for a variety of psychophysiological problems (heart palpitations, ulcers, etc.). He had, in spite of a very traumatic childhood, been attempting ROLE relationships until the break up of an important relationship with a woman. Shortly after this ROLE relationship ended, George became a "born again" Christian. He did not worry about relationships anymore: God would give him a girlfriend when He wanted George to have one. Further, if he prayed long enough and hard enough, God might decide that he could have a new stereo. When friends and relatives tried to get George to look at religion more humanistically, George stated that Satan was working through them, they needed saving, and that he would pray for them. As his friends withdrew, George prayed more fervently.

MYSTICISM AND ROLES

People can also avoid ROLEs through mysticism. Like the authoritarian religious person, the "mystical retreater" tries to find a simple, clichéd answer rather than struggle with the effort and terror of understanding other live, struggling people. The person may either become a "guru" in an attempt to maintain limited ROLE relationships or a "guru follower" for the same purpose. Unfortunately, truisms, no matter how true, are experienced by people as hollow in the sense that they are stated without a profound understanding of the other's core ROLE constructs. This phoniness results in other people withdrawing from the mystic in confusion, discomfort, or suspicion.

Paul, a mental health worker from a neighboring city, entered treatment to help his suicidally depressed son. Earlier in his career, he had been a sensitive and effective psychotherapist. As the effects of dealing daily with the terrors of ROLEs with clients made themselves felt, Paul began to desperately search for the *answer* to mental illness. His search led him into existentialism and Eastern psychologies and religions. Paul then established a group of "existentialistic–Hinduistic–Zen Buddhistic" psychotherapists. He was the leader, the great therapist, whom they followed blindly. Clients or therapists who questioned his insights were either defensive, resistant, or lacking in integrity (see also Timerlin and Timerlin, 1982).

SEXUALITY AND ROLES

Although sex is a biological act, sexuality has to do with what sex means to the person (Luria and Rose, 1979). A person can use sex to express intimacy or to retreat from ROLE relationships. When used to retreat from ROLEs, sex helps define the relationship on solely physical grounds and allows the participants an opportunity to escape the terrors associated with ROLE relating.

Joan was a young woman who came into treatment for "memory blocks" covering several parts of her adolescent development. Her relationship with her family had been filled with the invalidation of any attempts at ROLE relating. Her parents, for example, would buy her anything but would not give her much in the way of emotional understanding. Her mother would confide about how "brutal" men were and that "all a man wanted was sex." This was exemplified in the parents' relationship by a father who was cold and domineering while the mother sacrificed her individuality. Thus, my client associated relationships with sacrificing her independence as a person. Joan was in quite a dilemma when, in adolescence, young men began to express an interest in her. Her resolution to this dilemma was to become quite promiscuous sexually. This kept the young men around, validated her mother's words (which was, by the way, a hostile avoiding of ROLEs), and defined the relationship in exclusively physical terms. In this way, she did not have to sacrifice her independence as a person. This pattern reached its conclusion on the night of her sixteenth birthday party when, in order to have some young men at her party, she wound up "servicing" several of them in her house.

Tim was a "womanizer" who enjoyed chasing women, getting them into bed, and dumping them. After "conquering" a woman sexually, he would quickly lose interest in her. Obviously, this sort of relating involves little in the way of understanding the experiences of the women involved. After 6 months of therapy, Tim started a session by stating, "You know, I met a woman the other night. She is really beautiful person trapped inside an ugly body." This statement signified a new phase in therapy—women were people and had, therefore, to be understood as experiencing human beings. This experiment with ROLE relationships concluded when he married the woman.

As a final example, consider Mike, a young man who sought therapy for a variety of reasons, not the least of which was having seven personalities (six of them female). After a very rough childhood involving an alcoholic, abusive father and a sexually unfaithful mother, Mike fell in love with a man. This man "used, abused, and dumped" him. Subsequently, Mike became an expert on causal sex, often having relations with as many as 10 men a night. If a man began to care for him, Mike would arrange (quite deliberately) to be seduced by another man while the caring person watched helplessly. This, needless to say, hindered the development of any deep relationship with the caring man. In therapy, Mike began to struggle between two equally unpleasant (for him) alternatives: care for someone as a person (ROLE relating) and risk overwhelming pain (terror) versus not caring and "having loneliness and emptiness eat away at my soul like a cancer."

LITERALISM AND ROLES

Landfield (1980a) has described a pathological way of organizing experience known as literalism. Landfield defined literalism as "a way of thinking, feeling, or doing which implies the restricted and absolute interpretation of an event or a relationship" (p. 315). Literally relating feelings, values, and behaviors (e.g., a feeling of sexual attraction is the same as having acted out sexually and being a "bad" husband in one's value system) has been associated with certain forms of psychopathology (Leitner, 1981a, b). Further, most forms of psychotherapy challenge literalisms in the client (Leitner, 1982).

Literalism would also make ROLE relationships most difficult. If feelings and values cannot be differentiated, to feel angry means that one is a "terrible" person in one's value system. For such a person, the realization that someone else felt angry would cause massive shifts in the personal construct system (threat) as the person reconstrued the basic worth of the other individual. The literalist would then be caught between not acknowledging the anger or stubbornly insisting that the person is terrible for having such a feeling. Both of these reactions illustrate the refusal to reconstrue characteristic of hostility. The link between hostility and retreating from ROLEs has already been discussed.

For example, Tom was referred for therapy due to lifelong feelings of inadequacy. He exemplified a person who literally related feelings, values, and actions. He could not feel anything other than love without believing he was a "terrible son of a bitch." (He had been called this by his parents in the past when he exhibited "negative" emotions. For example, when scared and sick with the flu, he had heard his mother say, "That God-damned son of a bitch. I'll never get any sleep if that fucker keeps vomiting.") Not by coincidence, Tom could not allow others deep access into his core ROLE as they would see the feelings which made him such an awful person. Further, he could not get to know others due to the possibility of reciprocity in ROLE relationships. His life, without deep ROLE relationships, was empty and lonely.

CHAOTIC FRAGMENTALISM AND ROLES

Landfield (1980a) also described chaotic fragmentalism as a pathological way of organizing experience. Chaotic fragmentalism was defined as "an unorganized complexity of thinking, feeling, or doing which implies an unrestricted, loose, undirected, and shifting interpretation of an event or a relationship" (p. 316). The chaotic fragmenting of values and behavior can be seen in the person who professes to be a "good mother" (value) although she has been objectively judged to physically and emotionally abuse her children (behavior). Serious psychopathology (e.g., schizophrenia) has been linked to the chaotic fragmenting of feelings, values, and behaviors (Leitner, 1981a, b). Further, many forms of psychotherapy can be viewed as challenging chaotic fragmentalism (Leitner, 1982).

Chaotic fragmentalism also makes ROLE relationships difficult. Because ROLE relationships involve construing and construing involves organization (Kelly, 1955), the chaotic fragmentalist does not engage in elaborate ROLEs. The confusion and disorganization associated with chaotic fragmentalism makes it difficult (if not impossible) to understand the construing process of another. Further, this amount of confusion will hinder others in their attempts to understand the fragmentalist (Landfield, 1977).

One example of chaotic fragmentalism can be seen in the client who believed he had been forced to have sex with a German girl while both of them were kidnapped by Serpentines (green snake-like creatures that reproduce through anal sex) in flying saucers. The chaotic fragmentalism manifested itself when he met a girl in a neighboring town with the same name as his "partner." He became convinced that they were in love and had shared many intimate moments. Nothing the woman said or did changed his mind. (A feeling—love—is unrelated to the woman's behavior.) In this example, there is no attempt to reconstrue the experience of the woman when she tried to invalidate his construing. This, once again, is hostility which has already been tied to the retreat from ROLEs.

ROLE Relationships and Psychotherapy

So far this chapter has focused on the pathological impoverishing of ROLE relationships. Psychotherapy may be defined as the attempt to change pathological ways of organizing experience through the use of an interpersonal relationship. As such, psychotherapy must deal with the terror of ROLEs. In the following discussion of therapy and ROLEs, we will, for purposes of simplicity, focus on individual psychotherapy with adults, although the basic points are applicable to other types of therapy. In the interactions between the members of the therapy dyad, the client is generally seeking help from the therapist. The difficulties the client has in ROLEs will most likely be manifested in the relationship with the therapist. Further, the therapist, by virtue of his or her humanity, is also well aware of the potential terrors inherent in any ROLE relationship established with the client. Thus, both client and therapist will simultaneously show the desire for ROLEs as well as the tendency to withdraw from ROLEs. While aspects of the therapy process will be discussed as if they are manifestations of the client or of the therapist, we recognize that, in reality, the division of the therapy relationship into these categories is somewhat forced and arbitrary.

THE THERAPY PROCESS, THE CLIENT, AND ROLES

Resistance and Defensiveness

If ROLE relationships are terrifying and if withdrawing from ROLE relationships leaves one vulnerable to issues of meaninglessness, a person is hard pressed to find a satisfactory compromise between these two options. Because therapy attempts to allow the client to develop new ways of relating, the terrors involved in treatment may be most upsetting to the client. One may be risking the terror of ROLEs as well as looking at the meaninglessness of one's past life. It is not surprising that, on occasion, a client may decide that this is more trouble than it is worth. When the client makes this decision, the therapist will sometimes say that the client is "resisting." (We will see later that "resistance" and "defensiveness" may be more related to the therapist's avoidance of ROLEs than to the client's.) Thus, resistance may be the client's solution to the dilemma of both terror and meaninglessness.

For example, Theresa sought treatment for a variety of reasons, most notably bulimia and depression. Her background included a stereotyped, upper-middle-class family in which everyone had their roles yet were without ROLEs. Father, a physician, was the breadwinner while Mother and daughters spent the money on a variety of material objects. Father had preached to the family that any emotional insecurities were signs of weakness and that his family was "too strong for that." Any emotional issue could be handled by "positive thinking." For Theresa, then, committing herself to therapy implied that she was too weak to be a part of her family. However, terminating therapy left her facing the implications of a life without extensive ROLE relationships. Her ambivalence about therapy was an understandable resolution to this dilemma.

Transference

Transference can also be viewed as both an attempt by the client to bring a ROLE relationship into therapy and an impoverishing of a ROLE. Kelly (1955) states both sides of this aspect of the client–therapist relationship: "Transference, as the term is reserved for use in psychotherapy, is based on ROLE constructs rather than constructs in general" (p. 664). He goes on to state, though, that the transference, because it is based on constellatory constructs, means that "the therapist soon finds himself cast into the form of a highly elaborated and vastly prejudicial stereotype" (p. 666). As the following example shows, the transference, if dealt with appropriately, allows the person to experience and struggle with the terrors associated with the invalidation of core ROLE constructs.

Joanne, a young black woman, sought therapy for "depression." During a substantial part of the treatment, Joanne acted polite, formal, and respectful. As I focused on this aspect of our relationship, the client began to elaborate on how I was probably a racist like all other "white guys." This led us into her fear of me as a white male and into her belief that a white man could never understand the experiences of a black woman. I commented on what it must be like to feel so alienated from so many other people (all white males). Joanne became quite tearful as she recalled incidents where white men had called her "Nigger," used her sexually then deserted her, physically assaulted her relatives, and burned crosses on her grandparents' yard.

THE THERAPY PROCESS, THE THERAPIST, AND ROLES

The therapist also struggles with the terrors of ROLEs. Generally, the term *countertransference* is used in describing this struggle. When experiencing countertransference, the therapist distances him or herself from the client. Countertransference can be overpowering when the therapist feels particularly anxious, threatened, and so forth by the client. In this situation, the countertransference difficulties may become so severe that the client (quite intelligently) terminates the treatment. Alternatively, countertransference problems may be less severe yet more subtle. In order to use countertransference effectively, the therapist must be alert enough to recognize these subtle cues. Let us now consider some of the many ways in which the therapist avoids ROLE relationships.

Resistance and Defensiveness

As implied earlier, terms like *resistance* and *defensiveness* may say more about the therapist's terror of ROLEs than the client's. The therapist who uses such terms may have a ready-made justification for any misunderstandings of the client's inner world. If the client does not do as expected, it is not the therapist's construing which is at fault; the client is obviously "resisting." If the client does not feel the way she or he "should" feel in a situation, the therapist has not misconstrued the situation; the client is "defending" against his or her "real" feelings. Thus, terms like resistance and defensiveness may offer the therapist a rationale for refusing to reconstrue when invalidated. In other words, these terms can reveal a therapist's hostility toward clients.

In this context, Landfield (personal communication, 1978) has described the evaluation of a child who had been severely abused by his father. The boy reported experiencing no anger toward his father. The clinicians assigned to evaluate this case concluded that the child was "repressing" his "real" feelings toward his father. They then decided on an extensive battery of psychological tests that also failed to demonstrate the existence of the "unconscious rage" against which the child was defending himself. Finally, in desperation, they decided to ask the client *why* he did not hate his father. The client told them that, first, his father's beatings were "fair" (i.e., he was only beaten when he disobeyed the rules in the house). Furthermore, each time he was beaten, it proved to his peers how "tough" he was. In this child's neighborhood, to be tough meant to be respected and to survive without being assaulted. By abandoning the concepts of defense, resistance, and unconscious, a more profound understanding of the client was achieved.

Sexual Attraction

A therapist's feelings of sexual attraction toward a client can also be a way of avoiding the terrors of ROLEs with the client. When this occurs, the client may become a sexual object more than a person struggling with the agonies over ROLE relationships in the outside world. Let us consider two cases of sexual feelings between therapist and client. In the first example, the therapy was seriously damaged. In the second case, the feelings were used to increase the growth occurring in therapy.

Marie sought treatment due to chronic marital unhappiness. Each time I began to see derivatives suggesting that a positive transference was developing in the therapy, I would receive a call from a psychiatrist colleague informing me that Marie had admitted herself to a state hospital. Because these were unexpected and serious ruptures in the therapy relationship, I sought consultation from a colleague. Neither of us could understand the causes of the ruptures. Upon discharge, Marie always returned to therapy and reported seeking the hospitalization after "waking up one morning and feeling suicidal." As she described her experiences during her third hospitalization, she mentioned being sexually attracted to a technician.

At this point, several things fell into place for me (the positive transference, feeling sexually attracted to a mental health professional, and the fact that Marie's previous therapist had been rumored to engage in sexual activities with his clients). I then asked about other times she had been sexually attracted to mental health professionals. Marie assumed a fetal position, began a rocking motion, and discussed her sexual encounters with her previous therapist. As the details emerged over the weeks, these encounters included making love in his house, performing fellatio during her "therapy" sessions, and his attempting to convince Marie to leave her husband and move to another state with him. Because positive feelings implied seduction and desertion, it is no surprise that, whenever the possibility of caring about our relationship emerged, Marie became agitated, suicidally depressed, and escaped from therapy to the state hospital. (I do not think, by the way, that I was of much help to Marie. I do not know if my ineffectiveness was due to the effects of the seduction, my limitations as a therapist, her leaving the area 6 months later, or some combination of these factors.)

As a second example of sexual feelings by a therapist, consider the case of Alice, an attractive young woman who entered therapy due to feelings of depression. We had been working together for about 18 months when, following a period of profound personal growth, a mutual decision was made to terminate treatment in 2 months. In a subsequent session, as Alice expressed her gratitude to me for being of help to her, the thought, "Where did I park my car?" quickly flashed through my mind. I recognized this as a distancing of myself from Alice—a manifestation of countertransference. This made me wonder *why* I had suddenly become anxious with Alice when she expressed gratitude toward me. As Alice continued, I became aware of being sexually aroused. (It was my anxiety about my sexual feeling that resulted in my quick thought about my car.) In this context, I reviewed my current life situation, my typical reactions to female clients, and what I knew of Alice as a person. During this review, I recalled that, until 6 months into therapy, Alice had not had a significant ROLE relationship with a man. Rather, she used sex to keep men interested in her.

Based upon this analysis of my countertransference reaction, I intervened by reflecting Alice's experience of gratitude. After she validated my reflection, I asked about what it was like to contemplate our relationship ending. This was quite painful, according to Alice. I then asked about any fantasies she may have had about the relationship continuing. In response to this question, Alice brought up some sexual dreams and fantasies she had been having about me. Because this was, once again, the use of sexuality as a way of stopping a man from deserting her, I stated, "It would be easier to give yourself to me sexually than to deal with the pain of therapy ending." Alice became quite tearful and began to talk openly about the loss she was experiencing. It reminded her of the death of her father when she was little. Since then, sex had always been a way of avoiding losing men. Further, she was terrified that a man would not care for her as a *person* as she had always been a sexual *object*.

Roles

The therapist can also retreat from the terrors of ROLEs by adopting a role in therapy. The therapist can, for example, be very formal in interactions with clients. The therapist may not be as interested in construing the client's experiential world as in being a "professional." The client is treated as an object to be probed and explored—not somebody to be understood in fundamental ways.

For example, Jim was a severely depressed young man who was admitted to an acute care psychiatric ward. When electroconvulsive therapy (ECT) was decided upon, the client became quite frightened. The man's psychiatrist stated, "I don't want to hear about his feelings. I just want the release papers signed so we can treat him."

Alternatively, a therapist can avoid ROLEs with clients by adopting an informal role. Here, the therapist comes across as "one of the guys" and is generally liked by the client. The therapist appears down to earth, warm, and charismatic. However, this sort of therapist, while emphasizing the commonality of his or her exerience with the client, is not subsuming the client's experience within a professional personal construct system. This lack of subsuming the client's ROLE constructs due to the assumption of commonality can lead to very serious disruptions in the therapy, according to Kelly (1955, p. 672).

In this context, Cal was seen one afternoon complaining of "emptiness" and "not knowing what is reality." The therapist, rather than exploring what these issues meant for Cal (which would have been an attempt to subsume Cal's construction process and establish a ROLE relationship), responded by agreeing on the emptiness and unreality of existence. The therapist then gave Cal a "pep talk," essentially stating that one must go on with life in spite of the meaninglessness of it. Later that evening, Cal deteriorated and was hospitalized with hallucinations, delusions, and other paranoid features. One can only speculate on the relationship between the therapist's official "confirmation" of the unreality of existence and Cal's subsequent deterioration.

Diagnosis

The therapist can also retreat from ROLEs through the use of a diagnostic nomenclature. The problem is particularly acute given that the current psychiatric nosology (Diagnostic and Statistical Manual for Psychiatric Disorders [DSM] -III) focuses on the construing of symptoms—not the construing of persons. The clinician, then, may be more interested in completing a checklist of symptoms than in understanding the inner experience of the person. Further, many of the suggested alternatives to DSM-III (e.g., behavioral checklists) also avoid construing the inner person.

Alternatively, the therapist may *assume* knowledge of the inner person based upon the diagnosis. This is qualitatively different from risking invalidation while attempting to establish a ROLE relationship with the client. A classic example is an individual who behaves in a way diagnosable as paranoid. This person will be assumed, by clinicians of certain orientations, to have an inadequate sexual identity resulting in a fear of homosexual impulses. Rosenhan (1973) gives many examples of clinicians falsely assuming knowledge of the client based upon standard diagnostic information.

To illustrate this point, consider Mildred, a woman referred to therapy because of alcohol abuse. This women would not talk about her life experiences in therapy. As we explored the reasons for this, Mildred informed me that I would not believe her. When I asked *why* I would not believe her, she stated a previous therapist had not only diagnosed her as a ''paranoid schizophrenic'' but also told her that, because of her illness, everything she told him was a delusion. She described incidents in the treatment where the therapist said, ''I don't believe that. After all, you're a paranoid schizophrenic.'' (If one were to use DSM-III to categorize this woman, the most appropriate diagnosis would be borderline personality disorder, *not* paranoid schizophrehnia.)

Kelly was well aware of the problems of current diagnostic systems: ''Much of the reform proposed by the psychology of personal constructs is directed toward the tendency for psychologists to impose preemptive constructions upon human behavior. Diagnosis is all too frequently an attempt to cram a whole live struggling client into a nosological category'' (1955, p. 775). Kelly urged that the therapist use a set of professional constructs to construe the construction process of the client. Kelly's term for establishing this sort of ROLE relationship was *transitive diagnosis.* In discussing transitive diagnosis, Kelly urged the therapist to both construe the client's construction process and to *act* based upon that construction. ''The client does not ordinarily sit cooped up in a nosological pigeonhole; he proceeds along his way. If the psychologist expects to help him he must get off his chair and start moving along with him'' (Kelly, 1955, p. 775). He then goes on to state, ''In transitive diagnosis the clinician, instead of preoccupying himself with the question, 'In what category should this case be classified?' immediately addresses himself to the question, 'What is to become of this client?' '' (1955, p. 776). Thus, according to Kelly, a clinician should use diagnosis to establish a more extensive ROLE relationship with the client.

Biochemistry and Genetics

Resorting to biochemical and/or genetic explanations of an individual's problems, although possibly useful in certain cases, may also be used by the therapist to retreat from ROLEs. By construing the client's problems as nonpsychological, the therapist does not have to struggle with understanding the *person* in distress. The drugging, shocking, and lobotomizing of clients may be as much related to the clinician's terror as the client's pathology. As a matter of fact, by focusing on non-ROLE reasons for emotional difficulties, these procedures may be a conspiracy between the therapist and the client for avoiding terror (Langs, 1982).

In this context, Ed (discussed earlier under ''Roles and ROLEs'') had been seen by a psychiatrist earlier in his life. The weekly interviews consisted of the psychiatrist asking if Ed felt better followed by the prescribing of a new medication when the answer was no. At one point Ed was taking eight medications simultaneously. The effects of the medications were such that Ed was often sent home from work because he was unable to function effectively. Ed reported one experience where, when changing residences, he packed a "whole shoe box full" of the psychotropic medications he was currently taking. Obviously, the use of medication hindered significant interpersonal understanding in the clinical relationship.

Alternatively, some clinicians attempt to totally ignore biochemistry and genetics. In so doing, they may remain "true" to their theory but seriously damage the person in distress. To take an extreme example, I have known a therapist who tried to cure mental retardation through client-centered therapy. The raising of hopes and the subsequent feelings of depression among clients, families, and friends were not considered. In this case, the clinician was following a non-biological theory in spite of the problems this caused the *person* being treated. This can be just as much an avoidance of ROLEs as being "quick on the draw" with the prescription pad.

Psychotherapy Schools

Many clinicians, in attempting to follow a "school" of psychotherapy, focus on things like external events, past events, behavioral responses, or unreasonable thinking; they do not attempt to construe the ROLE constructs of the person. If this is carried to an extreme, the clinician may be more interested in a specific therapeutic technique than in understanding the person seeking help. If a theory of psychotherapy does not permit technical flexibility, the clinician runs the risk of rigidly following the theory in spite of the needs of the client (Leitner, 1982). When this occurs, the client may remain emotionally impoverished even though symptoms "improve." The client is "cured" in the sense that she or he will use a more "normal" way of retreating globally from ROLEs.

For example, Joanne (discussed above under "Transference") had originally been seen by another mental health professional. Joanne's problem had been diagnosed as "passivity." Rather than struggling with her terror around ROLEs, the therapist treated Joanne with assertiveness training. This resulted in Joanne becoming quite assertive in her interpersonal behavior. However, the experience of inner emptiness and meaninglessness due to the lack of ROLE relating continued. In other words, Joanne's behavior was cured although she continued to exist without extensive ROLE relationships. Langs (1982) gives many examples of ROLE-avoiding therapy (which he terms *lie therapy*).

Some Concluding Thoughts

This chapter, by paying attention to Kelly's sociality corollary, discusses personal construct theory in a way that seriously challenges the "too cognitive" criticism of the theory (Bruner, 1956; Rogers, 1956). We attempt to show the potential of the theory to understand the passions of the human heart. Our desire for ROLEs, the potential terror of ROLEs, and our experience of emptiness and meaninglessness if we retreat from ROLEs are central aspects of our humanity.

This chapter is not the definitive elaboration of the sociality corollary, however. As a matter of fact, many personal construct theorists may elaborate the corollary in totally different ways. (Believing in the philosophy of constructive alternativism, we hope this is the case.) Further, as mentioned earlier, we make a deliberate error in defining ROLEs as all-or-none experiences. In reality, the intermediate levels of ROLE relating are critical for the human enterprise. As a matter of fact, rather than discussing the avoidance of ROLEs, we would be more accurate if we discuss the *limiting* of ROLEs. ROLE relationships exist for the cases we discuss; they just are not developed as extensively as possible.

In spite of this error, the chapter says some useful things about ROLEs, psychopathology, and psychotherapy. It obviously takes tremendous courage to develop extensive ROLE relationships. This implies that the task of the therapist is not simply to attack the person's "irrational" constructs or to modify his or her behavior in the hope of indirectly changing the construct system. Rather, the personal construct therapist should sensitively and cautiously approach an understanding of the uniqueness, integrity, and terrors of the inner core of each client. In this way, the therapist, in addition to "curing" a symptom, may have the opportunity to touch another human life.

Acknowledgments

I would like to thank Ann Fuehrer, Roger Knudson, Alvin Landfield, Karen Maitland-Schilling, and Cecilia Shore for their comments on earlier drafts of this manuscript. I would especially like to thank Andrew Garrison for his help, encouragement, and support. All of the cases discussed in this paper have been provided with both false names and falsifying information in order to protect the identities of the individuals involved. In the final analysis, these individuals, more than anyone else, demonstrated the relationships between terror and sociality. I would like to express my deepest gratitude to these clients for teaching me so much.

References

Bannister, D. (1977). *In* "New Perspectives in Personal Construct Theory" (D. Bannister, ed.), Academic Press, New York and London, pp. 21–38.

Bruner, J. S. (1956). *Contemporary Psychology,* **1,** 355–357.

Buber, M. (1970). "I and Thou", Charles Scribner's Sons, New York.

Fromm, E. (1950). "Psychoanalysis and Religion", Yale University Press, New Haven.

Kelly, G. A. (1955). "The Psychology of Personal Constructs", Vols. I and II, Norton, New York.

Kelly, G. A. (1969a). *In* "Clinical Psychology and Personality: The Selected Papers of George Kelly" (B. Maher, ed.), Wiley, New York, pp. 7–45.

Kelly, G. A. (1969b). *In* "Clinical Psychology and Personality: The Selected Papers of George Kelly" (B. Maher, ed.), Wiley, New York, pp. 165–188.

Landfield, A. W. (1954). *Journal of Abnormal Social Psychology*, **49**, 529–532.

Landfield, A. W. (1955). *Journal of Abnormal Social Psychology*, **51**, 434–438.

Landfield, A. W. (1977). *In* "Nebraska Symposium on Motivation" (J. K. Cole and A. W. Landfield, eds.), Vol. 24, University of Nebraska Press, Lincoln, pp. 127–178.

Landfield, A. W. (1980a). *In* "Personal Construct Psychology: Psychotherapy and Personality" (A. W. Landfield and L. M. Leitner, eds.), Wiley Interscience, New York, pp. 289–320.

Landfield, A. W. (1980b). *In* "Personal Construct Psychology: Psychotherapy and Personality" (A. W. Landfield and L. M. Leitner, eds.), Wiley Interscience, New York, pp. 122–140.

Landfield, A. W. and Leitner, L. M. (1980). *In* "Personal Construct Psychology: Psychotherapy and Personality" (A. W. Landfield and L. M. Leitner, eds.), Wiley Interscience, New York, pp. 3–17.

Langs, R. (1982). "The Psychotherapeutic Conspiracy", Jason Aronson, New York.

Leitner, L. M. (1980). *In* "Personal Construct Psychology: Psychotherapy and Personality" (A. W. Landfield and L. M. Leitner, eds.), Wiley Interscience, New York, pp. 102–121.

Leitner, L. M. (1981a). *Journal of Personality Assessment*, **45**, 539–544.

Leitner, L. M. (1981b). *British Journal of Psychiatry*, **138**, 147–153.

Leitner, L. M. (1982). *British Journal of Medical Psychology*, **55**, 307–317.

Luria, Z. and Rose, M. D. (1979). "Psychology of Human Sexuality", Wiley, New York.

Mair, J. M. M. (1977). *In* "Nebraska Symposium on Motivation" (J. K. Cole and A. W. Landfield, eds.), Vol. 24, University of Nebraska Press, Lincoln, pp. 243–290.

McCoy, M. M. (1977). *In* "New Perspectives in Personal Construct Theory" (D. Bannister, ed.), Academic Press, London and New York, pp. 93–124.

Rogers, C. R. (1956). *Contemporary Psychology*, **1**, 357–358.

Rosenhan, D. L. (1973). *Science* **179**, 250–258.

Stringer, P. and Bannister, D. (1979). *In* "Constructs of Sociality and Individuality" (P. Stringer and D. Bannister, eds.), Academic Press, London and New York.

Timerlin, M. K. and Timerlin, J. W. (1982). *Psychotherapy: Theory, Research, and Practice*, **19**, 131–141.

7

How Parents of Young Mentally Handicapped Children Construe Their Role

Helen McConachie

Alex to me is just Alex. I can't really describe what she is.
She's not sort of like a normal child, but on the other hand,
she's not abnormal, if you know what I mean, in my eyes.

In this chapter, I do two things, First, I discuss what it might mean to be the parent of a young mentally handicapped child (for example, to the father quoted above). Second, I suggest how a personal construct theory analysis can elucidate the parent–child relationship.

Families of mentally handicapped children are no more homogeneous a group than they were before the child was born. A banal comment, perhaps, but one that requires constant emphasis to professionals bound up in public service definitions of "needs" of families, and medical pathology definitions of "mental handicap". Until the late 1960s, professional ideas of parents of handicapped children consisted largely of stereotypes about "guilt", "shame", "ambivalence", "rejection", and so forth (Wolfensberger, 1967). There followed a phase in which parents' strengths were given greater emphasis, and many have been trained by professionals as "co-therapists", learning techniques for teaching their children and managing behaviour problems (Gath, 1979; O'Dell, 1974; Yule, 1975). More recently, this one-way flow of information has been questioned and models of "partnership" discussed. "One of the foundations of partnership between parents and professionals lies in the recognition of how much they have in common and how much they have to learn from one another" (Mittler and Mittler, 1983, p. 10). Goals for the future include understanding the individuality of parents and of families, their differences and changes in feelings, life style, and priorities, in such a way that they become central to the planning of services.

My own experience is as a professional, first, as a behaviourally trained clinical psychologist working with parents on programmes to facilitate their child's development, and later as a research worker. From the beginning, I was struck by the differences between families and by the unpredictability of the nature of their adjustment to the child. One family with a mentally and physically handicapped child, both parents unemployed, an overcrowded house, other young children, would appear to enjoy life and undertake teaching programmes apparently effortlessly; another family, with a less-handicapped child, more money, babysitters and short-term relief care in a hospital unit available, would find life very stressful and consistent teaching impossible. In general, advice on teaching their children is a type of service valued highly by parents, satisfying their desire for detailed and continuing support (e.g., Wishart, Bidder, and Gray, 1980). But we know much less about those parents for whom it "misses the point".

In my research I aimed to study those differences between parents which might have the most relevance for the success or failure of early intervention. My guiding assumption was, as personal construct theory suggests, that I could only understand those differences in terms of individual meanings and interpersonal action, and that group results are inappropriate guidance for clinical prediction and practice. I chose to look at mothers' and fathers' own styles of teaching their children (McConachie and Mitchell, 1985) and at family patterns of child care in the daily routine (McConachie, 1982). I also attempted to explore with repertory grids how parents construe their interaction with their child, and in particular how integral teaching is to their perception of their role (McConachie, 1983). The way in which these strands might mesh together for individual parents and families forms the final stage of the research.

Through experience, my construing of parents of mentally handicapped children has been elaborated and reorganised almost beyond recognition. I invite the reader to explore his or her own constructs of mental handicap and of parent–child interaction. However, in this chapter, I am able only to raise in passing a variety of issues which merit fuller exploration; I have selected those which seem to lead to implications for a reworking of the relationship between parents and professionals.

What Does It Mean to Have a Handicapped Child?

Fundamental to personal construct theory is the contention that all people

> can be said to be "scientists" in the sense that they have theories about their universe (not as systematic or sophisticated as the theories of professional scientists but theories nevertheless), and on the basis of these theories they have particular hypotheses (expectations) which are fulfilled or not fulfilled, and in the light of the outcome of their "experiments" their views are modified.
>
> (Bannister, 1966, p. 362)

The process of becoming a parent is one of the most common and yet also potentially one of the most profound experiments in living which a person can conduct. This will be true for both mothers and fathers. The mother's physical experience of pregnancy and child-birth must make more immediate for her the concurrent changes in self-construing and the anticipatory construing of the child. However, Lewis (1982) and Scott-Heyes (1982) have illustrated that it is a time of significant psychological (as well as social and economic) change for fathers. I shall therefore carry on talking about "parents", while not intending to deny in any way the primacy of the woman's experience.

We might consider three aspects of the changes in construing around the time of birth of a first child. First, becoming a parent will involve a significant shift in core role structure. Such a shift is likely to involve anxiety, threat, even guilt: that is, feelings of profound disturbance as well as feelings of joyful accomplishment and anticipation. Second, new mothers and fathers will already have available to them constructs of what babies are like, what mothers are like, what fathers are like, derived from their own experience as children in relation to their parents, from their experience of their contemporaries who have children, and so on. Third, the transition to parenthood is not a complete metamorphosis: the parent retains preoccupations and relationships other than with her or his child. The meaning of the transition is thus structured uniquely by each parent out of past experience and present circumstances (O'Reilly, 1977). All three aspects of change also have relevance, though perhaps to a lesser degree, for subsequent pregnancies; for example, parents will probably have clearer expectations of themselves as parents, and of the possible characteristics of the baby.

When we consider the initial reactions of parents to the birth of a handicapped child, we may tend to overlook the fact that the parents have also been involved in the ordinary anticipatory processes outlined above. For example, they have imagined getting to know the new child, and what their life together will be like. They may have imagined how they will be "good" parents, and elaborated that construct for themselves in various ways. When parents are given the diagnosis of a handicapping condition in the child shortly after birth, the continuity and predictability of events are rudely interrupted.

Several parents have documented vividly the feelings they went through at such a time. Hannam (1975) described rage, aggression, thoughts of killing his child, guilt, feelings of failure, and fear at the strength of what he was going through. In personal construct theory terms, these would seem to represent "the awareness of imminent comprehensive change in one's core structures" (Kelly, 1955, p. 489). The *threat* generates active and dramatic attempts to resist all change, and yet perhaps at the same time also to extend the range of one's construing so as to begin to encompass and make meaningful the new and challenging events. What any new parent might feel is taken to an extreme, with additional themes particular to the situation. Parents may feel *guilty*, reacting "in ways they have never reacted before, or could envisage themselves acting" (Davis, 1983). Other parents have described feelings of grief, as if needing to mourn for the child who was anticipated, before beginning to accept the child who is now theirs (Corney, 1981). Fathers may describe immediate worry about the future:

> I was not much concerned because I would not be able to tell my friends what a clever son I had. I was, however, extremely depressed by the prospect of the sheer disorganisation and disturbance that seemed to be involved. Bernard would almost certainly have to be looked after indefinitely.
>
> (Wilks and Wilks, 1974, p. 9)

I interpret this father's *anxiety* as being not only about practical circumstances in the future but also as not really knowing what the future will hold, an awareness that he does not know what present events imply. The anxiety may lead to reliance on previous, tighter patterns of construing, "safer" predictions, temporarily drawing back from the elaborated systems the individuals have developed with growing maturity. Also, there is likely to be constriction in what the parents find meaningful, an attempt to minimize apparent incompatibilities between constructs. A narrowing of the perceptual field is reported commonly by mothers after child-birth, for example, becoming absorbed in the child's routines and losing interest in a paid job which might at other times have been vitally important in how they defined themselves. Under the perceived threat of the child's handicap, the tendency to a narrowed focus may be even greater:

> I was sleeping badly and tried to forget about the problem by working hard and investing more and more energy in it. It must have been infinitely harder for my wife. For me there was an abnormal child only when I came home in the evening.
>
> (Hannam, 1975, p. 19)

> My husband worried a lot about the future but I shut that out of my mind and lived one day at a time.
>
> (Spain and Wigley, 1975, p. 78)

Another strategy for dealing with anxiety and confusion may be to adopt constructs proffered by others, trying to find the "right way" to deal with this child who is "different". Most of such advice and "knowledge" is likely to be unhelpful and not flexible enough to guide the new parents in how to make sense of the diagnosis and how to react moment by moment to the child. The most helpful person at this time may be another parent of a handicapped child, who is able to construe more accurately what will reassure and guide the parents (Pugh, 1981).

Individual reactions will vary, depending partly on how the parents have been told of the diagnosis. Parents who say they were told "well" tended to have been together at the time, with the child present and in privacy; they were told by someone who conveyed sympathy and concern, and who was ready to talk with them again when they were able to absorb the information a little and to think of what questions they wanted to ask (Cunningham, 1979). When reassured of continuing support in the future, parents may then be allowed to experience some of the ordinary positive feelings about the birth of a child; for example, the quite ordinary though intensified desire to help the child on in life will be recognised and validated.

Reactions will also vary with how parents have construed themselves before:

> Mr. Peters saw himself as the "male" and "tough" member of the family and thought it was right he had been told [on his own, and rather abruptly]; Mrs. Peters was cast in the weak and feminine role and was allowed at least the "luxury" of breaking down. The man had to carry the burden.
>
> (Hannam, 1975, p. 29)

However, there are many ways of "carrying the burden", and one might instead interpret the situation as Mrs. Peters having taken on herself the grieving for both of them during her 6 months' breakdown (Bentovim, 1972).

For many mentally handicapped children, the acknowledgement of delayed development comes at some time after birth. In this case, it is often the parents who have first suspected that all is not as it should be. They may act on their suspicions and seek medical advice. A very difficult time will then follow for many, during which they are officially "reassured" that all is as normal whereas their own alternative constructions are becoming firmer through experience. Eventual confirmation may come partially as a relief, making sense of the parents' perceptions. For others it will, however, still come as a severe shock, if the diagnosis is of severe handicap and they had allowed themselves only to construe the child as "slow".

Alternatively, parents may not perceive that anything is wrong. One example is where it has already been established that the child has one form of disability, and only later is it suggested that the child is also mentally handicapped. Parents have reported this extra shock as the more shattering, perhaps because the blow is delivered to a tentative and newly forming system of construing. There are some similarities with the situation of parents whose child is developing well, and is then damaged by meningitis, fits, or some other trauma.

Some parents may ignore slowly accumulating evidence. In this case they are likely to react with hostility to professional suggestions that there is a problem. In personal construct theory terms, *hostility* is defined as the continued effort to extort validational evidence in support of a theory or expectations which are no longer tenable (Kelly, 1955). Parents may do this by stressing how wide the range is in normal achievement of developmental milestones (Booth, 1978), or by relying on benign constructions, such as, "She's a good baby" or "He's just lazy". They may seek reassurance from friends, relatives, and perhaps other professionals. To label such parents as "difficult" is to fail to understand the self-preserving function of their behaviour, that is, that they are trying to avoid for the time being the chaos which might result from abandoning central expectations about their lives. Denial that anything is wrong may be a more likely reaction of fathers than of mothers, especially if they have missed out on professional consultations and concentrated observation of and interaction with the child.

Whether the label of "mental handicap" is conferred quickly or slowly, the child's status is ambiguous. A mother of two severely handicapped sons put it this way:

> They say to you your child will be handicapped. It doesn't dawn on you really . . . they were a totally unknown quantity when they were so small and doing nothing and I thought, "Well, I don't even know what the handicap means"
>
> (Booth, 1978, p. 218)

The everyday acts of caring for the child do not readily fit the officially provided construct of handicap, and the future is opaque.

THE CONSTRUCTION OF "HANDICAP"

The medically based construction of "mental handicap" is the most commonly held culturally. It is viewed as a fixed attribute of the person which intrudes on all aspects of living, that is, a construct which is both preemptive or constellatory and also superordinate. As Bannister (1981) points out, the implicit contrast pole—"able"?, "normal"?—is too sweeping to be defined adequately. Most people have not had a breadth of individual experience through which to elaborate and individualise the construct; as, for example, brothers and sisters of handicapped children have done, so that for them it ceases to have stereotyped implications or to mean "nothing but handicapped".

What meanings did "normality" have for the parents before the child was born? Did "abnormality" hold any implications? Does the construct become fixed immediately in superordinacy by its extreme relevance to their experiences, and by other people's reactions? I think it must; it will rarely become a marginal construct. However, its elaboration takes time. At first some parents, for example, parents of Down's syndrome babies, may in fact be struck more by similarities than by differences—"She's just like my other children really". The relative slowness in development may only become obvious toward the end of the first year when "parents will quite suddenly 'see' the handicap" (Cunningham, 1983, p. 105).

How does the parent's construction of handicap affect the child? The following quotation from a physically handicapped adult reflecting on her childhood illustrates the above questions, and also the problems which may arise when parents overemphasize their educational role.

> Something happens in a parent when relating to his disabled child; he forgets that they're a kid first. I used to think about that a lot when I was a kid. I would be off in a euphoric state, drawing or coloring or cutting out paper dolls, and as often as not the activity would be turned into an occupational therapy session. "You're not holding the

scissors right'', ''Sit up straight so your curvature doesn't get worse''. That era was ended when I finally let loose a long and exhaustive tirade. ''I'm just a kid! You can't therapize me all the time! I get enough therapy in school everyday! I don't think about my handicap all the time like you do!''

(Diamond, 1981, p. 30)

So far I've considered the type of construct which handicap may be for parents. One further structural issue is the question of the range of convenience of their existing constructs. For example, can they describe the handicapped child easily in the terms they use for other children? As part of a small interview study of parents of young mentally handicapped children, I asked each mother and father separately to tell me ''what sort of child she (or he) is, what her personality is like''. The majority of the 22 parents had no difficulty in describing their children as happy, sociable, getting into mischief, placid, strong minded, full of fun, or whatever ''personality'' terms were appropriate. There seemed to be two main groups of parents who did not easily use such psychological constructs (beyond perhaps ''loveable''), and who gave their descriptions in terms of behavioural and physical constructs. First, there were three fathers who spent relatively little time with their child and even less in close interaction with him or her (McConachie, 1979). Second, there were the parents of two profoundly and multiply handicapped children, and of one child with very difficult behaviour. One mother said, ''I can see it showing through sometimes how he would have been. He would have been serious and loving, with a lot of patience''. But in her summary description of her son, his limited behavioural repertoire was more salient. Dobson (1980) did suggest a range of convenience problem for parents of older children in extending to the handicapped child the constructs which they used to describe other members of the family. She too suggested that behavioural and physical problems may affect in similar ways parents' construing of a mentally handicapped child. Perhaps we can conclude that, though the construct of handicap may be superordinate in the parents' view of their child, their ordinary range of constructs about people may be more immediately meaningful unless the child presents severe behavioural or physical problems.

To summarise so far: the discovery that their child is handicapped is a traumatic one for the parents. The initial stages are likely to remain a crisis for the psychological reasons outlined previously, whatever the future improvements in services and in public prejudice. To have a mentally handicapped child is a reversal of expectations, and a setting adrift into a sea of confusion about what the implications will be for themselves and for their child.

THE PARENT'S ROLE

As time passes, the parents gradually take on the role of ''parent of a mentally handicapped child''. Traditionally, *role* has been defined as a course of activity interlocked with that of others, or as a set of expectations held by others about a person's behaviour. In personal construct theory however, the individual is seen as more active and experimental in taking on a role, and to play a social role requires the individual to attempt to construe how others see the world.

> This isn't to say that he tries to conform to their outlooks, he may even try to stand them on their heads, but if he tries to understand others by putting on their spectacles and then does something, then that which he does could be considered as a role.
>
> (Kelly, 1966)

I would, however, suggest that the limits and nature of the experimentation involved in playing a role are somewhat determined by the first definitions, that is, the way ideologies within the society may determine real-life constraints such as the level of public services provided. Thus a family may be tired and strained to the limits of its resources by the needs of a severely mentally handicapped child, or alternatively may be able to play their roles more creatively together as a family if able to make use of a short-term care service, or other flexible provision.

Getting used to being parents of a mentally handicapped child will involve the parents in extending and realigning their constructs about their circumstances and themselves, so that they can begin to construe the immediate future in some detail. Radley (1974) suggests that this picture of the future must include positive elements in order for the first processes of change to occur. As change proceeds, the parent will seem to be acting out the role competently, but will still be feeling it as a strange one. Eventually, there is the stage of full congruence with core role structures. The implications of the new role are unique for each individual, as much to do with past relationships and experience as with present circumstances. Further, and here I refer to the commonality corollary of personal construct theory, parents will also be aware of how others construe the role of parent of a handicapped child. They can see both the private and public views. To some extent their actions may be affected by the discrepancy between what they know and feel about themselves personally, and what they consider others expect of them (Shotter, 1970). For example, they may feel the child's disabilities or deviant behaviour are a reflection on them as parents at the same time as "knowing" they are not.

Voysey (1975) has explored the negotiation between the public and private meanings of the parents' role. On the one hand, she describes the social forces which shape "the reconstitution of family life" (her book's subtitle), and on the other, she explores the ways in which individuals construct different meanings for their lives. They may portray themselves to themselves and others as "accepting the inevitable", "coping splendidly", "self-sacrificing", "making amends", "just as normal", and so forth. Voysey's analysis suggests that parents of handicapped children tend to adopt positive constructions, congruent with the normal order of child rearing. They may take whatever size of family they have as an advantage, finding other children a support and comfort, or being glad that they can concentrate on helping an only child.

> Overall the majority of parents claim that their disabled child has not had deleterious effects on their family life. The question is, how they construct such claims in the face of questioning which implicitly asserts the contrary. (pp. 26–27)

As interviewer, Voysey is at all points aware that what the parents say is a response, for example, to her seeming to assume that the central business of life is to bring up children and that parents should subjugate other interests to this. Helping professionals will also channel parents' possibilities for expression in such ways.

ACCEPTANCE

"Acceptance" refers to how parents take on the role of parent of a handicapped child, and it is generally given a lot of weight by professionals. However, it is hard to find an "official" definition, and in practice it seems a strangely tight construct.

In terms of psychological reality for parents, we might equate acceptance with the stage of congruence with core role structures mentioned earlier. But what is it that parents are expected to accept?

> Whilst the *child* may indeed be accepted, few parents will accept a *disability* and a constructive emphasis on adaptation and orientation is more productive and realistic.
> (Russell, 1983, p. 48)

This distinction may underlie some of the differences in interpretation of acceptance between parents and professionals. One measure sometimes used by researchers is parents' accuracy in assessing their children's current or predicted level of competence: parents tend to agree with professionals on the former but not on the latter assessment (Wolfensberger and Kurtz, 1971). If parents' central constructs about the child and aspirations for the child differ from those of professionals, then their ideas of appropriate school placements and other services are also likely to differ.

> I've always thought there's nothing wrong with him. You can see from his face he's Down's syndrome; but the way he carries on, his intelligence. . . .

This father (interviewed in McConachie, 1979) was reluctant to have his child go to school at the age of two and a half years, when a place was offered, as being too early. He construed his child first of all as a child, and not as a handicapped child. Are we then to conclude that he did not "accept" the child? Would the child benefit were he to focus more on the handicap? Attempts to define and insist on acceptance seem ultimately contradictory.

Parental reluctance to accept professionals' verdicts may have a number of meanings and effects. Some parents' ''non-acceptance'' may push them to prove the professionals' bleak prognosis wrong, or to demand provision of better services, for example, school places where there are none for multiply handicapped children (Schaefer, 1979). On the other hand, there may be negative effects, such as a father undermining a mother's appropriate attempts to facilitate the child's development (Corney, 1981). Once again this may be an outcome of lack of professional communication with the father, a failure to ensure joint planning of goals.

Some researchers have suggested later generalised differences between mothers and fathers in their reactions to the child's handicap. For example, it has been suggested that fathers are more sensitive to the possible social stigma of having a mentally handicapped child, particularly when the child's handicap is obvious from appearance (Cain and Levine, 1963; Tallman, 1965). It is also suggested that having a mentally handicapped son has a greater emotional impact upon fathers than having a daughter (Farber, 1959; Gumz and Gubrium, 1972). These findings have been interpreted as the fathers taking a more instrumental or externally oriented role in the family and having had aspirations for their sons' achievements in the world. Mothers, while perceiving more stigma for a boy than for a girl in being mentally handicapped, vary in reaction to the child more in terms of variables such as the child's competence rather than in terms of the child's appearance (Cain and Levine, 1963; Levinson and Starling, 1981). The mothers' construing seems to reflect their experience that the more handicapped the child, the greater the burden of care, and this burden will fall largely on their shoulders (Wilkin, 1979). Wolfensberger and Kurtz (1971) did not confirm these findings of differences between mothers and fathers, and between sons and daughters, and suggested that other variables such as social class and religion were of more relevance. For example, they found Protestants to be more ''realistic'' about the child's handicap than Catholics, but did not offer any explanation of this difference.

Group generalizations about reactions of parents to their child's handicap give little or no guidance in understanding the complexity of the process of adjustment of an individual parent or an individual family. Isolating particular variables does not suggest how professionals can most appropriately work with a Catholic mother, or parents of a boy, and so forth. A more useful way of understanding the complexity of parents' views is to relate them to an individual analysis of total family functioning. There are many functions which families fulfill, for example, economic, education, physical care, rest and recuperation, socialization, ideology, self-definition, affection, guidance, and vocational.

> No family can adequately attend to all functions. The issue is one of setting priorities for parents' attention and finding resources to assist the family with others. Every family should not emphasize the educational function—perhaps their time would be far more

effective in areas such as guidance, religion and affection. Intervention programs should
be sensitive to the natural rhythms and preferences of each family.

                    (Turnbull, Brotherson, and Summers, 1982, p. 8 of Part 2)

Such an analysis of family structure, roles, and functions seems a necessary
background to understanding what it might mean to a parent to have a mentally
handicapped child. At the present, professional helpers may focus solely on
parents' roles as educators and caretakers for their children. However, the above
quotation implies that, for some parents, resistance to professional concentration
on the child's cognitive development alone can be seen as a meaningful outcome
of their whole-family view, and one to be respected and worked with flexibly,
not dismissed as non-acceptance.

Providing an Enabling Structure

Kelly did not develop an elaborated account of child development, in personal
construct theory terms. However, lines along which parent–child relationships
may be understood as a joint experiment can be gleaned from his account of
psychotherapy. Both a therapist and a parent are ultimately more responsible for
enabling the interaction to take place, but the client and the child determine much
of the themes of the transaction.

From the beginning, babies are active, not passive, and their behaviour is
organized and has pattern; they bring even to their earliest social interactions
individual characteristics which will affect the behaviour of others towards them
(Schaffer, 1977). During early interaction, the parent ascribes meaning to the
baby's behaviour, and attempts to interpret what the baby is construing, that is,
what it is attempting to discriminate as different from other events. By highlight-
ing certain acts and not others, by timing their own activity to the pauses in the
child's activity, parents uniquely structure the child's developing perceptions.
Also the parents have things they want the child to do, and they use their
understanding of the child to achieve those ends through acting together (Shotter,
1974). We should note that construing is as much about acting as about feeling
and thinking, for both the young child and the parent. The only difference is that
we can also ask the parents why they do what they do.

I will examine two sets of questions about the interaction of mentally handicapped children and their parents: first, how interaction may be affected by the
parents' perceptions of the child as handicapped, and second, how it may be
affected by the particular nature of a mentally handicapped child's behaviour.

Salmon (1970) said of the first significant figures in a child's life, usually the
mother:

Her construing gives him the basis of his own however much he may later elaborate
his own view. It is she who provides him with the first dimensions for appraising his own
behaviour, just as the first role relationship he plays is played with her. (p. 216)

How do the parents' constructions of handicap affect how the child comes to see her- or himself? It is likely that the child will adopt into core role constructs much of how others react to him or her. If parents construe the handicap in terms of what the child is not and cannot do, then the child is likely to develop low self-expectations. However, the process is not inevitable and is one of continuous negotiation (Shotter, 1974); the child may rebel, as in the quotation from Diamond (1981) given earlier. What if parents have difficulty in construing the child along the dimensions they utilise in construing others? Can they begin to see how the child perceives the world? To the extent that parents lack shared content in their perception of themselves and of the child, then they lack a firm basis for their relationship, and the child will lack dimensions from which to elaborate his or her own construing (Salmon, 1970). From such a basis, we might then predict that the mentally handicapped child would develop a self-concept which is relatively unstable and not clearly related to his or her constructs about other people—as Wooster (1970) has found. These observations perhaps lead to some suggestions for intervention by professionals, that is, that it may be helpful to observe clearly with the parents the complexity of what the child does and can do, and to join with parents in interpreting the child along "normal" dimensions rather than attributing the child's behaviour to the handicap.

In what ways might the nature of the child's handicap affect how parent and child respond to each other? In order to answer this question, I will first suggest a definition of what *mental handicap* means in terms of what children do and think and predict. To some extent, it is the same exercise as defining how all children's construing differs from that of adults, except that the process of development is slower. Certainly very much the majority of young severely mentally handicapped children can be observed to make clear and consistent discriminations, and to predict successfully the habits of both objects and living things including other people. They learn to coordinate their activity within social interaction at an elementary level, and most begin to use spoken words to some degree of flexibility in communication. However, mental handicap is usually recognised to imply specific difficulties, in addition to slowness in development and to any direct impairment of sensory channels or limited mobility.

The World Health Organisation definition (1983) of mental handicap involves two essential components: first, intellectual functioning which is significantly below average and second, marked impairment in the ability to adapt to the daily demands of the individual's own social environment. Mentally handicapped children have been said to have a "relative inability to project from ordinary unstructured experience, a deficiency in spontaneous learning" (Clarke and Clarke, 1974, p. 371). This definition seems to suggest a specific difficulty in extending the number and range of convenience of constructs and in tightening the system or exploring the implications between constructs. This difficulty will affect both intellectual tasks and social interaction. We can take this description further by looking at research into the interaction of parents and young mentally handicapped children to see how it might differ from that of parents and non-handicapped children.

ANTICIPATION IS FUNDAMENTAL

The majority of comparative studies have found differences in the details of parent–child interaction. For example, in the case of vocal communication, Berger and Cunningham (1983) observed mothers and Down's syndrome children from 1 to 6 months of age, and found that over that period "the mutual adaptation, and regulation of the handicapped dyads' vocal behaviour was becoming less successful than in their non-handicapped counterparts" (p. 329). Jones (1977) studied mothers and slightly older Down's syndrome children, matched on developmental age with non-handicapped children, and found fewer initiations by the children, less feedback by the mothers, and less successful turn-taking in communication. However, other comparable studies have found greater similarity between the two groups in interaction (e.g., Buckhalt, Rutherford, and Goldberg, 1978; Vietze, Abernathy, Ashe, and Faulstitch, 1978). There may be an effect here of ability level: Vietze *et al.* did note that the most delayed children in their sample, aged 1 year, responded less reliably and quickly to their mothers' vocalisations, and they suggested that this unpredictability would eventually affect the interactive style of the mothers.

The observed differences are mainly of two kinds—the number of cues given by the child, and the success of "meshing" of the interaction. Impairment in the child will affect the cues available from which the parent can construe the child's intentions, for example, the cues given by blind children when listening are often ambiguous, and the movements of children with cerebral palsy are often jerky and misdirected. Smooth turn-taking by parent and child seems essentially to be a matter of anticipation and successful prediction by each partner to the interaction. A study of depressed mothers and their 2-year-old children has thrown light on the ways in which interaction may be relatively unsatisfactory to both sides (Puckering, 1982). Depressed and control mothers did not differ on a variety of indices, for example, in the amount of warmth and negative comments they expressed nor in the amount of time they were fully involved with the child. There were also no differences in the total time spent in play during the observations. However, depressed mothers generally spent more time unoccupied, more time in physically active play with their children, and the children were less likely to respond to the mothers' "link statements", that is, verbal or non-verbal additions to the interaction which are clearly linked to the content of the child's activity. It was suggested that mothers used physical playfulness as a generalised diversionary tactic to avoid having to control the child. Possible explanations for the difference in child responsiveness included the suggestion that depression in various ways discourages responsiveness in others. On the other hand, mothers were receiving less discriminating feedback from the children for their interventions, and so had less guidance for improving their meshing with the child.

A handicapped child's diminished or ambiguous cues may tend to have a similar depressing effect upon interaction. Reduced cues and responses from the child will lower the rewards of interaction for the mother, decreasing her ability to interpret and predict the child's behaviour. These characteristics of the interaction also pose difficulties for professional intervention. First, the professional who knows the child less intimately than the parent may find it even harder to interpret the fine detail of the child's behaviour. Second, he or she is asking the parent to concentrate effort in a situation which the parent perhaps finds less rewarding than it might be with a non-handicapped child.

All the research referred to in this section looks at mothers: what little research evidence there is on interaction between fathers and mentally handicapped children suggests that in general mothers and fathers are alike, both as groups and within couples, though the range of differences between couples is obviously large (Cheseldine, 1977; McConachie and Mitchell, 1985; Mitchell, 1980). In my own research, many couples were alike and some were different in their styles of interaction with the child. We might then speculate as to the differential effect on the individual children of similarity or difference: for example, as long as each parent is internally consistent and can be predicted by the child, the experience of differing styles may be beneficial in promoting flexibility in the child's construing.

PARENTS AS TEACHERS

One aspect of parent–child interaction of particular relevance for mentally handicapped children is the role of parents as teachers of their children. As children develop and their behaviour becomes more orderly and meshed with that of familiar others, those others begin to foster some aspects of behaviour in preference to others. For example, they begin to instruct the child in the requisite vocal skills for their own language, but not necessarily in any conscious and deliberate way. Bruner (1975) has described how parents "scaffold" the child's behaviour, limiting the degrees of freedom in a task and making perceptually obvious the associations the child needs in order to solve a particular problem. In this way, we might say that all parents are teachers. It is important to note that the child is a highly active participant in this process; a handicapped child may be a less active and equal partner, and need to have his or her experience structured for longer.

Much of the advice about teaching given to parents of handicapped children is based on applied behaviour analysis. The approach is essentially "remedial", that is, the behaviour of a mentally handicapped child is construed as problematic and unpredictable, and teaching involves bringing the child's behaviour under the stimulus control of the parent. Greater predictability of the child is the goal also of a personal construct theory approach, but in terms of the parent coming to construe how the child experiences events. The parent does not write the agenda for the interaction. Some parents have stressed the benefits to themselves in the flexibility they have acquired, for example, in dealing with their other children, through their experiences with the handicapped child.

Parents often do have explicit ideas about how and what they want to teach their child. Several studies have elicited parents' ideas and then looked for their reflection in the interaction with the child. McGillicuddy-De Lisi (1982) interviewed the mothers and fathers of non-handicapped 4-year-olds about hypothetical child-care situations, and found that their beliefs about the processes underlying child progress—such as direct instruction, self-regulation, identification, negative feedback, accumulation, and so forth—were related in a predictable and direct way to their teaching strategies. Demographic variables such as socio-economic status and family size were related only indirectly to teaching. Parents' beliefs were both a source and an outcome of experience. For example, parents of only children and of three children differed reliably in the types of beliefs they professed; parents of only children tended more to believe in the efficacy of direct instruction, whilst parents of three children cited self-regulation, impulsivity, and negative feedback as controlling processes. Identification of parental constructions such as these can therefore aid understanding of the variability in parental teaching styles which affect children's development. However, it should be noted that other similar studies show up different patterns, for example, finding clear relationships between how parents say they see their children and how they teach demonstrated only by mothers with girls (Davis, 1979) and by mothers of a higher educational background (Moss and Jones, 1977). One explanation of variation between studies may be that some tasks show up relationships differently from other tasks.

Another way of examining parents' construing in teaching is to look at decision points in the interaction and ask the parent to explain the option chosen. At least two studies of parents and mentally handicapped children have adopted this strategy (Mitchell, 1980; Mogford, 1979). Mogford was able to show that clashes in turn-taking occurred particularly when mothers attempted to initiate activity directed toward chosen therapeutic goals. They then would fail to monitor and respond to the cues given by the child. A secondary effect was that the demands made on the child were less likely to be adjusted to a suitable level as the mother would not be responding to feedback from the child's ongoing activity. The mothers who were didactic in this way gave various explanations, such as wanting the child to play with toys the "right" way, or letting the child learn by trial and error. However, many mothers showed a high level of sensitivity and skill in play with their child. By intervening in various ways they were able to expand the child's span of attention and to maintain interest in an activity, which are likely to be fundamental requisites for the establishment and elaboration of constructs. The mothers chose play things judiciously and kept each one accessible to the child, removing distractions. They anticipated and prevented disruption and failure, and pitched their suggestions for activities at a level just beyond that which the child could achieve easily.

I stated before that many of the programmes designed to help parents teach their young mentally handicapped children have had their roots in applied behaviour analysis. Some expansion in philosophy may be becoming evident. For example, Beveridge based a training course for parents on the observation of individual differences in natural style of interaction along a dimension of directiveness (Beveridge, Flanagan, McConachie, and Sebba, 1982). Directive parents seemed to be ready to intervene by physically manipulating their child to help him or her make a response. Less directive parents were more likely to sit back and ask the child to try again before actively intervening. Beveridge included in the course teaching techniques such as gaining attention and limiting choice which set the scene for a successful child activity, and also techniques such as verbal and physical prompting, feedback, and rewards which are more directly derived from behaviour modification. She found as hypothesised that there was merit in introducing parents first to those techniques which more readily fitted with their own style. She found there to be effective teachers amongst both the directive and the less-directive parents.

PARENTS AS EDUCATORS?

I have suggested so far that parents are naturally enablers and teachers, acting in joint exploration and experiment with their children. However, this is not the same as professionals' expectations that parents of young mentally handicapped children will deliberately adopt a role of "educator".

Parents in some countries at least are now frequently surrounded by exhortation and advice on playing with their child, from the moment the handicap is known, through television programmes, popular magazines, home visitors, and so forth. Some have even been told (with no foundation in truth) that their child will not learn anything after 5 years old, and so they must teach everything they can quickly. This pressure interacts with general western child-care values, particularly in the middle classes, which place high importance on conscious provision for children's play and adult participation in it. If such activity forms an important part of what parents construe as being a "good parent", then it is likely that having a child who finds play difficult will affect their outlook and satisfaction in the parental role, adding feelings of inadequacy to the pressure.

> I think you always are going to feel more pressure if your little one is handicapped, there's no way round it. When you get a little one that doesn't do anything until you're the catalyst . . . it almost becomes an obsession . . . because you feel like he'd be sitting there, and you know that you're either going to sew . . . or you could get him to learn his "k" sounds. (Winton and Turnbull, 1981, p. 15)

In personal construct theory terms, an obsession is tight construing in one part of the system with the remainder loose and confused. Are professionals' attempts to intervene in a helpful way potentially harmful, fragmenting further parents' attempts to make sense of their situation? This question of potential harm has rarely been admitted into professional discussion of early intervention.

Another potential source of miscommunication between parents and professionals is how they perceive "teaching", "learning", "parenting", and so forth. If they do not construe at least to some extent similarly, and do not spend time in negotiating expectations on which they can both agree, then they will be unable to develop a working relationship. For example, programmes currently offered by professionals generally suggest that parents adopt a teaching structure of short concentrated sessions with the child, in which they determine the nature and acceptability of the activity. Parents will feel out of step with the programme if intensive one-to-one sessions are not compatible with their own construing of teaching, or with their construing of parenting. Many parents report that they try to teach opportunistically, and programmes for parents could in theory encourage this by helping parents to internalise a teaching model and to react when appropriate to an initiation by the child.

> By interalize we mean that the parent has achieved a skill in applying the principles and concepts such that she . . . can "intuitively" react to the child and learning situation. (Cunningham and Jeffree, 1974, p. 7)

One further point to be made about intensive one-to-one sessions is that for those who do construe teaching in this way it may have negative implications—for example, like school homework when they themselves were young. Baker, Clark, and Yasuda (1981) looked at the relationship between parents' expectations and child progress after parent training. The degree to which parents perceived themselves as responsible for teaching did not relate to outcome, but parents' expectations of problems in teaching did (negatively). I think we might interpret this finding as parents feeling low in confidence, and perhaps out of step with the programme on offer, and their predictions being self-fulfilling.

Parents with whom I worked on a parent-teaching course (Beveridge *et al.* 1982) reflected a great variety of perceptions of teaching when interviewed afterwards:

> My normal way of teaching at home is whatever I'm doing, I try to involve him, like dusting and hoovering and so on. . . . He likes roaming round with me, and he's learning as he comes round.

> Obviously, I've never taught before. I mean I taught my children. But it wasn't really like teaching to me; it was just some sort of duty I think (laughs).

> A parent working with a child is not the same as a teacher teaching. As a parent you are also wanting to teach other things, for example, exercising choice, therefore you are not as strict as a teacher. (p. 59)

When I conducted repertory grids with mothers and fathers of young mentally handicapped children, I looked at the structure of implications of teaching for them and at how central or peripheral it was within their construing of their role with their child. One mother grouped together the constructs of teaching, treating the child as handicapped (rather than as normal), and ''I get harassed''. She seemed enthusiastic about undertaking a parent-teaching course but in subsequent discussion of the grid realised her ambivalence, which she could then discuss with the nursery staff in order to establish a shared meaning for their collaboration.

Parents and Professionals

> The framework that we bring to understand how families behave can facilitate or retard our work. If we have too narrow a view of family functioning, the types of questions, goals and strategies we can use become more of a disservice than help to families.
>
> (Freeman, 1976, p. 746)

A family has a pattern and a system—so too do the individual members of the family. In this chapter, personal construct theory is applied to understanding some aspects of the lives and concerns of parents of young mentally handicapped children.

What implications does this analysis have for the roles of helping professionals? Young children need a parent to reflect back the consequences of their actions, and thus to structure the perceptual features of objects and events, so that their significance can be construed. Likewise, parents need to reconstruct their perceptions and expectations of themselves and their lives, and construct a picture of their child who has been labelled ''mentally handicapped''. This process will be aided by having someone there to help in consolidating and then in elaborating new construing. Davis (1983) suggests that each family should be provided with an individual counsellor as soon as possible after the diagnosis is made known, and has outlined the ways in which the counselling might proceed. For example, the counsellor can help the parents to clarify their questions; the parents themselves will answer the questions through their experiences, which the counsellor can then help them evaluate.

Professionals will need to be as versatile in responding to parents as parents are in responding to their children, that is, responding in a variety of carefully chosen ways to each parent, and to different parents. Throughout the chapter I suggest tentative conclusions as to how certain professional strategies may be helpful. For example, the way in which parents are initially told of the handicap has great potential either for provoking lasting distress, or for sensitive understanding of parents' reactions (including hostility towards professionals). Jointly conducting with parents a detailed observation of the child's abilities may enhance construing of the child's intentions and may help elaborate positive construing of the child, as well as laying the basis for choosing appropriate teaching goals.

It is important for the future that the principles upon which services to the families of young handicapped children are based acknowledge the variety in individual people and in their systems of construing. For example, advice and training given to parents in teaching their children can undoubtedly be helpful in several ways; parents want to do something constructive for the child, and in seeing progress can reconstrue feelings of inadequacy and hopelessness. However, the strategies suggested to parents must be sensitive and complex in order that the child may develop its own construing flexibly. The strategies must also be tailored to the interpersonal style of the individual parent and child, and to how parents construe their role in the context of their whole family life.

References

Baker, B. L., Clark, D. B., and Yasuda, P. M. (1981). Predictors of Success in Parent Training. *In* "Frontiers of Knowledge in Mental Retardation", (P. Mittler, ed.), Vol. I, University Park Press, Baltimore, pp. 281–291.

Bannister, D. (1966). A New Theory of Personality. *In* "New Horizons in Psychology" (B. Foss, ed.), Penguin, Harmondsworth, pp. 361–380.

Bannister, D. (1981). Construing a Disability. *In* "Handicap in a Social World" (A. Brechin, P. Liddiard, and J. Swain, eds.), Hodder and Stoughton, London, pp. 230–236.

Bentovim, A. (1972). Emotional disturbances of handicapped pre-school children and their families: Attitudes to the child, *British Medical Journal*, **3**, 634–637.

Berger, J. and Cunningham, C. (1983). The development of early vocal behavior and interactions in Down's syndrome and non-handicapped infant–mother pairs, *Developmental Psychology*, **19**, 322–331.

Beveridge, S., Flanagan, R., McConachie, H., and Sebba, J. (1982). "Parental Involvement in Anson House", Anson House Preschool Project Paper 3, Dr. Barnardo's, Barkingside.

Booth, T. (1978). From normal baby to handicapped child: Unravelling the idea of subnormality in families of mentally handicapped children, *Sociology*, **12**, 203–221.

Bruner, J. S. (1975). The ontogenesis of speech acts, *Journal of Child Language*, **2**, 1–19.

Buckhalt, J. A., Rutherford, R. B., and Goldberg, K. E. (1978). Verbal and non-verbal interaction of mothers with their Down's syndrome and non-retarded infants, *American Journal of Mental Deficiency*, **82**, 337–343.

Cain, L. F. and Levine, S. (1963). "Effects of Community and Institutional School Programs on Trainable Mentally Retarded Children" (Research monograph), Summarized in D. Pilling (1973), "The Handicapped Child: Research Review", Vol. 3, National Children's Bureau and Longman, London.

Cheseldine, S. (1977). "Parent-Child Interaction and Language Facilitation with the Mentally Handicapped", Unpublished doctoral dissertation, University of Manchester.

Clarke, A. M. and Clarke, A. D. B. (1974). "Mental Deficiency: The Changing Outlook" (3rd ed.), Methuen, London.

Corney, M. (1981). A lost child lives on. *New Forum*, **7**, 54–56.

Cunningham, C. C. (1979). Parent Counselling. *In* "Tredgold's Mental Retardation" (12th ed.) (M. Craft, ed.), Ballière Tindall, London, pp. 313–318.

Cunningham, C. C. (1983). Early Support and Intervention: The HARC Infant Project. *In* "Parents, Professionals and Mentally Handicapped People" (P. Mittler and H. McConachie, eds.), Croom Helm, London, pp. 91–110.

Cunningham, C. C. and Jeffree, D. M. (1974). "The Organization and Structure of Workshops for Parents of Mentally Handicapped Children", Paper presented at the British Psychological Society Conference, Bangor, Wales.

Davis, H. (1979). "An Exploration of Possible Relationships between Maternal Constructs and Behaviour", Unpublished doctoral dissertation, University of London.

Davis, H. (1983). Constructs of handicap: Working with parents and children, *Changes*, **1**, 37–39.

Diamond, S. (1981). Growing Up with Parents of a Handicapped Child: A Handicapped Person's Perspective. *In* "Understanding and Working with Parents of Children with Special Needs" (J. L. Paul, ed.), Holt, Rinehart and Winston, New York.

Dobson, C. (1980). "Parental Perceptions of Mentally Handicapped Children", Unpublished master's thesis, University of Leicester.

Farber, B. (1959). Effects of a severely mentally retarded child on family integration, *Monographs of the Society for Research in Child Development* (no. 71).

Freeman, D. S. (1976). The family as a system: Fact or fancy? *Comprehensive Psychiatry*, **17**, 735–749.

Gath, A. (1979). Parents as therapists of mentally handicapped children, *Journal of Child Psychology and Psychiatry*, **20**, 161–165.

Gumz, E. J. and Gubrium, J. F. (1972). Comparative parental perceptions of a mentally retarded child, *American Journal of Mental Deficiency*, **77**, 175–180.

Hannam, C. (1975). "Parents and Mentally Handicapped Children". Penguin, Harmondsworth.

Jones, O. (1977). Mother–Child Communication with Pre-linguistic Down's Syndrome and Normal Infants. *In* "Studies in Mother-Infant Interaction" (H. R. Schaffer, ed.), Academic Press, London, pp. 379–401.

Kelly, G. A. (1955). "The Psychology of Personal Constructs", Vols. I and II, Norton, New York.

Kelly, G. A. (1966). Cited *in* D. Bannister and F. Fransella (1980), "Inquiring Man" (2nd ed.), Penguin, Harmondsworth.

Levinson, R. M. and Starling, D. M. (1981). Retardation and the burden of stigma, *Deviant Behavior*, **2**, 371–390.

Lewis, C. (1982). "A Feeling You Can't Scratch"?: The Effect of Pregnancy and Birth on Married Men. *In* "Fathers: Psychological Perspectives" (N. Beail and J. McGuire, eds.), Junction, London, pp. 43–70.

McConachie, H. (1979). "Mothers' and Fathers' Daily Involvement with their Handicapped Children", Paper presented at I.A.S.S.M.D. 5th Congress, Jerusalem, Israel.

McConachie, H. (1982). Fathers of Mentally Handicapped Children. *In* "Fathers: Psychological Perspectives" (N. Beail and J. McGuire, eds.), Junction, London, pp. 144–173.

McConachie, H. (1983). Fathers, Mothers, Siblings: How Do They See Themselves? *In* "Parents, Professionals and Mentally Handicapped People" (P. Mittler and H. McConachie, eds.), Croom Helm, London, pp. 124–137.

McConachie, H. and Mitchell, D. (1985). "Parents Teaching their Young Mentally Handicapped Children". *Journal of Child Psychology and Psychiatry*, **26**, (in press).

McGillicuddy-De Lisi, A. V. (1982). The Relationship between Parents' Beliefs about

Development and Family Constellation, Socioeconomic Status and Parents' Teaching Strategies. *In* "Families as Learning Environments for Children" (L. Laosa and I. Sigel, eds.), Plenum, New York, pp. 261–300.

Mitchell, D. (1980). Down's Syndrome Children in Structured Dyadic Communication Situations with Their Parents. *In* "Advances in Mental Handicap Research" (J. Hogg and P. Mittler, eds.), Vol. I, Wiley, London, pp. 161–194.

Mittler, P. and Mittler, H. (1983). Partnership with Parents: An Overview. *In* "Parents, Professionals and Mentally Handicapped People" (P. Mittler and H. McConachie, eds.), Croom Helm, London, pp. 8–43.

Mogford, K. (1979). "Interaction and Communication between Handicapped Children and their Parents: A Study of Remedial Play", Unpublished doctoral dissertation, University of Nottingham.

Moss, H. A. and Jones, S. J. (1977). Relations between Maternal Attitudes and Maternal Behavior as a Function of Social Class. *In* "Culture and Infancy: Variations in the Human Experience" (P. H. Leiderman, S. R. Tulkin, and A. Rosenfeld, eds.), Academic Press, New York, pp. 439–467.

O'Dell, S. (1974). Training parents in behavior modification: A review, *Psychological Bulletin,* **81,** 418–433.

O'Reilly, J. (1977). The Interplay between Mothers and Their Children: A Construct Theory Viewpoint. *In* "New Perspectives in Personal Construct Theory" (D. Bannister, ed.), Academic Press, London, pp. 195–219.

Puckering, C. (1982). "The Impact of Maternal Depression on Young Children", Paper presented at D.C.P. symposium Problems of Parent–Child Relationships, Manchester.

Pugh, G. (1981). "Parents as Partners", National Children's Bureau, London.

Radley, A. R. (1974). The effect of role enactment upon construed alternatives, *British Journal of Medical Psychology,* **47,** 313–320.

Russell, P. (1983). The Parents' Perspective of Family Needs and How To Meet Them. *In* "Parents, Professionals and Mentally Handicapped People" (P. Mittler and H. McConachie, eds.), Croom Helm, London, pp. 47–61.

Salmon, P. (1970). A Psychology of Personal Growth. *In* "Perspectives in Personal Construct Theory" (D. Bannister, ed.), Academic Press, London, pp. 197–221.

Schaefer, N. (1979). "Does She Know She's There?", Futura, London.

Schaffer, H. R. (1977). "Studies in Mother-Infant Interaction", Academic Press, London.

Scott-Heyes, G. (1982). The Experience of Perinatal Paternity and Its Relation to Attitudes to Pregnancy and Childbirth. *In* "Fathers: Psychological Perspectives" (N. Beail and J. McGuire, eds.), Junction, London, pp. 23–42.

Shotter, J. (1970). Men, the Man-makers: George Kelly and the Theory of Personal Constructs. *In* "Perspectives in Personal Construct Theory" (D. Bannister, ed.), Academic Press, London, pp. 223–253.

Shotter, J. (1974). The Development of Personal Powers. *In* "The Integration of a Child into a Social World" (M. Richards, ed.), Cambridge University Press, Cambridge, pp. 215–244.

Spain, B., and Wigley, G. (eds.). (1975). "Right from the Start", National Society for Mentally Handicapped Children, London, pp. 75–80.

Tallman, I. (1965). Spousal role differentiation and socialization of severely retarded children, *Journal of Marriage and the Family,* **27,** 37–42.

Turnbull, A. P., Brotherson, M. J., and Summers, J. A. (1982). "The Family's Influence on the Development of Independence: Rationale, Design and Methodology, and Conceptual Framework", Paper given to A.A.M.D. conference, Boston, Massachusetts.

Vietze, P. M., Abernathy, S. R., Ashe, M. L., and Faulstitch, G. (1978). Contingent

Interaction between Mothers and Their Developmentally Delayed Infants. *In* "Observing Behavior" (G. P. Sackett, ed.), Vol. I, University Park Press, Baltimore, pp. 115–132.

Voysey, M. (1975). "A Constant Burden: The Reconstitution of Family Life", Routledge and Kegan Paul, London.

Wilkin, D. (1979). "Caring for the Mentally Handicapped Child", Croom Helm, London.

Wilks, J. and Wilks, E. (1974). "Bernard: Bringing Up Our Mongol Son", Routledge and Kegan Paul, London.

Winton, P. J. and Turnbull, A. P. (1981). Parent involvement as viewed by parents of preschool handicapped children, *Topics in Early Childhood Special Education*, **1**, 11–19.

Wishart, M. C., Bidder, R. T., and Gray, O. P. (1980). Parental responses to their developmentally delayed children and the South Glamorgan Home Advisory Service, *Child: Care, Health and Development*, **6**, 361–376.

Wolfensberger, W. (1967). Counselling the Parents of the Retarded. *In* "Mental Retardation: Appraisal, Education and Rehabilitation" (A. A. Baumeister, ed.), University of London Press, London, pp. 329–400.

Wolfensberger, W. and Kurtz, R. A. (1971). Measuring of parents' perceptions of their children's development, *Genetic Psychology Monographs*, **83**, 3–92.

Wooster, A. D. (1970). Formation of stable and discrete concepts of personality by normal and mentally retarded boys, *Journal of Mental Subnormality*, **16**, 24–28.

World Health Organisation (1983). "Mental Handicap", Report commissioned from the Joint Commission on International Aspects of Mental Retardation, World Health Organisation, Geneva.

Yule, W. (1975). Teaching psychological principles to non-psychologists, *Journal of the Association of Educational Psychologists*, **10**, 1–12.

8

Couples' Constructs: Personal Systems in Marital Satisfaction*

Greg J. Neimeyer and Jean E. Hudson

Einstein's recognition that "it is the theory which decides what we can observe" (Heisenberg, 1972, p. 77) is as relevant to our implicit personal theories as to their more formal scientific offspring. As personal scientists we choose those alternatives which appear to offer the greatest opportunity for elaborating our understandings. It has been argued that we choose relationships for the same reasons: to extend and define our understanding of experience (Duck, 1979; R. Neimeyer and G. Neimeyer, 1982). Nowhere is this more clear than in the choice of a marriage partner. As Kelly (1955, p. 523) noted, "Other things being equal, the man confronted with the alternative of marriage will choose marriage if that appears to provide him with an opportunity to enlarge or secure his anticipatory system."

But the selection of a particular mate simultaneously opens and closes new doors: at once enabling and disabling the further investigation of particular alternatives. The decision to marry a concert pianist, a professional athlete, or a practicing psychologist carries major implications for the nature and direction of personal elaboration. But these implications cannot be fully appreciated on a prenuptial basis. They emerge only as *lived* anticipations (Radley, 1977) which take form as the relationship itself is forged. In this sense love may not be blind but it is at least shortsighted.[1]

The fact that all the implications of marriage are not knowable at the outset, however, does not deter the general conviction that marriage will open more doors than it closes; that through marriage the world will become more meaningful, predictable, and understandable. Just as importantly, the choice of a particular partner reveals quite clearly *which* doors the individual wants to open; that is, which aspects of the self the individual chooses to elaborate. It is no

*Note: We would like to acknowledge gratefully the assistance of all those who helped in the preparation of this work. Very special thanks go to Martha B. Cousar for her contribution throughout the entire project.

[1]One of the primary goals of premarital counseling is to help the partners to overcome this shortsightedness. This is accomplished by having them trace the implications of their decision to marry, often by anticipating the nature of their relationship in specific areas of core role structure (e.g., religious upbringing, childrearing, etc.).

ISSUES AND APPROACHES
IN PERSONAL CONSTRUCT THEORY

127

accident that intake interviews for marital therapy routinely ask spouses what first attracted them to each other (Satir, 1967). Answers reveal not only specific attractions ("It was his carefree, devil-may-care outlook"), but also networks of anticipations regarding the nature of the subsequent relationship ("I thought life would never get us down, never get too serious"). These anticipations often signal directions which the individual views as optimally elaborative. It is no subtle irony that it is these very characteristics which so often become the presenting problems for therapy. This volte-face is a product of reconstruing the desired characteristics in light of their actual day-to-day implications. This invalidation of elaborative anticipations can be quite dramatic. So it is that the attractive "devil-may-care" outlook on life becomes reconstrued as an attitude of "blatant irresponsibility."

But there are many ways of frustrating productive role relationships. This chapter discusses some of those ways. Processes which distinguish satisfied from dissatisfied couples are addressed in a general model of close relationships, and the model is tested on a sample of 20 couples. Therapeutic implications of the findings are also noted.

A Model of Marital Relationships

First, what defines the marital relationship as unique from other forms of role relations? Given the notion that relationships in general are pursued on the basis of their elaborative potential, what is special about the marital partnership? One answer is that the nature of any specific relationship is defined by the particular construct subsystems which it involves (R. Neimeyer and G. Neimeyer, 1982). In this way we develop "colleagueships" with others whose professional constructions we engage without them necessarily becoming our friends, per se. Friendship might emerge to the extent that the development of our professional understandings begins to spill over into the interpersonal arenas. In this case the "trajectory" (Delia, 1980) of the relationship changes as the interactants engage new (interpersonal) construct subsystems. In much the same way the course of a role-bound social exchange with a grocery clerk can be altered by asking about his or her family (always good for a startle response) or by asking for a date. The point is that the areas of potential construct system elaboration (e.g., professional, interpersonal, spiritual, recreational) determine the particular type of relationship. Marital relationships are no exception.

Unlike relationships in which the systems employed are fairly circumscribed or superficial, marriage involves the development of many different subsystems at varying levels of intimacy. The elaboration of sexual, emotional, recreational, and social frontiers, among others, says something about the comprehensive nature of marital relationships. In particular, the marital partnership may be defined by the *depth* and *breadth* (constructs borrowed from Altman and Taylor's [1973] social penetration theory) of potential construct system development. In this way marriage can be viewed as a vital form of intimate colleagueship in which two personal scientists develop an enduring collaboration with respect to one another's important life projects. Such a collaboration brings to light at once both the tremendous possibilities and the potential liabilities of this form of role relation. Full development of these possibilities requires that each spouse both supports and extends the other's way of viewing the world. At least two distinct processes are involved in this venture: validation and extension.

Validation occurs when individuals obtain evidence in favor of their social hypotheses. The effect of validation is to secure the system of understandings by tightening the relationships among its constructs (Bannister, 1960; 1963). Psychologically, validation assures individuals of the usefulness of existing constructs. Individuals may obtain this validation by developing relationships with similar others (Duck, 1973). For example, they may marry someone who shares their religious convictions.

A certain amount of validation encourages the development of the systems by assuring the workability of existing structures. This validation provides a degree of security which enables individuals to venture more boldly in the elaboration of their systems (Goldstein and Rosenfeld, 1969). This explains why the attractiveness of similarity waxes and wanes over the course of relationship development (McCarthy and Duck, 1976). By subsuming one another's differing viewpoints, individuals extend their own personal construct systems. As Duck (1979) has noted, it seems likely that successful long-term relationships are characterized by a recurring pattern of validation and extention such that tentative structures are first confirmed and then actively elaborated.

The remainder of this chapter details the processes of validation and extention. Empirical and clinical evidence is offered to support the view that satisfying marital relationships involve a continuous and reciprocal process of personal elaboration. Some implications of these findings for therapeutic interventions with distressed couples also are discussed.

Studying Marital Relationships

As part of a larger study, 20 married couples (mean number of years married = 2.7; SD = 1.5) were solicited through a newspaper article to participate in "a study of marital relationships." Couples were given theatre tickets in exchange for their participation in completing the Areas of Change Questionnaire and an exchange form (Thomas, 1979) of the retest. Couples first were administered the Areas of Change Questionnaire which consists of 34 behaviorally specific items (e.g., assuming more financial responsibility, conducting household chores). For each item spouses are asked to indicate on a 7-point continuum the degree and direction (more or less) of changes they would like to see in their partner's behaviors. Significant desired changes are tallied and summed for the husband and wife. The total summed score reflects the degree of marital distress (possible range = 0 to 64). Higher scores indicate greater dissatisfaction. Normative data indicate that non-distressed couples seek an average of 7.6 (SD = 6.4) changes in their relationship whereas distressed couples seek an average of 26.5 changes (SD = 11.4) (See Weiss, Hops, and Patterson, [1973] for validity and details of scoring).

The 20 couples in the sample chosen for this study had scores ranging from 2 to 46. Wives did not appear to want more change in their relationships ($\bar{X}$ = 9.4; SD = 7.02) than did husbands ($\bar{X}$ = 9.0; SD = 6.28). The bimodal distribution of the scores made the designation of "satisfied" (n = 10; $\bar{X}$ = 8.2; SD = 4.1) and "dissatisfied" (n = 10; $\bar{X}$ = 27.8; SD = 10.2) groups an easy task.

Following the completion of the Areas of Change Questionnaire, couples were instructed to complete a series of 6 × 6 exchange grids (Thomas, 1979). Using both spouses and their parents as elements in the grid, six constructs were elicited from each partner. Then they were asked to rate each of the elements along each of their own constructs using a 7-point Likert-type scale (e.g., affectionate 3 2 1 0 1 2 3 distant), and to predict their spouse's ratings along those same constructs. Partners then exchanged grids and (without access to one another's ratings) were asked to repeat the procedure: first completing their own ratings and then predicting their partner's ratings. Lastly, each person was asked to rank order his or her *own* constructs from 1 (most important in judging my close relationships) to 6 (least important). The three constructs ranked most important were designated *superordinate* and the three ranked least important were designated *subordinate*.

On the basis of the model discussed above, predictions were made concerning differences between satisfied and dissatisfied spouses in terms of their ability to validate and elaborate one another's construct systems.

Validation

Validation can occur at several levels (cf. R. Neimeyer and G. Neimeyer, 1982). Construct similarity refers to the amount of commonality which occurs in the *content* of the spouses' constructs. It was measured using Duck's (1973) conceptual criteria. Scores could range from zero (no construct similarity) to 6 (sharing all constructs). Actual scores ranged from zero to 4.

Functional similarity (Neimeyer and Neimeyer, 1981) refers to the degree of similarity in *applying* the constructs to particular others. Spouses can validate one another not only by sharing a similar structure for anticipating experience (construct similarity), but also by applying that structure in a similar way to mutually know others (functional similarity). Functional similarity was measured by summing the absolute values of the discrepancy between husbands' and wives' rating of the six role titles. Lower scores indicate higher functional similarity. Assuming that satisfied couples share higher levels of validation in their relationships, it was predicted that they would display greater construct and functional similarity than dissatisfied couples.

TESTING CONSTRUCT SIMILARITY

A chi-square statistic first was applied to the distribution of construct similarity for satisfied and dissatisfied couples at superordinate and subordinate levels of construing. Overall, satisfied couples showed greater construct similarity ($\bar{X} = 2.0$; $SD = 1.37$) than did dissatisfied couples ($\bar{X} = 1.2$; $SD = .79$), $\chi^2_{(1)} = 8.42$, $p \leq .01$. This was a function of different levels of subordinate similarity between satisfied ($\bar{X} = 1.2$; $SD = 1.2$) and dissatisfied ($\bar{X} = .5$; $SD = .71$) couples, $t_{(18)} = 1.79$, $p \leq .05$. No difference in construct similarity was found at superordinate levels (satisfied couples: $\bar{X} = .8$; $SD = .78$; dissatisfied couples: $\bar{X} = .7$; $SD = .67$).

Assuming that subordinate constructs are more readily accessible (cf. R. A. Neimeyer, 1981) to the spouses, an interesting and clinically useful interpretation suggests itself. Marital dissatisfaction stems, in part, from not feeling validated on a day-to-day basis in the relationship. This is consistent with clinical experience.

Couples seeking therapy often present a general concern (e.g., "We're just not getting along anymore;" "We no longer have anything in common,") which can be linked to specific behaviors (e.g., "She's such a messy housekeeper;" "He never pays the bills on time"). From a behavioral perspective, the counselor may arrange a simple contingency contract (Margolin and Weiss, 1978) which establishes a quid pro quo (e.g., she keeps house if he pays the bills).

The simplicity of the approach is appealing but has certain disadvantages. Among them is the potential danger of circumventing issues involving core role structure by focusing attention exclusively on subordinate issues. Rather than dealing at the level of subordinate constructions, the construct therapist might prefer to trace the implications of the spouses' complaints to their core role relationship. This can be accomplished by means of Hinkle's (1965) laddering technique.

Imagine the couple seeking therapy as being separated from one another by a towering brick wall (an apt metaphor for anyone who has done marital counseling). Part of the therapist's job is to assist the couple to overcome that obstacle. In response to the question, "Why is it important that your partner keep the house clean," or whatever, the couple will quickly ladder upwards toward such *shared superordinates* as, "because it shows that he or she appreciates me, respects me, or loves me." Metaphorically, this is analogous to propping ladders on either side of the hypothetical wall which separates them. At ground level (subordinate constructions) the ladders are farthest apart, but each rung of the ladder brings the spouses closer together until they meet at the top (superordinate constructions). Partners are often suprised and relieved to learn that they really desire much the same things from their relationship at superordinate levels.

This intervention can be followed up in at least two ways. The first continues to focus on the *content* of the presenting (subordinate) problems. Often even simple interventions, such as asking the spouses to consider three things they might do to show their appreciation for one another, can have a marked impact on the relationship by increasing the levels of validation at subordinate levels.

The second alternative is to focus on the *process,* rather than the content, of presenting issues. By standing back and reflecting on the laddering process itself, couples can see that subordinate complaints are meaningful only insofar as they carry superordinate implications. This can be illustrated by asking them how upset they would be over their presenting concerns if they felt genuinely loved and respected in their relationship. Reflecting on the process in this way also helps the spouses to see that very superficial behaviors are used as a springboard for far-reaching inferences concerning deeper levels of core role structure (cf. Duck and Craig, 1977).

TESTING FUNCTIONAL SIMILARITY

In contrast to construct similarity, functional similarity (G. J. Neimeyer and R. A. Neimeyer, 1981) refers to the extent to which two individuals actually *apply* their constructs similarly to particular elements of experience. For example, both spouses may evaluate others in their lives along the dimension, "trustworthy versus untrustworthy," but may disagree as to *which* of their acquaintances are worthy of trust. This represents a case in which the two individuals consensually *validate* the *content* of one another's construct, but *invalidate* its *application.* Stated differently, this would be an instance of construct similarity in the context of functional *dis*similarity (R. Neimeyer and G. Neimeyer, 1982).

The prediction that satisfied couples would show higher levels of functional similarity than dissatisifed couples was supported by an analysis of the data, $t_{(18)}$ = 1.85, $p \leq .01$. Satisfied partners applied their constructs more similarly ($\bar{X}$ = 86.4; SD = 11.8) than dissatisfied couples ($\bar{X}$ = 90.0; SD = 24.2).

A breakdown by construct ordination indicated no significant difference between satisfied ($\bar{X}$ = 44.6; SD = 12.0) and dissatisfied ($\bar{X}$ = 45.9; SD = 15.3) couples at subordinate levels. There was a tendency, however, toward the more similar application of superordinate constructs by satisfied ($\bar{X}$ = 41.8; SD = 7.3) than by dissatisfied ($\bar{X}$ = 44.0; SD = 10.3) couples, $t_{(18)}$ = 1.66, $p \leq .06$.

This result extends the findings regarding construct similarity. It suggests that satisfied relationships are characterized by higher levels of validation not only in the content, but also in the application, of their construct systems. It seems likely that it is especially important that couples "see eye to eye" at superordinate levels of construing, though this interpretation is supported only by a tendency in the predicted direction.

Clinically, functional dissimilarity can be a complex issue. More often than not, however, experience has shown that spouses are more upset when they believe the other misunderstands them (lack of sociality) than when the other disagrees with them (functional dissimilarity). It follows that spouses can more easily tolerate disagreement if they feel their partner has accurately subsumed their differing constructions. This clinical insight is consistent with the findings of some empirical work.

Harvey and Wells (cited in Harvey, Wells, and Alvarez, 1976) concluded from a study of 72 high-conflict couples that "*a lack of understanding of divergence* is as critical or more critical to the viability of close relationships than is actual divergence itself" (original emphasis, pp. 247–248). This is supported by the experimental work of Aderman, Bryant, and Domelsmith (1978) which noted that training individuals to understand and anticipate disagreements was a useful means of inducing a greater tolerance to differences. In other words, functional dissimilarity may be an especially important factor insofar as it interacts with sociality. When the spouse feels genuinely understood, he or she is more accepting of the other's differing viewpoint. This process is reflected in the widely accepted cardinal rule that the therapist "support before confronting"; that is, validate (to lessen the threat), then elaborate (suggest alternative perspectives, etc.).

Extention

Although similarity in the content and application of the individual's system enhances its validity, similarity alone is insufficient for continued relationship development. Camus (1956) characterized hell as a place in which one's identity was permanently fixed and unchanging. Construct theory acknowledges the need for continued growth of the personality. Because Kelly's (1955) personal scientist model implies that individuals seek not only to confirm, but also to extend their interpretive frameworks, it becomes important to study those processes by which they enlarge their existing network of constructions. Interpersonal understanding or *sociality* (Kelly, 1955, pp. 95–103) represents one vehicle for this personal elaboration.

There is little doubt that Kelly (1955) envisioned sociality as the primary inroad to a psychology of close relationships. The sociality corollary stipulates that genuine role relations are limited by the interactants' degree of understanding; that is, by their ability to subsume one another's constructions. This suggests that a major factor in the development of interpersonal relationships is the amount of understanding between interactants.

By subsuming the viewpoints of others, individuals have available simultaneously two systems for construing social experience (Thomas, 1979). This increases the comprehensiveness of the meaning structures on which they can rely for interpreting social experience, while at the same time assuring a high level of understanding of the person whose constructions they subsume. The positive impact of understanding on successful relationship development is underscored in the literature on successful marital relationships (Christensen and Wallace, 1976; Laing, Phillipson, and Lee, 1966). These studies support the argument that a "critical factor in the development of productive role relations . . . lies in the ability of one or both participants in a dyadic relationship to subsume the points of view of the other person" (Landfield, 1971, p. 7).

In contrast, ineffective understandings jeopardize interpersonal development. Two mechanisms which relate to misunderstanding are threat and anxiety. Major misconstructions at relatively superordinate levels of the system produce threat. Threat is regarded as "the awareness of imminent comprehensive change in one's core role structure" (Kelly, 1955, p. 489). It damages a relationship by implying the need for major reconstruction of superordinate understandings. For example, the wife whose core role structure involves trusting her spouse is likely to be critically threatened when she learns of her husband's infidelity. This sudden dose of invalidational evidence results from an inaccurate superordinate construction of her role relations with her husband. It jeopardizes her most central constructions of her relations and forces massive reconstruction of her system.

A second mechanism that influences interpersonal understandings is anxiety. Anxiety represents the recognition that "the events with which one is confronted lie outside the range of convenience of one's construct system" (Kelly, 1955, p. 495). In other words, anxiety results from an inadequate or underdimensionalized understanding of impending experience. The young adolescent is anxious regarding the very first date because she or he has no system within which such experience can be meaningfully construed. Anxiety manifests itself in the marital relationship when interactants recognize that they no longer can accurately understand or predict one another. "I just don't know what has happened to the person I married; we can't even talk anymore," is a statement which typifies anxiety-laden relationships. Because such relationships are relatively asocial, there is very little grounds for anticipating mutual elaboration.

Threat and anxiety have an impact on marital relationsips at all stages of development, beginning with the choice of a particular partner. As Kelly (1955, pp. 523–524) details,

> Marriage might place the man [sic] in a world where everything would be unpredictable and where his carefully wrought prediction system would, as a system, be wholly obsolescent. If he thinks he can come to understand his girl friend better and better, he is challenged by the prospect of marriage. If he is persuaded that she would never make any kind of sense and that, if married to her, he himself would not either, his answer is likely

to be, "No!, No!, No!." A mysterious or unpredictable girl may evoke a passing interest; but if she shows no promise of ever making any more sense than she does at the moment, the man will not wish to bind himself to her. Furthermore, if he finds that he himself makes less and less sense while in her company, he is likely to seek to extricate himself from the relationship.

In summary, threat and anxiety are two mechanisms which frustrate interpersonal development; threat by jeopardizing the validity of the system's superordinate dimensions, and anxiety by removing the construct system of one or both interactants from within the other's range of convenience. This reasoning implies that successful intimate relationships are accompanied by greater interpersonal understanding.

Richardson and Weigel (1971) developed a similar rationale when they suggested that the crucial component in satisfactory marriages is the extent to which partners can adopt one another's viewpoint. But they also argued that a basic commonality between spouses construct systems may facilitate understanding, a viewpoint shared by Duck (1973, 1979) in relation to friendship. Unfortunately, there is neither a strong theoretical, nor empirical warrant for this assumption.

Theoretically, Kelly (1955) is explicit about the *incidental* relationship between similarity (commonality) and understanding (sociality). He emphasized that "there is a difference between two people's holding the same construction system and two people's understanding each other so they can play roles in relation to one another. Simply stated, one does not have to be like certain people in order to understand them" (Kelly, 1955, pp. 100–101).

This incidental relationship also is reflected in the inconsistency of the empirical literature. Smail (1972) found support for the positive relationship between similarity and understanding in a psychotherapy group. In contrast, the results of his research on 20 married couples led Corsini (1956) to conclude that "there is no evidence that understanding the mate is a function of the similarity of the selves of the mates" (p. 232). This inconsistency in empirical findings concerning the relationship between similarity and understanding challenges the intuitively compelling assertion that "commonality of constructs makes them easier to understand" (Duck, 1979, p. 282; cf. Adams-Webber, 1979).

For this reason research has begun to measure understanding more directly. Understanding is measured by assessing the accuracy with which individuals predict one another's construct ratings. This predictive accuracy score (Landfield, 1977) is calculated by summing the absolute difference between the spouses' own ratings and their partner's predictions of their ratings. Lower discrepancy scores indicate higher understanding.

The general assumption that satisfied partners understand one another more accurately than do dissatisfied partners received strong support in our own sample of 20 couples, $t_{(18)} = 6.7$, $p \leq .001$. This difference was due to the greater understanding of satisfied spouses at superordinate levels ($\bar{X} = 81.9$; $SD =$

18.9), relative to dissatisfied spouses ($\bar{X} = 88.5$; $SD = 18.4$), $t_{(18)} = 3.47$, $p \le$ .001. There was no significant difference between the groups at subordinate levels (satisfied: $\bar{X} = 90.8$; $SD = 18.2$; dissatisfied: $\bar{X} = 92.3$; $SD = 22.2$). This finding supports the notion that spouses' understanding of one another, especially along important constructs, is a critical factor in successful marital relationships (cf. Wijesinghe and Wood, 1976).

In addition to the overall level of understanding in a relationship, support for the importance of *reciprocal* understanding can also be found within construct theory. As Duck (1979) has noted, it is possible to have a unilateral understanding of someone without developing a *mutually* elaborative relationship.

There are two ways to delineate this mutuality. The first way concerns the balance between the husband's and the wife's understanding. Grossly asymmetrical understanding (for example, when the wife understands the husband much better than he understands her) should be associated with marital dissatisfaction. In such cases, spouses do not afford one another an equal opportunity for elaboration. The lopsided nature of the role relations prevents reciprocal development.

In order to test this first hypothesis, we examined the discrepancy between the wife's understanding of the husband and vice versa. Lower scores indicated greater mutuality. As predicted, satisfied spouses where characterized by lower discrepancy in their understandings of one another ($\bar{X} = 10.2$; $SD = 4.66$) than were dissatisfied partners ($\bar{X} = 22.5$; $SD = 14.22$), $t_{(18)} = 8.98$, $p \le .001$. Symmetrical understanding does seem to be associated with marital satisfaction.

The second way in which mutuality can be viewed concerns the utility of the construct systems themselves. Imagine the case in which both the husband and the wife understand one another more accurately along his constructs. They have an effective grasp on one another's viewpoints only when operating within his system. When they attempt to anticipate experience from within her system, the world is confused, disorganized, and unpredictable. The construct systems themselves are differentially useful. This inequity may create dissatisfaction because it limits the partners' ability to simultaneously understand and elaborate both construct systems. The spouses are psychologically cramped because they can understand one another accurately along only one network of dimensions.

Results of analyses supported this reasoning. There was a greater discrepancy in the accuracy with which the husbands' and wives' construct systems were used for the dissatisfied couples ($\bar{X} = 14.5$; $SD = 8.5$) than for satisfied couples ($\bar{X} = 10.0$; $SD = 8.19$), $t_{(18)} = 3.49$, $p \le .001$. Perhaps satisfactory marital relationships require not only that spouses are equally able to understand one another, but that they can operate with equal facility from within one another's network of understandings.

Clinically, there are many means of facilitating sociality in the marital relationship. Any procedure which enhances "metaconstruing" (construing the construction processes of one another) is likely to be helpful. Three general strategies suggest themselves. The first is direct communication skills training. Gottman, Notarius, Gonso, and Markman (1980) outline a useful structured approach to enhance sociality in this way. These techniques are designed to facilitate metaconstruing by having couples successively approximate an understanding of one another's position on various issues.

The second means of enhancing sociality is through role play. A rich and diverse set of tacit constructions (R. A. Neimeyer, 1981) can be portrayed and subsequently articulated in this fashion. Kelly's (1955, pp. 1141–1154) own discussion of role playing procedures is a useful guide in this regard and can be augmented by discussions of family sculpting (Constantine, 1978; Papp, Silversmith and Carter, 1973) and psychodrama (Moreno, 1976).

A third approach to improving sociality concerns developing what the ego analysts designate as a "relationship ego." The concept refers to the couple's ability to step outside of their individual positions and to comment on the relationship as if from a third-person perspective. This means developing a shared set of metaconstructions which help the spouses clarify and anticipate their experience as a couple. The objective is to dislodge them from their individual perspectives by inviting them to collaborate in the development of a *common* system of understandings: a shared theory of their relationship (Wile, 1981). Although our own work in this regard is still in formative stages, we have found two techniques useful for this purpose.

The first is Kagen's Interpersonal Process Recall (IPR) technique (Kagen, 1972; Schauble, 1973) in which couples are first videotaped in discussion and then invited to observe and comment on (process) their behaviors. There are multiple variants of the IPR procedure. Its flexibility allows it to be tailored to particular issues and interaction styles. The spontaneous articulation and elaboration of relationship constructions (e.g., "We're so cruel to each other!") is an exciting process to facilitate.

The second technique for developing relationship constructs is an adaptation of Kelly's (1955, pp. 319–359) self-characterization technique. Here spouses are asked *individually* to write a brief sketch of their relationship from the third-person perspective of an "intimate and sympathetic friend." They then share the characterizations and discuss their similarities (validating their relationship constructs) and their differences (elaborating those constructs). The use of double dyad grids in which relationships instead of individuals serve as elements (Ryle and Breen, 1972a; 1972b) provides a more structured variant of this approach and a means for collecting empirical data.

Summary

This chapter sketches some of the implications of personal construct theory for understanding marital relationships. Like other forms of role relations, marriage represents an elaborative choice. Individuals choose to develop particular relationships in an effort to render their experience more meaningful and understandable. The enduring and intimate nature of the marital relationship distinguishes it as central to this project.

Successful marriages have been characterized as mutually elaborative. Partners encourage each other's development by validating and extending their systems of understanding. The empirical evidence presented here is generally consistent with this formulation.

In particular, satisfied spouses are more validating and understanding in their relationships than are dissatisfied partners. Consistent with a parallel literature in friendship formation (Duck, 1973; Duck and Allison, 1978; Duck and Spencer, 1972; G. J. Neimeyer and R. A. Neimeyer, 1981), satisfied couples are more similar in the content and application of their construct systems. As with friendships (cf. R. A. Neimeyer and G. J. Neimeyer, 1983), it seems likely that satisfied couples also structure or organize their construct systems in similar ways. Each of these types of similarity validates an aspect of the construct system. As partners become more convinced of the validity of their views, they are better able to subsume one another's differing viewpoints.

This is supported by the findings that more satisfied spouses are better able to understand one another, especially along more important constructs. They also show more *mutual* understanding. Dissatisfied spouses are more discrepant in their understandings of one another and in their abilities to use both construct systems with equal facility. This lack of mutuality jeopardizes interpersonal elaboration by limiting the partners' ability to contribute to their joint development in a continuous and reciprocal way.

Some implications of these findings for therapeutic interventions also are noted. But no attempt is made to embed these techniques within the context of a more complete approach to marital therapy. Although useful extrapolations can be made from Kelly's (1955, Volume II) original discussions of the psychotherapeutic process, and from the reflections of R. A. Neimeyer (1980) and Epting (1984), no work to date has described in detail the nature of marital therapy from a personal construct perspective. This is surprising because marital relationships provide a ''living laboratory'' for the design of social experiments bearing on the spouses' role relationship. Much of the therapist's task might be aimed at fostering collaboration between the marital partners in the design and implementation of relevant social tests.

As an example, a case developed in which anger and physical abuse were presenting problems. The wife, frightened by her husband's explosive episodes, withdrew from him for fear of triggering his violence. He, of course, was incensed by her withdrawal. Each partner viewed two alternatives as available: withdrawal or violence. Both alternatives were seen as unsatisfactory, though they ''slot-rattled'' (Kelly, 1955, p. 938) freely between the two. Following a discussion of their shared dilemma, the spouses were invited to brainstorm for "a variety of creative ways that couples could express their anger." They became somewhat playful in this task and generated several inventive means of expressing anger. Among them was the suggestion that they keep an aerosol can of whipped cream in the refrigerator and whenever they began to feel upset they could use this can to "vent their anger" on the unsuspecting spouse. A characteristic uneasiness (anxiety) was expressed when the couple was asked to anticipate the impact of this new behavior on their own relationship. But their willingness to try this new form of expression proved quite useful. The couple learned that anger itself is an acceptable part of a relationship and that it does not *necessarily* carry implications for emotional distance or physical abuse. This intervention is by no means a general prescription for abusive spouses, but it does illustrate the experimental nature of behavior (Kelly, 1970). In particular, it demonstrates how spouses can jointly formulate and conduct experiments which yield new data to be integrated into their role relationship.

By encouraging partners to collaborate in testing alternatives to unproductive behaviors, the therapist promotes a continued process of shared experimentation. Gradually, this helps the spouses to develop an increasingly accurate theory of their own relationship (cf. Wile, 1981) which is useful in anticipating experience. A fuller discussion of the means by which this could be accomplished would represent a valuable contribution to personal construct therapists working with dissatisfied couples.

References

Adams-Webber, J. (1979). "Personal Construct Theory: Concepts and Applications", Wiley, New York.

Aderman, D., Bryant, F. B., and Domelsmith, D. E. (1978). Prediction as a means of inducing tolerance. *Journal of Research in Personality*, **12**, 172–178.

Altman, I. and Taylor, D. A. (1973). "Social Penetration: The Development of Interpersonal Relationships", Holt, Rinehart & Winston, New York.

Bannister, D. (1960). Conceptual structure in thought disordered schizophrenics. *Journal of Mental Science*, **106**, 1230–1249.

Bannister, D. (1963). The genesis of schizophrenic thought disorder: A serial invalidation hypothesis. *British Journal of Psychiatry*, **109**, 680–686.

Camus, A. (1956). "The Fall", Knopf, New York.

Christensen, L. and Wallace, L. (1976). Perceptual accuracy as a variable in marital adjustment. *Journal of Sex and Marital Therapy*, **2**, 130–136.

Constantine, L. (1978). Family sculpting and relationship mapping techniques. *Journal of Marriage and Family Counseling*, **4**, 13–23.

Corsini, R. J. (1956). Understanding and similarity in marriage. *Journal of Abnormal and Social Psychology*, **52**, 327–332.

Delia, J. G. (1980). Some tentative thoughts concerning the study of interpersonal relationships and their development. *The Western Journal of Speech Communication*, **44**, 197–203.

Duck, S. W. (1973). "Personal Relationships and Personal Constructs", Wiley, London.

Duck, S. W. (1979). The Personal and the Interpersonal in Construct Theory: Social and Individual Aspects of Relationships. *In* "Constructs of Sociality and Individuality" (P. Stringer and D. Bannister, eds.), Academic, London, pp. 279–298.

Duck, S. W. and Allison, D. (1978). I liked you but I can't live with you: A study of lapsed friendships. *Social Behavior and Personality*, **8**, 43–47.

Duck, S. W. and Craig, G. (1977). The relative attractiveness of different types of information about another person. *British Journal of Social and Clinical Psychology*, **16**, 229–233.

Duck, S. W. and Spencer, C. P. (1972). Personal constructs and friendship formation. *Journal of Personality and Social Psychology*, **23**, 40–45.

Epting, F. R. (1984). "Personal Construct Counseling and Psychotherapy", Wiley, London.

Goldstein, J. W. and Rosenfeld, H. M. (1969). Insecurity and preference for persons similar to oneself. *Journal of Personality*, **37**, 253–268.

Gottman, J., Notarius, C., Gonso, J., and Markman, H. (1980). "A Couple's Guide to Communication", Research Press, Champaign, Illinois.

Harvey, J. H., Wells, G. L., and Alvarez, M. D. (1976). Attribution in the Context of Conflict and Separation in Close Relationships. *In* "New Directions in Attribution Research" (J. Harvey, W. Ickes, and R. Kidd, eds.), Erlbaum Associates, Hillsdale, New Jersey.

Heisenberg, W. (1972). "Physics and Beyond", Harper Torchbooks, New York.

Hinkle, D. (1965). "The change of personal constructs from the viewpoint of a theory of construct implications", Unpublished doctoral dissertation, Ohio State University, Columbus.

Kagen, N. (1972). "Influencing Human Interaction", Michigan State University, East Lansing.

Kelly, G. A. (1955). "The Psychology of Personal Constructs", Volumes I and II, Norton, New York.

Kelly, G. A. (1970). Behavior is an Experiment. *In* "Perspectives in Personal Construct Theory" (D. Bannister, ed.), Academic, London, pp. 255–269.

Laing, R. D., Phillipson, H., and Lee, A. (1966). "Interpersonal Perception: A Theory and a Method of Research", Springer, New York.

Landfield, A. W. (1971). "Personal Construct Systems in Psychotherapy", Rand McNally and Co., Chicago.

Landfield, A. W. (1977). Interpretive Man: The Enlarged Self-Image. *In* "The Nebraska Symposium on Motivation 1976" (A. W. Landfield, ed.), University of Nebraska Press, Lincoln/London, pp. 126–177.

Margolin, G. and Weiss, R. (1978). Comparative evaluation of therapeutic components associated with behavioral marital treatments. *Journal of Consulting and Clinical Psychology*, **46**, 1476–1486.

McCarthy, D. and Duck, S. W. (1976). Friendship duration and responses to attitudinal agreement-disagreement. *British Journal of Social and Clinical Psychology*, **15**, 377–386.

Moreno, Z. T. (1976). Psychodrama. *In* "Group Psychotherapy: Theory and Practice" (Mullan and Rosenbaum, eds.), Free Press, London, pp. 252–376.

Neimeyer, G. J. and Neimeyer, R. A. (1981). Functional similarity and interpersonal attraction. *Journal of Research in Personality*, **15**, 427–435.

Neimeyer, R. A. (1980). George Kelly as Therapist: A Review of His Tapes. *In* "Personal Construct Psychology: Psychotherapy and Personality'' (A. W. Landfield and L. M. Leitner, eds.), Wiley-Interscience, New York, pp. 74–101.

Neimeyer, R. A. (1981). The Structure and Meaningfulness of Tacit Construing. *In* "Personal Construct Psychology: Recent Advances in Theory and Practice'' (H. Bonarius, R. Holland, and S. Rosenberg, eds.), Macmillan, London, pp. 105–113.

Neimeyer, R. A. and Neimeyer, G. J. (1983). Structural similarity in the acquaintance process. *Journal of Social and Clinical Psychology*, **2**, 1–6.

Neimeyer, R. and Neimeyer, G. (1982). "Interpersonal Relationships and Personal Elaboration: A Construct Theory Model'', Paper presented at the International Conference on Personal Relationships, Madison, Wisconsin.

Papp, P., Silversmith, O., and Carter, E. (1973). Family sculpting in preventive work with "well families''. *Family Process*, **12**, 197–212.

Radley, A. (1977). Living on the Horizon. *In* "New Perspectives in Personal Construct Theory'' (D. Bannister, ed.), Academic, London, pp. 221–249.

Richardson, F. C. and Weigel, R. G. (1971). Personal construct theory applied to the marriage relationship. *Experimental Publication System*, **10**, (MS. 371-5).

Ryle, A. and Breen, D. (1972a). A comparison of adjusted and maladjusted couples using the double dyad grid. *British Journal of Medical Psychology*, **45**, 375–384.

Ryle, A. and Breen, D. (1972b). The use of the double dyad grid. *British Journal of Medical Psychology*, **45**, 383–389.

Satir, V. (1967). "Conjoint Family Therapy'', Science and Behavior Books, Inc., Palo Alto, California.

Schauble, P. (1973). Facilitating Conditions: Basic Dimensions for Psychological Growth and Effective Communication. *In* "Sexual, Marital and Familial Relations'' (R. Woody and J. Woody, eds.), Thomas, Springfield, Illinois, pp. 65–121.

Smail, D. J. (1972). A grid measure of empathy in a therapeutic group. *British Journal of Medical Psychology*, **45**, 165–169.

Thomas, L. F. (1979). Construct, Reflect and Converse: The Conversation Reconstruction of Social Realities. *In* "Constructs of Sociality and Individuality'' (P. Stringer and D. Bannister, eds.), Academic, London.

Weiss, R. L., Hops, H., and Patterson, G. R. (1973). A Framework for Conceptualizing Marital Conflict, a Technology for Altering It, Some Data for Evaluating It. *In* "Behavior Change: Methodology Concepts and Practice'' (L. A. Homerlynch, L. C. Handy, and E. J. Mash, eds.), Research Press, Champaign, Illinois.

Wijesinghe, O. B. A. and Wood, R. R. (1976). A repertory grid study of interpersonal perception within a married couple's psychotherapy group. *British Journal of Medical Psychology*, **49**, 287–293.

Wile, D. B. (1981). "Couples Therapy: A Nontraditional Approach'', Wiley, New York.

9

Problems and Prospects in Personal Construct Theory

Robert A. Neimeyer

The limitations of [a] theory can be accounted for by its context of origin. . . . This means that the present condition of personal construct theory can be explained by *sociopsychological analysis*. In other words, it is possible for personal construct theory to "know itself" by the application to it of a developed form of the *sociology of knowledge*. This is [a] stronger form of reflexivity that provides a basis for radical criticism.

(Holland, 1981, p. 25)

One of the distinctive characteristics of Kelly's (1955) psychology of personal constructs is its *reflexivity*, that is, its capacity to interpret within its own theoretical framework the very theorizing (construing) activity that led to its formulation. As Oliver and Landfield (1962) have noted, this self-referential character of the theory enables it to avoid "the fallacy of reflexivity," which is entailed when a theorist propounds a general system of psychology that excludes the psychological processes by which it was derived. For example, a theory of radical behaviorism that refuses to account for the creative cognitive activities of its author would be fallacious in this sense.

Put forward in this way, reflexivity operates as a *logical criterion* by which the adequacy of psychological theories can be judged. Thus, the psychologist cannot afford "to forget that he is an observing, thinking, calculating being, and that whatever he says about the mind and its activities must not be permitted to deny this" (Oliver and Landfield, 1962, pp. 122–123). As a logical criterion, the demand for consistent reflexivity is a minimal one; certainly it is met (at least in a loose sense) by most personality theories (Oliver and Landfield, 1975). But it is also possible to construe reflexivity in a second, deeper sense, as a *self-critical* activity that applies the concepts and methods of social scientific thought to the study of a given branch of social science, in the hope of understanding and perhaps surmounting its current limitations. Holland (1981) has suggested that this kind of self-critical reflexivity can be practiced at two main levels, the personal and the social. At the personal level, construct theorists might be encouraged to interpret their own theoretical shortcomings in the terms of their theory: Is their failure to build a comprehensive social psychology a result of the individualistic "focus of convenience" of their theoretical constructs? Does their heavy reliance on the repertory grid represent a form of methodological "con-striction," motivated by the "anxious" awareness that data gathered by other methods may fall outside the purview of their present conceptual system? By using the resources of the discipline in this critically reflexive way, it may be possible to move the theory toward greater scope and clarity, toward increasing extension and definition.

The second level at which reflexive self-study can be practiced is the social. Questions posited at this level are more molar, and pertain less to the functioning of the individual scientist than to the scientific community as a whole or to particular collectivities of scientists pursuing joint research: To what extent are the methods and content of science conditioned by the social, economic, and political forces operative in a given society? What social factors facilitate or impede the development of a particular scientific specialty? Tentative answers to such questions can point up limitations imposed on the course and direction of intellectual inquiry by factors extrinsic to the scientific enterprise itself. By taking into account such influences, practicing scientists may be able to circum-vent certain barriers to knowledge production that otherwise might operate out-side their awareness.

Historically, these second-level questions have been formulated most clearly within the sociology of science, a field that originated in the work of Marx (1904) and Durkheim (1915), and that was brought into focus in the 1950s by Merton (1945/1973) and Mannheim (1952). My own interest in the sociology of science stemmed from a curiosity about the social processes at work in the development of personal construct theory. It seemed to me that a reflexive, critical study of the social evolution of the theory might elucidate its current status and future directions in a way that the more usual intellectual critique of the theory might not. What followed was an attempt to characterize the so-ciohistorical development of construct theory in terms of the model outlined by Mullins (1973). It may be useful to review the results of this earlier study briefly before examining from a sociological standpoint several problems that currently confront construct theorists, the primary task of the present chapter. Readers interested in a more detailed report of these findings are urged to consult the original study (R. A. Neimeyer, 1983, 1985a).

The Development of Personal Construct Theory

Essentially, Mullins' (1973) model traces the progress of the nascent "theory group" (i.e., a coherent group of scientists sharing a common theoretical orien-tation and interest in a related set of problems) as it gradually differentiates from its parent discipline and eventually matures to become a specialty in its own right. The basic feature of this process is the changing *pattern* of *communication* within the emerging group. Connections between members of a theory group, like those between scientists in the general scientific communication structure, consist of four types of professional–social relationships: (1) *communication,* serious discussion about ongoing research; (2) *coauthorship,* a more intimate form of association in which two or more scientists jointly publish a theoretical, practical, or research contribution; (3) *apprenticeship,* the training of a student by his or her teacher; and (4) *colleagueship,* two scientists working at the same institution (Mullins, 1973, p. 19).

As a theory group congeals, less formal communication ties (often with persons outside the scientist's focal area of interest) are augmented by closer coauthor, apprentice, and colleague relations among group members. Of course, any given scientist will continue to form and break many such ties during the course of her or his research career. But the degree of cohesion in the communication structure linking group members as an aggregate will suggest the amount of social structural progress made by the theory group. Additionally, Mullins holds that certain specifiable intellectual developments accompany the social communicative changes undergone by the emerging group. For the sake of conceptual clarity, he segments this continual evolutionary process into the following four stages, a scheme I have found helpful in organizing an account of personal construct theory's development.

NORMAL STAGE (TO 1955)

Prior to 1955, personal construct theory existed only in a germinal sense. Supported by few students and no significant coauthor and colleague ties, Kelly worked in virtual isolation at Ohio State University to establish the outlines of his distinctive approach to clinical psychology and personality theory. As Figure 1 indicates, publication of intellectual materials during this phase was quite limited, consisting of an occasional repertory grid study or theoretical paper. Thus, both the early scientific communication structure and the early literature in construct theory displayed the relatively low degree of organization that Mullins (1973) and Kuhn (1970) associate with fields in the normal science phase of development.

NETWORK STAGE (1955–1966)

The transition to network status was catalyzed by the publication of Kelly's (1955) *Psychology of Personal Constructs,* which provided both an exciting theory and a suggestive program statement around which like-minded clinicians and researchers could gather. Members of the incipient theory group began conducting discussions more with one another than with researchers whose major interests lay elsewhere, thereby producing a "thickening" of the scientific communication structure. By the mid-1960s, a handful of American and British universities had joined Ohio State as training and research centers, and a number

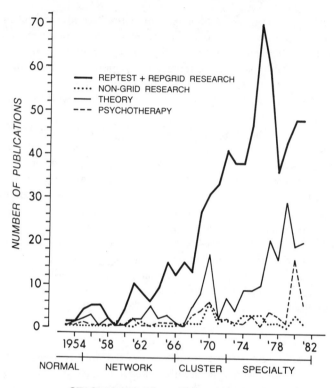

Figure 1. Number of publications in construct theory by category and year, 1953–1981. (Note: The apparent decline in number of publications in later years is artifactual; it results from a delay in incorporating references into the bibliography on which the figure was based.)

of important collaborative ties were cemented by coauthorship. This development was especially vigorous in England, owing largely to the efforts of Bannister and his colleagues at the University of London.

As consensus as to the shared aims of the group began to develop, the published output of the group began to increase steadily. This was particularly true of repertory grid studies on clinical psychological topics, many of which relied on computerized analysis packages designed by Slater (1965) and distributed throughout the United Kingdom (see Figure 1).

CLUSTER STAGE (1966–1972)

By the late 1960s, a stable and productive cluster of personal construct researchers had assumed faculty positions at the University of London and had begun to share with Bannister a measure of the social and intellectual leadership of the rapidly expanding British wing of the theory group. The appearance of earlier scientific successes attracted new students and colleagues to the major English and Scottish research centers. This triggered a "publication explosion" on the British front, a fainter echo of which could be discerned in the American literature as well. As Figure 1 illustrates, the great majority of these articles employed adaptations of repertory grid technique. This accords with Mullins's (1973) observation that the availability of suitable methodological resources is a primary factor influencing the rate at which a theory group develops.

Predictably, communication during the cluster stage became even more in-grown, as apprentice and colleague relationships continued to displace the informal relations characteristic of earlier stages. The proportion of citations to work generated by other theory groups further declined. Coauthorship networks in Great Britain grew in complexity and stability. This produced a degree of scientific focus and communicative cohesiveness not found in the more fractionated American community, which had lost its social and intellectual leader with Kelly's death in 1967.

As the young theory group gained visibility through its published literature and its social-organizational efforts, critical work related to its emphasis began to appear. Though not without ambivalence, the British psychological community accorded personal construct researchers a measure of professional respect, and repertory grid studies were granted a niche beside more traditional investigations in elite British journals. In the United States, on the other hand, the theory group was more often regarded as either revolutionary or foolish for its rejection of traditional theoretical formulations. Partly for this reason, the bulk of the U.S. work was published outside mainstream American journals, thereby decreasing its salience to the parent discipline. As I later suggest, an appreciation of the differential rate of social structural progress in the two major branches of the theory group is essential to understanding the dilemmas that it currently faces.

SPECIALTY STAGE (1972–PRESENT)

Ironically, as the successful British clusters grew in visibility and importance, their stability was increasingly jeopardized by the hiring efforts of groups at competing institutions. Over the decade of the 1970s, most of the large British research centers declined markedly in membership as promising students and faculty moved on to take positions elsewhere. In contrast, American research and training centers began to grow over this same period, both in membership and intellectual output. Thus, just as social communication patterns in the United Kingdom began to assume once again the informal pattern of normal science, their counterparts in the United States began to thicken to network levels. In large part, this discrepancy was the result of the differential degree of institutionalization of the theory in the two countries. By the early 1970s, construct theory had established a place for itself in the literature, curriculum, and political structure of British psychology, and could afford to relinquish some of the powerful apprentice, colleague, and coauthor ties that had made it such a tightly knit scientific community during the cluster phase. In the United States, on the other hand, institutionalization proceded more slowly, necessitating the close student–teacher and colleague–colleague basis of the group.

As Figure 1 indicates, the total intellectual output of the group continued to grow early in the specialty stage. But the character of this work differed in important respects from the ground-breaking successes of the cluster stage. Proportionately more secondary materials (edited volumes, review articles, and textbooks) appeared in order to preserve the distinctiveness of construct theory, and at the same time to grant outsiders some familiarity with its content. Despite these efforts, the intellectual production of the group continued to diversify, because it had become too large to be held to a dogmatic line by "the immediate mechanisms of conversations and lectures" (Mullins, 1973). This movement toward differentiation of interests was given further impetus by researchers outside the United States and the United Kingdom, who began to enter the theory group in significant numbers as the group moved into specialty status in the early 1970s.

Problems and Prospects

The completion of this sociohistorical study affords me an opportunity to reflect upon some of the unique issues that confront personal construct theory (PCT) at this point in its development as a discipline. Like developmental crises in the lives of individuals, these issues represent important problems, the adequate resolution of which ultimately can strengthen the prospects for the theory group's healthy maturation. Because of their imminence, I choose to focus upon four such problems: the intellectual isolationism of the theory, its "crisis of methodology," its relation to the new "cognitive" therapies, and the formation of an international organization for construct theorists. In taking up each of these topics, I refer to the opinions of major figures within the theory. Unless otherwise noted, such citations are based upon their personal communications to me in the context of tape recorded, structured interviews conducted from the summer of 1979 through the fall of 1980.[1]

[1] I would like to express my appreciation to the following persons, who granted me interviews or responded in writing to the interview questions. *From the United States:* J. Bieri, W. Crockett, R. Cromwell, F. Epting, A. W. Landfield, L. Leitner, J. Mancuso, G. Neimeyer, and S. Rosenberg. *From Great Britain:* D. Bannister, S. Duck, F. Fransella, R. Holland, J. M. M. Mair, A. Radley, A. Ravenette, D. Rowe, A. Ryle, P. Salmon, P. Slater, and P. Stringer. *From the Netherlands:* H. Bonarius, P. Dingemans, and P. Rathod. *From Canada:* J. R. Adams-Webber. *From Hong Kong:* M. McCoy.

THE INTELLECTUAL ISOLATIONISM OF PERSONAL CONSTRUCT
THEORY

By the term *intellectual isolationism* I mean to refer to the tendency of theory group members to disaffiliate themselves from other traditions of thought, and instead perpetuate a relatively "ingrown" pattern of communication with one another. This tendency has its origins in Kelly's dismissal of the formulations of his predecessors as if they were wholly irrelevant to his own theory-building efforts. In the eyes of his most sympathetic critics, this isolationism is noted simply as a curiosity. Reviewing Kelly's 1955 work, Bruner (1956, p. 356) remarks, "With respect to ancestry, Professor Kelly seems to care little for it. One misses references to such works as Piaget's *The Child's Construction of Reality,* the early work of Werner and the writings of Harry Stack Sullivan, Lewin, and Allport—all of whom are on his side and are good allies to boot." For reviewers working in those traditions (e.g., the psychoanalytic) from which Kelly borrows, but at the same time condemns, Kelly's failure to reference others becomes a reason to minimize the import of his work. McArthur (1956, p. 307), also reviewing *The Psychology of Personal Constructs,* states that "the reader is left with a feeling of irritation at finding billed as new discoveries things he can find almost word for word in the earlier works of Freud or in the later works of those who concerned themselves with the psychodynamics of normal personality." At his worst moments, Kelly not only ignores but caricatures the image of persons offered by competing theorists (cf. Holland, 1970) in such a way that the genuine humanism and reasonableness of his own position stand out in even sharper contrast. Such tactics lead his most caustic critics to infer that

> [Kelly] is exercised over a problem of his own making, for his broadsides are against a piece of psychoanalytic theory that was discarded in the 1920's. . . . It is incumbent upon a serious contributor to personality theory to know the dominant theory, especially if he criticizes it and erects his ostensibly new one on the basis of this criticism. Kelly writes as if he knows psychoanalysis, but he does not.
>
> (Appelbaum, 1969, p. 21)

Appelbaum then goes on to conclude—unfairly, I think—that whatever popularity Kelly enjoyed could be attributed to clinical psychology's need for a "savior" during its early years of development.

> We are regularly offered a self-advertised advant-garde which all too often is merely reactionary and uninformed. Kelly apparantly believed that he had to make up his own system, to start anew, to gather around him those who had the same complaints he had. He was a prophet with honor but little prophesy, a spokesman more than a speaker, his eminence an accident of time.
>
> (Applebaum, 1969, p. 25)

We need not agree with these conclusions in order to recognize the ease with which Kelly's manner of presentation leads members of other theory groups to dismiss the significance of his theory. Indeed, major figures *within* PCT (e.g., Salmon, Stringer) also have been critical of Kelly's failure to acknowledge his historical roots, in part because this leaves the theory more vulnerable to serious philosophical criticism (Adams-Webber).

Later construct theorists have been accused of perpetuating this isolationism, thereby weakening their position by ignoring work conducted by other camps. Thus Pervin (1973, p. 112), in his review of Bannister and Fransella's (1971) *Inquiring Man,* states, "The major limitation of the book is that the constructs used by the authors are at times . . . so tight and preemptive as to preclude incorporation of valuable insights from other theoretical points of view." Ryle, from his position on the periphery of the theory group, puts it more bluntly:

> [PCT's] main weakness is in its isolation, its self-isolation. Kelly's rather cavalier dismissal of everybody else, particularly psychoanalysis and behaviorism, seems to have been taken on board by most personal construct theorists, and a serious attempt to relate the theory to other attempts at dealing with human behavior has not taken place.

What these observers consistently (and rightly) point out is the extent to which PCT's insularity renders it less adequate as a comprehensive theory than it could be, were it to take into account work arising from other tradtitions. What is missed in such accounts, however, is an appreciation of the important so-ciological function served by such isolationism, both at the theory's inception and in its later development. Holland (1977) touches upon the former when he explains,

> The emergence of new personality theories is accompanied by ambivalence towards predecessors as the new theorists filter out what they need from the past and construct around it a new position. . . . For a new discipline to emerge it is necessary for strong expectation to be created that particular methods pursued in a certain theoretical direction will lead to new knowledge. (pp. 131–132)
>   In the continuous process of competition between intellectual formulations attached to various groups. . . . groups sharing the same sphere of potential influence . . . will be at great pains to claim distinctiveness for themselves. (pp. 163–164)

As Holland demonstrates, the textbook description of scientific progress as a dispassionate and objective process of theorizing and experimentation fails to take into account the complex social processes actually involved in knowledge production. One such social factor is the need of the theorist to attract adherents with sufficient commitment to the new perspective to perform the laborious tasks of applying it, testing its implications, and so on. Thus, although Kelly's failure to credit his intellectual predecessors may have resulted partly from his limited exposure to their work,[2] it also served to emphasize the distinctiveness, and therefore the attractiveness, of his own formulations.

---

[2]This benign interpretation is supported by Kelly's own "bootstrap" educational history (Thompson, 1968), during which he earned a patchwork of degrees in physics, mathematics, and education before studying psychology—for a single year—and completing his PhD at the State University of Iowa in 1931.

Nor is it surprising, from a sociology of science perspective, that later construct theorists have helped perpetuate this isolationism. British observers have noted that Bannister's publically advertised disdain for "orthodox" British psychology helped attract to PCT the students needed to pursue the group's research program. But a tendency toward intellectual insularity is by no means a unique feature of PCT: it is a quite regular occurrence in the course of disciplinary development. Lemaine, MacLeod, Mulkay, and Weingart (1976, p. 6) observe that as a field grows, "the proportion of references to papers by authors not centrally engaged in the field declines markedly." Similarly, Mullins (1973) takes this inattention to work conducted outside the theory group to be a defining characteristic of cluster level activity. As such, it serves a purpose, facilitating more cohesive communication ties and focusing the developing group's efforts on a manageable set of theoretical problems.

Yet, a recognition of the adaptiveness of isolationism at early stages of the group's development does not imply that the theory should not attempt to transcend such ingrown communication patterns as it matures to specialty status. What is understandable (perhaps even necessary) for first generation network members can be a serious failing among second or third generation specialists. The challenge facing PCT at the present historical moment is no longer that which confronted the theory group in 1955 or even in 1970. Rather, the present challenge is that of revitalization through integration with other disciplines.

Fortunately, many present day construct theorists recognize this requirement. One promising frontier for such integrative efforts (cited by Ryle and Adams-Webber among others) is the modern cognitive work being done by experimental psychologists. Crockett articulates the need for construct theorists to explore this domain:

> People in construct theory feed on each other's work, and have not been influenced to the extent I think they should have by advances in cognitive psychology in particular. That, it seems to me, is changing, as people like Rosenberg move into the PCT framework, and as people who have been in PCT since it began, for example Mancuso, begin to adopt some of the tenets of current cognitive psychology.[3]

Construct theory could be enriched by taking into account work in other fields as well, particularly developmental psychology (Salmon, Mancuso), linguistics (Adams-Webber) social psychology (Duck), and even physiological psychology (Fransella). Moreover, the possibility of theoretical and metatheoretical cross-fertilization exists with such diverse fields as the new philosophy of science

---

[3]Mancuso and Adams-Webber's edited volume *The Construing Person* (1982) represents a major attempt to bring the methods and findings of modern cognitive psychology to bear on the basic framework of construct theory. See particularly the chapters by Mancuso and Adams-Webber (on memory and attentional processes), Gara (on the study of prototypes), Crockett (on schemata), Adams-Webber (on information theory and linguistic marking), and Mancuso and Eimer (on features analysis). In a similar vein, I have found that studies of "the self as a cognitive prototype" are immensely suggestive for a personal construct conceptualization of depression and suicide (Neimeyer, 1984, 1985b).

(Mair), sociology and (even) psychoanalysis (Holland). Holland summarizes PCT's current shift from a more isolationist to a more integrationist stance:

> I think there is new evidence, very fresh evidence at this point, that the theory is becoming so well established that it can begin to notice some of its limitations and some of the wider contexts that have to be linked into if the theory is to have a wider influence than just in psychotherapy or the very personal one-to-one situation.

THE "CRISIS OF METHODOLOGY"

It is generally true of scientific activity that research areas tend to develop in response to major innovations, particularly technical innovations (Lemaine *et al.*, 1976). Yet, as Holland (1977, p. 132) points out, "There may be limitations on discovery imposed by the particular repertoire of techniques available to the investigator." For this reason, critical attention should be aroused in cases when a specialty comes to rely heavily upon a single method or closely related set of methods, because such reliance tends to restrict both the type of questions the specialty addresses and the range of knowledge it ultimately produces.

From 1954 to 1981, members of the theory group associated with personal construct psychology have published 964 books, book chapters, and journal articles, 707 of which are empirical (data-based) research reports. Of these, 677—or *over 96%*—have employed some variant of repertory grid technique as their primary (or more often their only) means of operationalizing the variables being studied.[4] This degree of methodological constriction is remarkable, and may be paralleled in the history of psychology only by Skinnerian behaviorism's reliance on the operant conditioning chamber and psychoanalysis' confidence in the psychoanalytic method as research paradigms that pre-empt all others. Given construct theory's singular devotion to grid technique, it is hardly surprising that the "major forcus of research within the framework of PCT has been the formal analysis of conceptual structures and their evolution" (Adams-Webber, 1979, p. 42). (In practice, virtually all grid work focuses upon "the formal analysis of conceptual structures." Serious studies of their "evolution" are relatively rare.) For a theory that claims to be a "total psychology" (Fransella, 1978), this constriction in subject matter is appreciable.

Because of the several problems with grid technique—the restriction it places on research style and direction being only one—I believe that PCT presently is confronted with a *crisis of methodology*. Moreover, I believe it is one which is recognized (at some level of awareness) by many theory group members, though they differ, depending on their philosophical and empirical predilections, on the avenues they see leading toward its adequate resolution. I later sketch the situa-

---

[4]For detailed discussion of repertory grid technique and illustrative applications, see Bannister and Mair (1968), Fransella and Bannister (1977), and G. J. Neimeyer and R. A. Neimeyer (1981).

tion as it is seen by the two major camps, and then venture a prediction concerning the likely outcome of the present situation.

Before doing so, however, I should at least mention my own basic enthusiasm for grid technique. It seems to me to be a method that deserves a place in the armamentarium of personal construct theorists, and perhaps of psychologists more generally. Elsewhere (G. J. Neimeyer and R. A. Neimeyer, 1981) I have summarized what I believe to be the major strengths of the method, though not all of them are used to full advantage in the existing literature. These include (1) its applicability to longitudinal and developmental research, (2) its ability to tap multiple levels of construing, both verbal and nonverbal (cf. R. A. Neimeyer, 1981), (3) its usefulness in studying relationships between constructs (and between constructs and elements), (4) its considerable flexibility, (5) its elucidation of idiographic data in easily quantifiable form, and (6) its capacity to be adapted to the study of interpersonal, as well as individual topics.[5] A final advantage of grid technique, its articulation with PCT itself, is considered further below.

But grids also have their problems, which can be classed roughly into two sets, the psychometric and the theoretical. Although the persons voicing these sets of criticisms do not cleanly divide into mutually exclusive categories, they do tend to fall into two identifiable clusters, the "grid methodologists" and the "PCT purists." Each cluster tends to perceive and emphasize a different set of concerns.

From the vantage point of the grid methodologists, the most significant problems with the technique concern its lack of psychometric soundness. Bavelas, Chan, and Guthrie (1976) exemplify this position. These authors conducted an extensive investigation of various "traits" (e.g., cognitive complexity, identification) derived from repertory grid matrices, both those generated by actual human subjects and those simulated by computer programs designed to produce matrices varying in their degree of randomness. They concluded that little evidence existed for the reliability and (convergent) validity of any of the trait measures. These concerns are echoed by some who are closer to the PCT purist camp. Adams-Webber (1979, p. 213), for example, concludes his review of the empirical literature by noting that "considerable confusion has arisen because of a general disregard for basic issues of reliability and validity in developing operational definitions for specific constructs, such as differentiation, within PCT." A related issue has to do with the external validity of grids, that is, the degree to which they are predictive of other behavior. As Adams-Webber (1979) points out, the evidence linking grid scores to specific observable behavior is quite sparse.

---

[5]For an excellent illustration of the use of grids to study dyadic processes—an underdeveloped but exciting research front—see Chapter 8 on marital satisfaction by Neimeyer and Hudson (this volume).

A number of other problems are posited at the psychometric level, for example, the potential restriction of the subjects' response entailed by grids requiring dichotomous classification or rank ordering of elements (Collett, 1979). A more general experimental criticism concerns the common failure to assess the "reactivity" involved in grid studies. Thus, Collett (1979, p. 248) remarks that

> The investigator may choose whether to accept the completed matrix as a summary of the subjects' actual opinions or as some convenient expression of what the subject assumes to be required in that situation. The delicate task of deciding between these conceptions is seldom aired by those who work with the grid. . . . There is absolutely no justification for assuming that the grid method is somehow immune to these reactive processes.

Ravenette (1977) concedes this point when he suggests that the constructs a subject records on the grid are not *elicited* from some pre-existing repertoire, but are *created* in response to experimental demands.

The solution to these problems, from the grid methodologist perspective, is most likely to come from increased attention to the principles of sound experimental design (Bonarius) and further refinement in grid technique itself (Collett, 1979). Rathod is one of the most visible representatives of this point of view. In a report (Rathod, 1980, p. 333), for example, he argues that "an idiographic instrument is reliable to the extent that the interpretations based on it remain invariant over differences in sampling information." He then examines the reliability of principal components solutions of grids of various sizes, concluding that they are "considerably invariant over the sampling of additional grid data." Elsewhere, Rathod (1981) critically evaluates several methods for analyzing grids that vary in their level of mathematical and technical sophistication, and makes the case that construct theorists could upgrade their methodology by incorporating the insights of statisticians and numerical taxonomists who work with similar data matrices.

From the vantage point of PCT purists, the problems with grid work are more basic than can be solved by further methodological refinements, or even by the development of more rigorous experimental designs which control for reactivity, demonstrate the relation of test scores to behavior, and so forth. As it is usually articulated, the basic problem is that psychologists have become so fascinated with grid-induced riddles—"griddles," to use Little's (1979) apt phrase—that they fail to ground their increasingly esoteric methods in a suitable comprehensive theory, preferably PCT. Thus Adams-Webber (1979, p. 20) traces the confusion that surrounds many grid measures to the fact that "investigators and clinicians have employed forms of grid test in research and assessment which have no logical relation to the principles of PCT." Similarly, Landfield (1980, p. 67) cautions that "it should be kept in mind that the use of a construct technique does not necessarily mean that it is being used in the best spirit of the theory." In opposition to figures like Collett (1979), Slater, Ryle, and Rathod (1980, 1981), who hold that grids can be used meaningfully independently of PCT, purists contend that such use not only vitiates grid technique itself but detracts from the theory-building efforts that are, or should be, the construct theorist's major task (Duck, Landfield, Bannister, Fransella). It follows from this that methodological ambiguities can only be resolved by tethering technique more closely to theory.

A second, and perhaps even deeper-going criticism to be voiced from this general point of view corresponds to the sociological observation with which this section opened: that the characteristics embodied in a theory group's technical resources subtly shape the sort of questions it asks. The elemental, verbalized antonyms invoked by the subject to compare and contrast elements on a standard repertory grid undoubtedly conduce to an interpretation of construing as a highly cognitive affair. Thus, Mair (1977, p. 141) rhetorically asks, "How much of PCT research has focussed explicitly on constructs as conceptual templets rather than as guides to action?" Bannister gets to the heart of the problem:

> One of the things that jammed the theory down a bit was that, despite all the developments in the grid—which are in some ways admittedly impressive—we've still been using, as it were, rather static, cross-section methods. We've found ways of cutting in, putting the slide under the microscope. . . . But we haven't found ways of following process, seeing flow, and making sense out of it, which is very dangerous when you're dealing with something that is essentially *about* flow, essentially about people living over time.

The most fundamental criticism from the purist perspective, then, is that grids reify precisely those aspects of PCT that are least adequate. By their very nature, they tend to obscure a conceptualization of construing as an essentially *temporal* rather than *spatial* affair (cf. Radley, 1977). But responsibility for this emphasis does not reside solely with technique; some responsibility must be shared by the theory which engendered it. As Mair observes:

> The presentation of PCT, I think, leads into ways of thinking that are very tight, rather than looser. "Structured," "bounded," I mean the whole adjective issue. . . . Adjectives have become almost gold as far as construct theory is concerned. But *verbs* don't get much of a look (laughs)! I mean it's a theory which, I think, is a theory of action, or process and the rest, and which doesn't get many verbs. . . . And why is that? It's because somehow in writing the theory—the particular example of the grid can be used—some kind of "cloppity-clop" notion, a cybernetic, information, trait-related notion, is still very much around. . . . A lot of people say this is a radical alternative psychology and so on. Mostly, I don't think it is that at all. I feel there are fingers stretched out, in Kelly, towards what *is* a radically different psychology, if you are to come to terms with a much elaborated and deeper sense of "knowing."

From this second, metatheoretical variant of the purist position, the crisis of methodology is resolvable neither by greater technical and experimental sophistication (the grid methodologists' solution) nor by simply tying method more firmly to theory (as advocated by most PCT purists). Neither solution is adequate, because *both* method and theory embody the same flaws. Kelly can be credited with having glimpsed the outlines of what psychology might one day become, and at his best moments even anticipated some of its contours (as in his treatment of loosening, threat, anxiety, etc,). But his writings, particularly his earlier ones, only begin to articulate the directions in which such an inquiry might lead. As such, they cannot be considered the criterion against which grid technique (or any other method) can be measured. In this light, the only adequate resolution of the present crisis will evolve slowly, from basic theoretical, meta-theoretical, and philosophical refinements. Ironically, it may hinge on the ultimate obsolescence of PCT as it now exists.

At the outset of this section, I promised to venture a prediction as to the outcome of the methodological crisis that now confronts the theory group. Unfortunately, I am not optimistic about the prospects for a healthy resolution. I believe the rift between the methodologists and the purists to be too deep and wide to be bridged, even at present, and indications are that it will continue to grow as the former become more mathematically sophisticated and the latter turn increasingly to (new) theoretical pursuits. Such diversification of group members typically accelerates when a group reaches specialty status. But in the case of PCT, the prospects of achieving a resolution that most group members could endorse is made still less likely by (1) the unevenness of social-structural progress displayed by PCT communities in various countries and (2) the (relatively) elite status accorded grid methodologists, at least in the United Kingdom. The first factor will serve to frustrate a widely agreed upon solution because the relative fragmentation of the theory group outside Great Britain will slow the dissemination of whatever methodological skills might eventually supplant or extend existing techniques. Even the widespread availability of intellectual materials concerning the new methods cannot be expected to counteract this effect, because the mastery of new technical resources seems to be transmitted mainly through direct apprenticeship. This is supported by the fact that existing state-of-the-art grid analysis methods, as represented by Slater's (1965; 1976) programs, have found only very limited use outside the United Kingdom and then principally by persons who have studied directly with him.

The second factor, that elite status tends to attach to sophistication in grid technique, further hampers movement toward crisis resolution. This is so because it is clear that a great many significant contributors are sympathetic to purist criticisms of the method, and hence are unlikely to rally around any solution that consists simply of a psychometric refinement of existing techniques. At the same time, the fact that grid users can claim at least a modicum of respectability within the (quantitatively oriented) parent discipline means that powerful social and professional inducements would have to be sacrificed in order for such techniques to be abandoned. Short of a complete "paradigm shift" in psychology as a whole, this seems unlikely to happen.

For these and other reasons, I believe a "methodological revolution" that would reunite PCT as a theory group to be a remote possibility. It seems far more probable that intragroup divisiveness will become increasingly apparent in the future, until the theory group as a specialty becomes so differentiated that it loses its distinctiveness, and gradually blends into the "normal science" scene once again. If this is the case, then methodological advances will be of local, rather than specialty-wide, interest. Of course, this does not mean that their intellectual significance is reduced. In fact, some such advances presently are taking place, and are beginning to attract the attention they deserve (e.g., Thomas' and Space's development of interactive computer administration of grids, Duck's and Viney's exploration of nongrid methods). The number of such innovations has grown, rather than declined, in recent years.

Finally, I close with one more remark about the future, putting forward a hope, rather than a prediction. If grid technique ultimately proves to be interesting, but too restrictive (and I believe it will), and if there are at least some seeds in Kelly's writing that deserve to be cultivated (and I believe there are), then I hope that a few construct theorists will begin to explore seriously the radically different methodologies that may enable them to do so. This exploration may well lead beyond the frontiers of psychology altogether, into fields as diverse as linguistics, ethnomethodology, symbolic interactionism, and cognitive anthropology. The obstacles to crossing such disciplinary boundaries are very great (Holland, 1977), but the dangers of methodological provincialism are far greater.[6]

RELATION TO THE COGNITIVE THERAPIES

Perhaps one of the most sweeping and widely publicized developments in the field of clinical psychology to take place since the mid-1970s has been the emergence of the various "cognitive therapies" (Kendall and Hollon, 1979). Historically, these therapeutic approaches represent a convergence of two major streams of influence, cognitive psychology and behavior modification. Starting in the late 1960s, behaviorists like Cautela (1967) and Ullman (1970) began

---

[6]My recommendation that construct theorists end their faithful marriage to the grid and become more methodologically promiscuous is in line with Feyerabend's (1978) argument that science is an essentially *anarchistic* enterprise. In essence, he argues that methodological prescriptions stultify, rather than advance, scientific progress, and that the only principle that does not inhibit such progress is: *anything goes.*

applying the principles of functional analysis to the study and modification of cognitive processes, construed as "covert behaviors." At about the same time, therapists like Ellis (1969) and Beck (1970) began to explore the relation between their avowedly rational or cognitive approaches and traditional behavior therapy. As Mahoney and Arnkoff (1978, p. 689) note, the general response to this merger "has been one of enthusiasm and fervid research," yielding works of major importance by Beck, Rush, Shaw and Emery (1979), Goldfried and Merbaum (1973), Bandura (1977), Mahoney (1974), Meichenbaum (1974), and many others.

When leading representatives of this cognitive behavioral movement reflect upon their intellectual heritage, they frequently credit Kelly's personal construct theory as having contributed importantly to their own work. Beck (1983), for example, credits his reading of Kelly in 1956 with reorienting him from an analytic perspective on the nature of psychopathology and psychotherapy to a cognitive perspective, one that has proven especially fruitful in the treatment of depression. Mahoney and Arnkoff (1978), more generally, regard Kelly as an "early cognitive-learning cultivator" who may have been one of "the founding fathers of our current trend" (p. 691). The fact that several cognitive–behavioral editors (e.g., Kendall, 1985; Mahoney, 1980; Merluzzi, Glass & Genest, 1981) have solicited book chapters from construct theorists further testifies to the congruence that cognitively oriented theorists see between their work and that being conducted within the framework of PCT.

My aim in this section is to address the relation that exists between construct theory and the cognitive therapies. In keeping with the social emphasis of this work, I concentrate on describing the reactions of members of the PCT theory group to these approaches, because this will suggest the extent to which an active collaboration between the two groups is possible.

A few theory group members perceive a basic compatibility between Kellian theorizing and cognitive therapeutic formulations. G. Neimeyer takes this position, and sees it deriving from their common intellectual ancestry:

> When I think of cognitive therapies, I think of Ellis' Rational Emotive Therapy, maybe some of Meichenbaum's work, Goldfried's rational restructuring, and Beck's work on depression. . . . And I think that they have a great deal in common with Kelly's construct theory. Most importantly, I think they probably draw from similar sorts of original sources (e.g., Korzybski's general semantics) and I think that these common sources of origin have not been sufficiently credited either by the cognitive approaches or by Kelly himself.

Bieri is in basic agreement with this point of view, observing that "there's no question that a lot of recent cognitive approaches in personality and psychotherapy . . . reflect some of the same concerns that [Kelly] had earlier elaborated''.

But this clearly is a minority position. G. Neimeyer is one of the few theory group members who sees "a possibility for an exciting interface" between PCT and cognitive therapy, and even he cautions that Kelly's fundamental conception of construing as a more than just a cognitive activity may become adulterated in the process.

A number of other figures (e.g., Landfield, McCoy) acknowledge a limited degree of correspondence between the two approaches, but believe that the later cognitive work has little to contribute to the more theoretically sophisticated PCT perspective. Cromwell articulates this sentiment:

> Obviously there are some commonalities here, but I believe anyone who has been thoroughly trained in a Kelly personal construct point of view winds up being a little bit disappointed in the approach of a lot of the cognitive therapies and cognitive personality theorists. . . . In dealing with the notions of affect, emotions, and feelings, it appears to me even now that Kelly was decades ahead of his time and the current cognitive theorists have not really caught up.

From this vantage point, personal construct theory is unlikely to be extended in any important way through its affiliation with cognitive therapy, although it may profit by gaining a wider audience (Dingemans, Landfield, Crockett). The clearly pragmatic basis for such an affiliation is suggested in a statement by Epting:

> My own interests lie in the direction of elaborating PCT in the direction of phenomenological and existential positions within psychology, just because I believe they're bigger ideas than the ones being pursued in cognitive psychology. Although the way to reach the rest of psychology is certainly through identifying with cognitive psychology, so that I can't argue with anybody who wants to take construct theory in that direction. But in truth, I don't really think that it has much to do with it, although Kelly wrote it initially so badly in some respects that it sounded like a cognitive theory. I think that was a mistake on Kelly's part, one that he later admitted, but one that he didn't have time to correct before his death.

Most PCT purists see Kelly's (sometimes inadequate) attempts to transcend the cognition–emotion–behavior trichotomy as the very essence of his theory, and hence experience some discomfort at being identified with an explicitly cognitive movement. Holland summarizes the current situation: "Cognitive psychologists are finding links [to PCT] to the embarrassment of personal construct theorists".

Although the above theory group members generally are willing to acknowledge *some* commonality between PCT and cognitive approaches (if only to "piggyback" their work to larger audiences), others are unable to concede even this degree of similarity between the two. Thus, Stringer states flatly that he sees "no relation here," and Mair adds, "I'm not aware of much in terms of cognitive behavior therapy and so on that says anything to me at all". The rejection of these new therapies by many in the PCT community is prompted not so much by technical differences between the two groups (e.g., in their psychotherapeutic procedures) but by their basic theoretical and metatheoretical incompatibilities. Salmon, for example, takes issue with the cognitivists' philosophical realism:

> I think behaviorism *a priori* defines reality independent of the perspective of the individual. And since cognition ought at least to be in some sense phenomenological, I see [cognitive behaviorism] as a doomed approach. If Kelly's approach is brought into this mishmash I should see no hope for any of it.

Leitner voices similar misgivings:

> I see very serious dangers in identifying ourselves too closely with these very recent cognitive approaches to personality and psychotherapy. . . . These "cognitive" positions are essentially behavioristic positions in sheep's clothing. I personally find many of these positions being in a sense very antithetical to construct theory when you look at the image of man implicit in them.

Fransella extends this criticism, and contends that the cognitive therapies incorporate Kellian insights, albeit in diluted form:

> They're subsumed by construct theory, aren't they? I mean, they're poor man's construct theories, basically. Aren't they? What do they do, except look at people in terms of how they construe things? . . . But they're behavior therapies, cognitive behavior therapies. Nowhere in those cognitive behavior therapist's "learning theory" is there anything that accounts for what they're doing. So they're cheating. . . . At a recent "Models of Man" conference, the Skinnerians there refused to say ultimately what their model of man was. They couldn't, because they couldn't keep doing what they're doing if they had to say, "Well, it's man-the-automaton." Because they know they're not automata. And until they come to grips with what they're talking about, I don't think they're going to get anywhere. I mean, if they want to cheat, fine, but I don't want anything to do with them.

Mancuso puts the rejection of the cognitive movement in its strongest form:

> These people who call themselves cognitive psychotherapists are full of hogwash. There is nothing cognitive about their work. They're very mechanistic. All they're saying is that if you talk to yourself and give yourself goodies, you're going to become a different person. I don't think they have a handle on it at all.

For the purposes of the present work it is unnecessary to assess the validity of any of these claims or counterclaims.[7] What is important is to realize that most leaders within PCT are at best lukewarm concerning the prospects for meaningful

---

[7]Of course, assessing the compatibility of cognitive therapeutic and personal construct approaches is *quite* important in its own right. In other writings (Neimeyer, 1984, 1985b; G. J. Neimeyer and R. A. Neimeyer, 1981) I have argued that although construct theory *does* differ in certain theoretical respects from many of the cognitive therapies, it is certainly related closely enough to them to permit cross-fertilization. In fact, the two theory groups already share a common interface, an interest in basic experimental work in cognitive psychology. Compare Merluzzi, Rudy, and Glass (1981), representing cognitive therapy, and Ryle (1978/1982) and Mancuso and Adams-Webber (1982) representing construct theory.

collaboration with cognitive–behavior theorists, and at worst are openly antagonistic to such collaboration. Rejection of the cognitive work, when it occurs, is
based on a critical evaluation, not of its clinical methods, but of its metatheoretical implications.[8] Construct theorists fear that the incorporation of their
formulations into a cognitive–behavioral framework will result in a distortion of
those tenets of PCT that are closest to the heart of Kellian theory: an image of
persons as active, interpretive agents, the impassioned nature of construing, and
so forth. Indeed, it seems *probable* that such unique features of the theory will be
missed by those who approach it from a more behavioral background. Consider
the following remarks by Rimm and Masters (1979, pp. 379–380):

> Kelly's (1955) fixed-role therapy bears a remarkable similarity to Rational Emotive
> Therapy in terms of its philosophical basis as well as its here-and-now action orientation.
> Nonetheless, Kelly's manner of presentation, while logically appealing, is quite esoteric,
> and this may in part account for why his impact on practitioners has not been nearly so
> great as that of Ellis.

These authors seem oblivious to the fundamental philosophical differences between the two therapies (e.g., in their advocacy of "rational" behavior), differences which are apparent even to construct theorists who are quite interested
in an Rational Emotive Therapy (RET) approach (Rowe). Moreover, they imply
that if Kelly's theory were less "esoteric," that is, if it were couched in more
common language, it would have greater impact. It is just this tendency to
"underdimension" PCT (e.g., by interpreting Kelly's "construct" as "cognitive") that leads PCT purists to shy away from close collaboration with the
cognitive–behavioral movement.

But this is not a unique failing of cognitive–behaviorists. It is generally
appreciated by sociologists of science that knowledge decays in the process of
standardization. As Mulkay (1979, pp. 58–59) explains:

> Meaning is lost by translation in science as well as in literature. Points of obscurity and
> conceptual difficulties are overlooked. The limitations of underlying assumptions are
> forgotten. And the balance and emphasis of the original formulation are altered to meet

---

[8]We need not accept this debate concerning the metatheoretical incompatibilities of the two
approaches at face value. As Ben-David (1978, p. 211) observes:

> The relationship to other groups working in the same or related areas will often be deter-
> mined by competition for scarce resources and rewards (such as recognition, appointments
> to positions, research grants, or honors). . . . Especially in nonexpanding systems, this
> competition may lead to conflicts, such as attempts by the well-established groups to
> suppress new ones, or attempts by the new groups to overthrow well-established ones.
> Although in the large majority of cases the conflict is over resources and rewards, and not
> about mutually exclusive explanations of the same phenomena, such groups will often try
> to present their views as a contradiction and refutation of those of competing groups and
> thus justify their claims for withholding rewards and resources from the latter.

the needs of new areas of application. In addition, because the knowledge, technical skills and standards of adequacy of the various audiences involved are likely to be quite diverse, the standardized version must be considerably simplified.

Therefore a certain loss of subtlety and meaning must be expected if construct theoretical formulations are to have a broad impact within the parent discipline. As a review of the foregoing remarks by major figures within PCT will disclose, there are broad national as well as individual differences within the theory group as to how much compromise of meaning should be allowed in order to assure the theory a wider audience. Specifically, proportionately more Americans seem willing to tolerate some loss of content, at least intially, in order to publish PCT work in cognitively oriented journals and potentially attract fresh interest in the theory. Major British figures, in contrast, are almost uniform in their rejection of such a position, largely because they fear the metatheoretical compromise that such a rapprochement might entail. In light of the differential degree of social-structural progress made by the theory group in the two nations, this divergence in opinion is not surprising. Construct theorists in the United States are hampered, both by the lower degree of institutionalization of their work and by their more "revolutionary" reputation, from having widespread impact on American psychology as a whole. For them, partial identification with a clearly "elite" group (like the cognitive–behavior therapists) at least assures them that their view will be heard, and perhaps even help shape the future of their parent discipline. Such a prospect is not fantastic, given the right social conditions. As Mullins (1973, p. 129) observes, a "small, coherent group can produce massive changes in the theoretical orientation of a field."

In the United Kingdom, on the other hand, the situation is very different. British theory group members have made considerable progress towards institutionalizing their position (on editorial boards, in the [BPS], etc.), and can claim a measure of elite status for their methodological prowess. Even the more unorthodox theoretical implications of PCT occasionally are aired in the classroom and conference hall. For British construct theorists, then, there is nothing to gain and much precious distinctiveness to lose by affiliating too closely with the cognitive behavioral tradition.

For this reason, the adequate resolution of PCT's problematic relation to the cognitive therapies necessarily will entail different courses of action for construct theorists in different countries. In particular, for Americans to refuse to dialogue with (receptive) cognitive therapists would be to perpetuate their intellectual isolationism which was previously discussed, and preclude their participation in the "cognitive revolution" that is changing the emphasis of mainstream psychology in the United States. Collaboration with the new approaches need not require American construct theorists to capitulate to a mechanistic paradigm, but it may require them patiently to emphasize and re-emphasize the metatheoretical commitments that inform their work. In the United Kingdom, on the other hand, this laborious but potentially fruitful task is less urgent, not only because PCT is more institutionalized in Britain, but because the cognitive therapies are less so. If the theory group is unable to tolerate different strategies for development in different nations, then its impact may be limited to those geographical regions where it is already best established.

FORMATION OF AN INTERNATIONAL ORGANIZATION

From a sociological point of view, resolution of this final problem is perhaps the most critical. It concerns the extent to which PCT, as a theory group, should seek to institutionalize its activity through the formation of its own professional organization. Of course, steps toward institutionalization already have been taken, especially in the United Kingdom, where PCT to some extent has penetrated existing societies and journals. But the present issue raises difficult, divisive questions not entailed in earlier British efforts, in large part because it lifts to a conscious level social organizational processes that ordinarily take place outside focal awareness. Thus, the decision to organize in a more formal way puts the question in crystalline form: should the theory group consciously seek to promote its own development?

The fact that these organizational issues did not emerge for PCT until it had passed from cluster to specialty status in the mid-1970s provides a kind of support for Mullins' (1973) model, because it would predict that heightened concerns about institutionalizing the theory group's work would coincide with the advent of looser social-structural ties among its members. The specific instigating context for this discussion was the Nebraska Symposium of 1975, later dubbed The First International Congress in Personal Construct Psychology. The apparent success of the congress prompted several practical questions: Would there be a second congress? When? Who would organize it? Where would it be held? Would it follow or diverge from the style set by the Nebraska example? Fransella, after some discussion with other prominent members of the PCT community (e.g., Bannister, Mair), announced that a second congress would be held 2 years hence in England. This announcement was received with general enthusiasm by construct theorists in England and abroad.

With the success of the Second Congress in 1977, it became clear that further conferences would be held at regular intervals, and that some mechanism for deciding where such "officially sanctioned" meetings would convene would be required. Again, an informal get-together of natural leaders (the group grew somewhat to include figures like Salmon, Epting, Bonarius, and Landfield) decided the issue, and the same mechanism served to establish the location of future congresses through 1983.

There has been little visible opposition to this informal decision-making arrangement. Nevertheless, the evident need of the theory group to decide the course of its own social–professional development and to settle competing interests (as in the case of two or more persons who want to sponsor the next congress) suggests the importance of asking the questions, ''What level of social-organizational development is appropriate for the theory group at this point in its sociohistorical development? Is it time to consider formalizing an organization of personal construct psychologists?''

I put this latter question to over two dozen major contributors in PCT in the course of personal or taped interviews with them and discovered that the theory group was sharply divided on the advisability of such a move. Those opposing formal organization (Mancuso, Ravenette, Ryle, Duck, Salmon, Rosenberg, Mair, Radley, Adams-Webber and Dingemans) frequently acknowledge that organizing could facilitate communication among group members, but fear that this communication would be too ingrown, ultimately reinforcing PCT's tendency toward insularity from the parent discipline. Duck emphasizes a related problem:

> As soon as you set up a separate organization, you're asserting a separate identity and so on and not being incorporated in things that people are doing. And it seems to me that one of the main problems with being a PCT person at this moment is that outsiders regard us as a separate group of people who are not to be dealt with necessarily.

Several of the remarks by this group also reflect a general suspicion regarding the effects of institutionalization itself. Adams-Webber, for example, contends that ''organizations may promote the status of a theory's adherents, but they do not foster the intellectual integrity of the people involved''. Furthermore, he stresses that ''theories should be evaluated on the basis of their logical validity and their usefulness in organizing empirical facts'', and suspects that formalizing social support for a position may detract from that process. Ravenette's remark exemplifies this more general concern:

> Institutions kill, and if they don't kill they change the emphasis to the preservation of the institution rather than the development of that for which the institution was formed. This is a very general statement, but I believe it to be true.

This sentiment finds its strongest expression in a statement by Mancuso:

> I'm totally opposed to formalizing organizations that are built around trying to pursue a particular line in psychology. . . . I think that if we can't make a dent on the field as a whole we have no business in the field. I enjoy our little get-togethers with people who are like-minded, the kind of thing we've been having in congresses and so on and those are fine. . . . But the minute this organization will become formal, the minute they talk about electing a president, that's when I quit.

A second sizable group (including Bieri, Crockett, Epting, Cromwell, Fransella, Holland, Rowe, G. Neimeyer, Leitner and Rathod) is generally supportive of constituting an organization with somewhat firmer structure and procedures than exist at present. Like those who oppose further institutionalization, this second group also takes into account the pros and cons of doing so, but concludes, on balance, that the former outweigh the latter. Epting is representative of this position:

> I can only see advantages. No, I can see some disadvantages if we were to solidify into a tight little group that would be very defensive and turn people off. . . . [But] an effective institution could develop that could promote the elaboration of construct theory, and I really think we can't avoid formalizing it. . . . If I had to come to a binary choice between whether to formalize it or whether not to, I would go on the side of coming up with some kind of organization.

A number of the theory group members who take this stand point out that it does not represent a sharp departure from tradition, but merely extends social processes that have been operative for some time. G. Neimeyer states:

> The reason that I would stand behind or back formalizing an international organization is that basically I would see that as doing little more than making explicit what's already happening on an implicit level. . . . There's a natural course of formalization going on, and I think that turning our attention to it and making that explicit may enable us to make some decisions consciously that otherwise we might just take for granted or make unconsciously.

He acknowledges one major drawback to this course of action, namely, that further formalization could foster intellectual inbreeding, and then continues:

> A second major disadvantage I would see is making explicit political struggles [within the theory group] that . . . are probably not as prominent under present conditions. . . . Thirdly, at the point that the theory becomes formalized there is going to be more and more of a critical reaction against construct theory.

Of course, this third disadvantage also has its positive aspects, as he points out: "The better target you give for someone to take aim at, the better criticism you're likely to get".

Those who advocate organization often point out that present arrangements, though adequate initially, are rapidly becoming outmoded as the theory group continues to increase in size. Thus Fransella, a member of the "natural leadership" since the beginning, remarked at the 1979 conference, "I feel very strongly that we need to come to some decision at this conference as to what is going to happen with an organization, because our group is just too big to go on with this." Holland adds sociological weight to this conclusion when he notes that

> it is a common problem for networks and social movements, that they reach a crisis point where they are so big that it is difficult to go on in an informal, haphazard, fashion. So I think that [PCT] is now beginning to organize.

If these observations are valid, that PCT has outgrown its existing informal structure or soon will do so, then the only option does not appear to be the overly-bureaucratized, self-perpetuating, intellectually stifling organization dreaded by so many theory group members. As Landfield points out:

> My own view is that what we need to do is to state our purposes. What is it that those of us in personal construct theory want to happen, and then do we feel that some kind of organization . . . with a little bit greater formality . . . will enhance the possibility of our doing whatever it is we want to do? . . . For example we might have a system where people would be nominated from different areas of the world. Perhaps there would be a committee of five people who would decide on their own chairman and then that committee would simply be responsible for finding someone to take over the responsibility of the congress every two years. They might eventually . . . have some jurisdiction over the Clearing House.

The principle being evoked here is one of *minimum sufficient organization* to achieve desired ends, a position advocated by the sociologist Becker at the Congress held in Holland in 1979. Framing the issue in this way permits us to explore the kinds of institutional structure that might support our intentions as a theory group. As Bannister emphasizes, there is ample room to create unconventional organizational alternatives compatible with the pluralistic philosophy of PCT itself.

> So I think we need to start, not with the question, "Can we organize in the traditional sense?" But if you want to get people interested in construct theory, how would we go about it—from a construct theory point of view? I'm not sure what the answer would be, but I'm sure it would be one that other people would see as looser, and more changing.

He goes on to voice his fundamental antagonism to traditional, hierarchical organizations:

> I am prepared to keep contending, that is, actively opposing and fighting against the tendency to simply replace me and my mob, if you like, by somebody else and some other mob. And I don't, in a sense, care whether they're better or worse qualified. The battle becomes about the way we are going to do things, not about who's doing them.

If reactions like Bannister's provide impetus for construct theorists to evolve a kind of organization which is less hierarchical and less restrictive than conventional alternatives, but which is nonetheless *sufficient* to the group's needs, then they will serve a useful end. But if they serve mainly to impede formalization, on the grounds that *any* institutionalization is inherently dehumanizing, then they may do more to stunt the development of PCT than promote it. It is worth realizing, with Mullins (1973), that specialty level development in a field necessarily entails the creation of a more bureaucratized communication structure than was characteristic of the earlier cluster stage, if only because the group has grown too large to conduct its affairs with the face-to-face informality that was possible when it had only a few members.

The Critical Upshot

In the foregoing pages, I presented four problems currently besetting construct theory: its intellectual isolationism, its crisis of methodology, its relation to the cognitive therapies, and its movement toward professional organization. By examining these issues against the backdrop of the theory group's sociohistorical development, I tried to demonstrate that each of these problems has a social dimension. Just as an individual's early spontaneous, egocentric development gradually yields to a more planful self-elaboration encompassing a keener awareness of the social context, so too the maturing theory group eventually may predicate its further development on a reflexive understanding of its sociological status. Perhaps personal construct theory has attained this level of disciplinary maturity.

A field takes on pertinence under a definite complex of social and intellectual conditions. For construct theory, these conditions included behaviorism's hegemony on the psychological scene, a condition that prevailed through the 1960s. In such a context, the rigorous personalism of Kelly's theory and its associated grid technique offered an alternative, both to the arid objectivism of behavioral formulations and to the abstruse subjectivism of "third force" psychologies. Introduced into a theoretical climate inimical to its survival, construct theory's self-reliant isolationism was both defensive and defensible.

But as Kelly (1955) has reminded us, the universe changes along a dimension of time. This is no less true of the universe of intellectual discourse. Certainly psychology as a discipline has changed since the 1950s, and has assimilated, consciously or unconsciously, many construct theoretical concepts in the process. If construct theory is to retain its vitality, it must be willing to move beyond its older Kellian knowledge claims and participate more fully in these broader developments. As I noted in my earlier discussion, there are signs that this reintegration is beginning to occur.

If this revitalization is to be sustained, however, social developments in the theory group must keep pace with the intellectual. This requirement follows from the reflexive nature of social science: we draft our theories in part as theories of our own lives. Thus, by perpetuating the small and intimate communication system characteristic of "the good old days of clusterhood," construct theorists organizationally reinforce the personalistic emphasis of the theory to which they subscribe. Were they seriously to elaborate their social-communicative network along more complex bureaucratic lines, they might more quickly confront the limitations of PCT as a theory of social life.

In the usual case, social science, as a body of knowledge, must adjust itself to fit the social reality it seeks to describe. Occasionally, however, a social scientific theory group must reverse this process, by adjusting its internal social reality (i.e., its communication processes and its organizational framework) to match its own knowledge output. Personal construct theory has not really matched the complexity and diversity of its own published literature, which meshes with numerous specialties in the social sciences, with a comparably complex social communication structure that would link it more firmly with other theory groups. However difficult these social adjustments may be, I believe they can, and must, take place.

References

Adams-Webber, J. R. (1979). "Personal Construct Theory: Concepts and Applications", John Wiley, Chichester, England.

Appelbaum, S. A. (1969). The accidental emminence of George Kelly. *Psychiatry and Social Science Review,* **3,** 20–25.

Bandura, A. (1977). Self-efficacy: Toward a unifying theory of behavioral change. *Psychological Review,* **84,** 191–215.

Bannister, D. and Fransella, F. (1971). "Inquiring Man: The Theory of Personal Constructs," Penguin, Harmondsworth, England.

Bannister, D. and Mair, M. (1968). "The Evaluation of Personal Constructs", Academic Press, London.

Bavelas, J. B., Chan, A. S., and Guthrie, J. A. (1976). Reliability and validity of traits measured by Kelly's repertory grid. *Canadian Journal of Behavioral Science,* **8,** 23–38.

Beck, A. T. (1970). Cognitive therapy: Nature and relation to behavior therapy. *Behavior Therapy,* **1,** 184–200.

Beck, A. T. (1983, March 3). Personal communication.

Beck, A. T., Rush, J., Shaw, B., and Emery, G. (1979). "Cognitive Therapy of Depression", Guilford, New York.

Becker, H. A. (1981). The Four Demons Chasing the Social Scientist. *In* "Personal Construct Psychology: Recent Advances in Theory and Practice" (H. Bonarius, R. Holland, and S. Rosenberg, eds.), Macmillan, London.

Ben-David, J. (1978). Emergence of National Traditions in the Sociology of Science. *In* "Sociology of Science" (J. Gaston, ed.), Jossey-Bass, San Francisso.

Bruner, J. S. (1956). You are your constructs. *Contemporary Psychology,* **1,** 355–357.

Cautela, J. R. (1967). Covert sensitization. *Psychological Reports,* **20,** 459–468.

Collett, P. (1979). The Repertory Grid in Psychological Research. *In* "Emerging Strategies in Social Psychological Research" (G. P. Ginsburg, ed.), Wiley, Chichester, England.

Durkheim, E. (1915). "The Elementary Forms of the Religious Life", Allen and Unwin, London.

Ellis, A. (1969). A cognitive approach to behavior therapy. *International Journal of Psychotherapy,* **8,** 896–900.

Feyerabend, P. (1978). "Against Method", Verso, London.

Fransella, F. (1978). Personal Construct Theory or Psychology? *In* "Personal Construct Psychology 1977" (F. Fransella, ed.), Academic Press, New York.

Fransella, F. and Bannister, D. (1977). "A Manual for Repertory Grid Technique", Academic Press, London.

Goldfried, M. and Merbaum, M. (1973). "Behavior Change Through Self-Control", Holt, Rinehart and Winston, New York.

Holland, R. (1970). George Kelly: Constructive Innocent and Reluctant Existentialist. *In* "Perspectives in Personal Construct Theory" (D. Bannister, ed.), Academic Press, London.

Holland, R. (1977). "Self and Social Context", St. Martins, London.

Holland, R. (1981). From Perspectives to Reflexivity. *In* "Personal Construct Psychology: Recent Advances in Theory and Practice" (H. Bonarius, R. Holland, and S. Rosenberg, eds.), Macmillan, London.

Kelly, G. A. (1955). "The Psychology of Personal Constructs", Vols. I and II, Norton, New York.

Kendall, P. (ed.). (1985). "Advances in Cognitive-Behavioral Research and Therapy", Academic Press, New York.

Kendall, P. C. and Hollon, S. D. (1979). Cognitive-Behavioral Interventions: Overview and Current Status. *In* "Cognitive-behavioral Interventions" (P. C. Kendall and S. D. Hollon, eds.), Academic Press, New York.

Kuhn, T. S. (1970). "The Structure of Scientific Revolutions" (2nd ed.), University of Chicago Press, Chicago.

Landfield, A. W. (1980). Personal Construct Psychology: A Theory to Be Elaborated. *In* "Psychotherapy Process" (M. Mahoney, ed.), Plenum, New York.

Lemaine, G., MacLeod R., Mulkay, M., and Weingart, P. (1976). "Perspectives on the Emergence of Scientific Disciplines" Aldine, Chicago.

Little, B. R. (1968). Review of Patrick Slater's *Explorations of Intrapersonal Space*, Vol. I. *Contemporary Psychology*, **22**, 759–761.

Mahoney, M. (1974). "Cognition and Behavior Modification", Ballinger, Cambridge, Massachusetts.

Mahoney, M. (1980). "Psychotherapy Process", Plenum, New York.

Mahoney, M. and Arnkoff, D. (1978). Cognitive and Self-Control Therapies. *In* "Handbook of Psychotherapy and Behavior Change" (S. Garfield and A. Bergin, eds.), Wiley, New York.

Mair, J. M. M. (1977). Metaphors for Living. *In* "Nebraska Symposium on Motivation" (A. Landfield, ed.), University of Nebraska Press, Lincoln.

Mancuso, J. C. and Adams-Webber, J. R. (1982). "The Construing Person", Plenum, New York.

Mannheim, K. (1952). "Essays on the Sociology of Knowledge", Routledge and Kegan Paul, London.

Marx, K. (1904). "A Contribution to the Critique of Political Economy", C. H. Kerr, Chicago.

McArthur, C. (1956). Review of G. A. Kelly, The Psychology of Personal Constructs. *Journal of Counseling Psychology*, **3**, 306–307.

Meichenbaum, D. (1974). "Cognitive Behavior Modification", General Learning Press, Morristown, New Jersey.

Merluzzi, T., Glass, C., and Genest, M. (eds.). (1981). "Cognitive Assessment", Guilford, New York.

Merluzzi, T., Rudy, T., and Glass, C. (1981). The Information Processing Paradigm:

Implications for Clinical Science. *In* "Cognitive Assessment" (T. Merluzzi, *et al.*, eds.), Guilford, New York.

Merton, R. K. (1945/1973). "The Sociology of Science: Theoretical and Empirical Investigations", University of Chicago Press, Chicago.

Mulkay, M. J. (1979). "Science and the Sociology of Knowledge", George Allen and Urwin, London.

Mullins, N. C. (1973). "Theories and Theory Groups in Contemporary American Sociology", Harper and Row, New York.

Neimeyer, G. J. and Neimeyer, R. A. (1981). Personal Construct Perspectives on Cognitive Assessment. *In* "Cognitive Assessment" (T. Merluzzi, *et al.*, eds.), Guilford, New York.

Neimeyer, R. A. (1981). The Structure and Meaningfulness of Tacit Construing. *In* "Personal Construct Psychology: Recent Advances in Theory and Practice" (H. Bonarius, R. Holland, and S. Rosenberg, eds.), Macmillan, London.

Neimeyer, R. A. (1983). The Development of Personal Construct Theory: Some Sociohistorical Observations. *In* "Applications of Personal Construct Theory" (J. R. Adams-Webber and J. Mancuso, eds.), Academic Press, Toronto.

Neimeyer, R. A. (1984). Toward a Personal Construct Conceptualization of Depression and Suicide. *In* "Personal Meanings of Death: Applications of Personal Construct Theory to Clinical Practice" (F. R. Epting and R. A. Neimeyer, eds.), Hemisphere/McGraw Hill, New York.

Neimeyer, R. A. (1985a). "The Development of Personal Construct Psychology", University of Nebraska Press: Lincoln.

Neimeyer, R. A. (1985b). Personal Constructs in Clinical Practice. *In* "Advances in Cognitive-Behavioral Research and Therapy" (vol. 2) (P. C. Kendall, ed.), Academic Press, New York.

Oliver, D. W. and Landfield, A. W. (1962). Reflexivity: An unfaced issue in psychology. *Journal of Individual Psychology*, **18**, 114–124.

Oliver, D. W. and Landfield, A. W. (1975). The fallacy of reflexivity: A reply. *Journal of Individual Psychology*, **31**, 183–186.

Pervin, L. (1973). On construing our constructs. A review of Bannister and Fransella's Inquiring Man: The theory of personal constructs. *Contemporary Psychology*, **18**, 110–112.

Radley, A. R. (1977). Living on the Horizon. *In* "New Perspectives in Personal Construct Theory" (D. Bannister, ed.), Academic Press, London.

Rathod, P. (1980). The reliability of the principal components of rep grid data. *Nederlands Tijdschrift voor de Psychologie*, **35**, 331–344.

Rathod, P. (1981). Methods for the Analysis of Rep Grid Data. *In* "Personal Construct Psychology: Recent Advances in Theory and Practice" (H. Bonarius, R. Holland, and S. Rosenberg, eds.), Macmillan, London.

Ravenette, A. T. (1977). Personal Construct Theory: An Approach to the Psychological Investigation of Children. *In* "New Perspectives in Personal Construct Theory" (D. Bannister, ed.), Academic Press, London.

Rimm, D. C. and Masters, J. C. (1979). "Behavior Therapy", Academic Press, London.

Ryle, A. (1978/1982). A common language for the psychotherapies? *British Journal of Psychiatry*, **132**, 585–594. *Reprinted in* "Converging Themes in Psychotherapy" (M. R. Goldfried, ed.), Springer, New York.

Slater, P. (1965). "The Principal Components of a Repertory Grid", Vincent Andrews and Co., London.

Slater, P. (ed.). (1976). "Explorations of Intrapersonal Space, Vol. I: The Measurement of Intrapersonal Space by Grid Technique", Wiley, London.

Thompson, G. (1968). George Alexander Kelly (1905–1967). *Journal of General Psychology*, **79**, 19–24.

Ullman, L. P. (1970). On cognitions and behavior therapy. *Behavior Therapy*, **1**, 201–204.

10

Relations with the Physical:
An Alternative Reading of Kelly

Phillida Salmon

In this chapter I consider some of the ways in which we understand the physical modality. Every kind of psychology must somehow acknowledge the fact that human beings are physical beings within a physical world. Because of its positivist character, traditional psychology has very much leant towards the bodily side of the mind–body dichotomy; and this orientation has, I think, taken two main forms. One is the assumption that there is an essential continuity between human and non–human animal species, and that our understanding of ourselves can be advanced by studying monkeys, rats, or pigeons. Since, like other animals, we are biological organisms, this does seem in many ways to make sense. As people, we are subject to the same basic physical laws as other species. We are born, we die, we reproduce ourselves. Like other animals, we need food and sleep; like them, we feel pain, and are subject to physical injury.

Yet somehow, despite these obvious truths, parallels with other species seem to fail in just those spheres of life which, in human terms, are the most significant. Britton once remarked, of Skinner's pigeons, that, while Skinner could succeed in training them to play ping-pong, he would never be able to teach them dissembling strategies, nor how to invent new rules for the game. If we look at human life in large-scale terms, it is difficult to see how it could be understood within the parameters that we apply to non–human animals. The great movements of people, which have altered the course of history and changed human civilization, cannot meaningfully be reduced to simple biological processes. Characteristically, they have involved the realm of the symbolic rather than the directly physical—meanings, images, ideas, convictions. Wars, for instance, which disrupt and shatter human lives, are sometimes explained in terms of parallels with non–human animal behavior. It is said that, like other animals, people fight over scarce physical resources, or to extend their territory. In this view, human wars are simply our version, writ large, of the battles for mastery of the herd fought out by rival stags at rutting time. If we examine this comparison, it cannot really stand, since it ignores certain essential aspects of human social behaviour. In human warfare, the causes with which individuals identify, and for which they willingly kill, suffer, and risk their lives, seldom involve any direct material advantage for them. Rather, wars typically involve something essen-

173

tially intangible and symbolic—a principle of some kind. If "conquest" is the cause, what is at issue is likely to be nominal rather than material. A flag is raised, an administration is taken over; but for the individuals who suffered for this cause, the physical space available has not been enlarged one whit. It is, in fact, hard to make sense of human social life in terms of the biological principle of self-preservation. There are many instances in history and in the contemporary world, of those who have chosen physical suffering and death, for a belief, a principle—religious martyrs, political dissidents, rebel groups, or hunger strikers. It is surely the symbolic self which people strive to preserve; and faith can keep people alive, just as shame and despair can kill them. Human life, at its most human, does seem qualitatively distinct from the lives of other animals.

A different way in which psychology has traditionally encompassed the physical in human life is in emphasising the biological basis of behaviour and experience. There are still many psychologists who believe that ultimately, psychological questions will be explained in terms of biological processes, although such people readily concede that that time is still a long way off. For me, what makes this expectation so alien is that it ignores a crucial qualitative difference between the two spheres of meaning. If I were to ask a friend what she thought of a novel we had both recently read, and she were to reply by describing the network of synaptic connections in an area of her brain, and the pattern of electrical activity within the network, this answer would leave my enquiry totally unsatisfied. Psychological questions seek psychological answers, and biological ones will not do.

More often than this complete reductionism, the biological is seen as partially helpful for understanding human life, in explaining particular aspects rather than its totality. For instance, psychologists often resort to biological explanations when they are considering behaviour which seems to have "gone wrong". What Kelly unkindly labelled "the search for the schizococcus" is one version of this. Perhaps the most serious objection to such an approach is that it confirms, and justifies, the exclusion of certain kinds of "deviant" people from the realm of ordinary human life, since there we do not generally make this recourse to special, biological explanations.

Another form of partial commitment to the biological is to see it as on a continuum with the psychological, as a more primitive, less-developed mode. Life is often viewed as initially biological, only later becoming psychological and social. Babies, in this view, start as physical organisms, and through socialization, gradually achieve a psychological character. To see them in this way is probably to deny the experience of most parents, who seem characteristically to encounter a *person* in their new baby. And increasingly, those who do research with infants have found it necessary to invoke psychological rather than biological processes; as the common currency has it, infants are active partners in the earliest social encounters.

The idea of a biological–psychological continuum can take another form, too. In an account of life such as Maslow's, the biological represents the more basic, the more primitive needs that must be satisfied before the more spiritual, creative, truly psychological needs can be expressed. Maslow himself (Frick, 1982), at the end of his life, reflected ruefully that this perspective seemed out of accord with contemporary American society. The material security and high standing of living which, by satisfying biological needs, should have guaranteed the development of higher motives, did not, in his experience, seem to have achieved this. It is a theme which many writers have dwelt on; for example, Hoggart (1962), who expounds the case that in post-war Britain, working class people "bought" material prosperity at the cost of much rich, shared meaning in their lives.

Our relations with our biology do, in fact, seem to be complicated. Food and sex, for instance, cannot meaningfully be reduced to the straightforward satisfaction of physical need. What we eat, when and in what order, how food is prepared, presented, and combined, our ways of eating, the social character of meals—all these things are governed by essentially symbolic meanings, from religious taboos to aesthetic preferences or the marking of family life. Human sexuality is similarly far from what we witness in other animal species—the simple living out, in appropriate contexts, of fixed mating patterns. Though probably in all societies, sexuality has been experienced as a powerful and significant aspect of life, it is difficult to see human sexual conduct as biologically "driven". It is not just that many people choose fidelity to a particular partner, while others choose celibacy. More fundamentally, we learn to feel sexually towards certain aspects of our experience, to define certain things as sexual; and these things are different in different societies. As Gagnon and Simon (1970) put it, "Sexual behaviour is socially scripted behaviour".

Nor do particular biological events apparently have a given, standard meaning. As the experiments of Schachter (Schachter and Singer, 1962) show, people define the emotional consequences of injected drugs by social clues from others thought to share the same situation. Even in relation to private physical events under our own skin, it seems that we look to others to help us define the experience we are having.

Most strangely of all, it is sometimes possible for human beings to transcend biological limits. In the stigmata of St. Francis, the feats of Indian fakirs, the imperviousness to pain or the production of physical deformations in deep hypnotic trances, people have shown the capacity to achieve what physiologically is "impossible".

Yet, despite the mysteriousness of our relations with our biology, we are as human beings deeply grounded in the physical. Most fundamentally, we are faced with the overwhelming physical facts of birth and death. We live in, and are part of, a natural world of great beauty, power, and strangeness, a world with its own forms and rhythms, a world which human beings did not create. In great works of art, with their enduring capacity to evoke feeling, their physical form is not merely the medium for something else; it is the actual embodiment itself, in sound, colour, form, or movement, which touches us so profoundly. The deepest levels of experience often seem to be carried by the physical mode. As Proust so richly illustrated, past experience, with all its intimate meaning, can suddenly be conjured up by a particular taste, a particular scent.

As human beings, we surely experience each other in the physical dimension. It is as physical presences that we encounter each other. When we lose someone we love, we lose their uniquely dear embodiment—in Tennyson's poignant words,

> But, Oh, for the touch of a vanished hand,
> And the sound of a voice that is still.

The language of the body, its bearing and carriage, are very personal. It seems to be true that, as Virgil believed, "the goddess is revealed by her gait". Experiments have shown that people are able to recognize those they know from photographic images that blur form, but show movement. When we first meet someone, we do not yet understand the particular meaning of his or her physical self, what it conveys. It is only as we come to know him or her that we learn the personal vocabulary of the person's form and bodily expressiveness—the meaning of facial details, gestures, expressions, and tones of voice.

What does psychology have to say about all this? Few theorists, or writers in psychology seem to have reflected on the uniquely human meaning of the physical modality. And it has to be said that this is true of Kelly. Apart from the essay he wrote about suffering a heart attack (Maher, 1979), Kelly himself did not apparently consider physical experiences in his writings. More seriously, it may seem that personal construct theory has no place in it for the physical. The main buzz words of this theory are theory, construe, construct, hypothesis, experiment. Its central image is man-the-scientist. What are the connotations of these words? They conjure up references to what is conscious, analytical, verbal, detached, planned, deliberate. The high level of abstraction at which Kelly's ideas are presented make, too, for a sense of remoteness; it is hard not to feel that the theory lacks earthiness. Certainly the sense that Kelly's approach is essentially cognitive and intellectual—a sense which prevents many people from embracing it personally—seems to bear this out.

The typical forms in which Kelly's theory is cast also tend to confirm such a picture. Grid-derived maps of semantic meaning, however intellectually intriguing, seem altogether distant from the world of feeling, and direct physical experience. Examining a principal components analysis of one's own constructs is far less powerful and personally involving than using the physically grounded methods of group sculpture, psychodrama, or two-chair confrontations.

As Mair (1976) has illuminatingly argued, metaphor is crucial in how we understand our lives. Perhaps what Kelly offered has been mistaken by the crystallization of his approach in the metaphor of man-the-scientist. If we were to adopt a different metaphor for encapsulating what is most significant in this approach, we might find a psychology quite unlike the one which people so often find over-intellectual, sometimes even dry as dust. I should like to suggest the kind of metaphor which that might be.

Basic to personal construct theory is the assumption that one can know others only through knowing one's own experience. The development of personal understanding, within this approach, is often taken very narrowly. Kelly's message is read as meaning triadic elicitation, applying elicited constructs to elements, feeding the grid into a computer, and inspecting the resulting statistical analysis. But, if we are really to enlarge our understanding of what is most deeply significant in our lives, perhaps we need to do something rather different from this—to pay close, careful, delicate attention to our bodily selves.

My own experience of trying to do this has been through the Alexander technique (Barlow, 1973). Working with this technique seems to illuminate many important things about human embodiment. The first of these is the sheer difficulty of certain kinds of contact with one's physical self. The technique demands an attention to each broad area of one's body in turn; but the attention involves no volition, no intention to alter or adjust what one focusses on. To achieve such an awareness and to sustain it without one's attention drifting away is extremely hard to do. This seems to relate to the unfamiliarity, for most of us, of becoming aware of things without some intention of directing them. Yet although the awareness sought is free from volition, it is itself not diffuse or open, since the technique channels one's consciousness into certain images. You are asked to become aware of your head as both forward and upward from your neck—to become aware of this without, however, altering the actual position of your head. You consider your neck as a long pillar extending all the way from the middle of the shoulder blades upwards to your head—again, without actually changing the position of the body parts involved in this image.

This process, in which images are central, is of course literally that of imagination. And in using imagination in this way, one discovers in it a mysterious potency. When I imagine my neck as a long pillar, I find that, without my *doing* anything, muscles in my back and my shoulders shift, relax, alter perceptibly. When I imagine my neck as free to turn my head to one side or the other, miraculously, physical changes take place near the front of my neck and under my chin, quite independently of any intention on my part. These changes involve muscles which I could not move if I were to try to do so deliberately, and sometimes take place in parts of my body in which previously I seemed to have little awareness.

Most immediately, what is at issue in this kind of exploration has to do with bodily positions, often of a quite subtle and intricate kind. One becomes aware, gradually, of particular ways in which one holds one's physical self—and in becoming aware, somehow comes to alter them, at least momentarily. At this level, the stuff of such inquiries is the pressing inward of an upper arm, the clenching of the shoulders, the weighing down on one side of the body, the head rigidly held, or the involvement of "irrelevant" parts of the body in a particular, specific movement. Yet more is involved in this developing awareness than the literally physical. Gradually, one comes to glimpse something of the deep personal meaning of physical posture. One finds, with time, that being aware of a particular angle of the arm involves being dimly aware of a characteristic stance, a posture, towards some aspect of one's life. And it is as if the body, of its own account, continues to think about this, so that in the course of ordinary living, one begins to notice oneself taking up that position as one experiences certain feelings, or undertakes certain kinds of thing.

All this, for me, sits closely with what I find most important in Kelly's approach. In what he looked to psychology to do, Kelly continually emphasised the need to go beyond what is commonplace, to enter the realms of the unknown. It seems to me that the kinds of exploration involved in using the Alexander technique potentially achieve this, and carry possibilities for real enlargement of psychological understanding. Kelly, who himself constantly tried to go beyond common sense, was well aware of how difficult it is to do so—a difficulty that using this technique certainly demonstrates. Core role constructs, as Kelly envisaged them, are both profoundly important in governing how we live, and also very difficult of access. It seems to me that it is in reaching just those spheres of ourselves that the Alexander kind of approach has such potentiality. But its definition of those spheres is quite differently framed from the usual definition of personal construct theory, and, for me, this suggests that we need a very different kind of metaphor for thinking about them.

In Kelly's language—a language characteristically used by those who adopt his approach—the central image is that of construing. Construing is seen as defining what human beings most fundamentally do. To construe means to order, to interpret, to evaluate aspects of one's experience within a universe of meaning. In suggesting an essentially disembodied mind engaging in its ordering activities, this image does not encompass the idea of an embodied self. Perhaps a much more fruitful image is that of people placing *themselves* in relation to aspects of their worlds. If we were to adopt this metaphor, we should see human beings as defining themselves by the ways they place themselves towards their experience. This would view people in terms of how they stand, in relation to their lives, and particular ways of being in the world, as essentially positions, postures, stances.

The essential accord between the Alexander and the Kelly approaches, and their potential mutual enrichment, is very strongly underlined, I think, by their seeing imagination as the route through which we enter the realms of the unknown. Kelly himself was surely very much concerned with the imaginative process. He valued the provisional, the playful, the alternative construction; he saw people's inventiveness and capacity for creation as their most precious, and their most human property. To me, it seems a pity that anticipation, rather than imagination, has generally been seen as *the* Kellian mode. The Alexander technique also gives a central importance to imagining, through which, in fact, the work of exploration proceeds. And, in such work, it becomes clear that imagination has power, leverage, and is not just an accompaniment to, or a preparation for action. Through using the technique, one finds, miraculously, that to imagine a thing is to create it. As Kelly demonstrated, in fixed role therapy, to try out a new view of life is actually to embody it, to live it out. The Alexander approach shows essentially the same thing to be true of bodily exploration: to reconstrue is itself to change, to imagine is to act.

I should like, however sketchily, to suggest what might be the consequences of reading Kelly's ideas in this way, for how we looked at two particular questions that seem socially and psychologically important ones. Following the Nazi persecution of the Jews, some psychologists, often through first hand experience, became much concerned with the phenomenon of racial hatred. In contemporary psychology, though the direction of work is somewhat different, there is growing concern with racism in our own society. Probably the dominant paradigm in such research is one that examines the meanings assigned to in-group and out-group members, particularly in relation to such factors as the person's own social situation, contact with the out-group, or experience of multi-cultural education.

Within this paradigm, personal construct theory has been seen by many as the approach to be adopted par excellence. Its focus on personal meaning—on how individuals define themselves and others—seems absolutely central to the questions involved. Grid methodology also seems a natural, in offering an exploration of the ways in which people define their own and other social groups—the categorizations they use, and the dimensions of meaning involved in these. It seems very promising, for instance, from this viewpoint to address questions about racism, and how to overcome it, by giving grids to children before and after a course of anti-racist teaching or multi-cultural education.

Sensible though such an approach seems, it may be altogether inadequate to provide a basis for effective social change. If racism could be equated with the personal attributes assigned to in-group and out-group members, would it be so very difficult to eradicate? Positions towards other kinds of people surely go deeper than this. As du Preez (1982) has argued, society can never be reconstructed until new kinds of awareness have been developed, and given form in social life. If psychology is to be socially effective, it has to develop more profound levels of awareness.

Yet Kelly's approach might be most fertile for approaching this question if we read it in the sorts of ways I have been suggesting. Racism would then be defined, not as a set of constructs applied to particular social categories, but as a personal stance taken towards one's social world. What might arise out of such a definition is, I think, suggested by the outcomes of using a less familiar form of Kelly's grid methodology—a form pioneered by Hargreaves (1979). In this version, the person simply arranges the self and other named people, groups, or social entities in relation to each other. This means placing a number of arrow-shaped slips somewhere on a large piece of paper—perhaps doing so several times. Only after making these spatial arrangements, is the person asked to try to explain them. What emerges from this cousin of the traditional rep grid form is something rather different from the usual outcomes. Instead of adjectives defining attributes of people, there are references to social relations, to the positions towards each other of social groupings, in a world of which oneself is part. These include such features as solidarity, belongingness, aspiration, exclusion, or lack of mutuality, for instance. These aspects, defining social orientation, and probably going very deep in personal experience, seem essentially to be about the stances which people take towards each other.

Another currently salient question—that of gender—might also appear rather different if it was approached in terms of this redefinition of Kelly. I think it is undeniable that by far the most illuminating work concerned with gender has been achieved in the United States and in Great Britain, not by academic psychology, but by the women's movement. The perspective and methods of this movement, if we examine them, seem to endorse the fertility of the approach I am suggesting. A fundamental concern is with consciousness-raising, which, meaning the developing awareness of fundamental, as yet inaccessible aspects of oneself, requires the use of deeply personal, intuitive methods rather than those of intellectual analysis. It is possible to see the slogan of this movement—personal is political—as one way of saying that, at its most profound and intimate level, personal experience is about the position one takes towards others. In that movement's perspective, only by becoming aware of their fundamental stance towards others can women free themselves of their inner imprisonment—their own maintenance of the social oppression they suffer.

For most psychologists, personal construct theory would probably be seen to offer to the examination of gender the same kinds of exploration which I suggested in relation to racism. This would mean looking at how, for instance, women generally construe themselves and others. There would be attention to questions about the supremacy of the male–female dimension, about the position of self, and ideal self, within the categories of masculine, or feminine, about the degree of exclusiveness of the two gender groupings, and about the kinds of dimensions which differentiated them. All these questions seem important. Yet, again, perhaps they fail to reach the most basic levels at which gender is experienced.

Of all aspects of our lives, perhaps gender is the most fundamental. As such, it may represent what, most fundamentally, most significantly, we embody. We might, therefore, come to understand its meaning better if we saw it, not as a pattern of constructs, but as an embodiment, and a way of placing ourselves in the world. Such a definition would lead to enquiries of a different kind, looking, closely and subjectively, at the personal language of the body. I find that I, like other women in the crowded Underground, sit and stand in particular ways that are unlike those of men. What does it mean, that we seem, relatively, to occupy less space than do men, that we take care, sitting next to a man, not to use the arm rest between seats, that we hold our legs closely together rather than spreading them? What is the personal significance of the differentiated bags and cases that men and women carry with them? Why is it alien to me—and apparently to other women—to carry papers in hard, rectangular cases, rather than the soft material and rounded forms we characteristically adopt? What are the subtle clues of body language which make it possible to identify someone as a man or a woman from the way they move, even if other physical indices are ambiguous? I remember reading once of a study in which people were asked what shape, and where in their bodies, they felt their real selves to be. Women characteristically referred to a sense of occupying the large part of the trunk, and being defined by a broad surface area presented to the world. Men generally felt themselves to be blade-shaped, edge to the front, and to reside within the head, neck, and upper chest. Fanciful though such images may seem to be, they perhaps offer important clues as to the most profound levels at which we experience our gender.

I do not know what Kelly himself would have said about this particular reading of his psychological approach. But, to me, the choice of a different metaphor from that of man-the-scientist promises a richer exploration of the most significant areas in human life. If we see people as embodying their experience, and as taking stances towards their lives, we can, I think, achieve a better understanding of what they do, since it is our position towards our lives which governs the kinds of engagements possible for us. Because Kelly saw inner meaning as central to human action, this redefinition of his approach may, ultimately, be truer to its essential spirit.

References

Barlow, W. (1973). "The Alexander Principle" (4th ed.), Arrow Books.
du Preez, P. (1982). "Social Psychology of Politics", Blackwell, Oxford.

Frick, W. B. (1982). An interview with Abraham Maslow, *Journal of Humanistic Psychology,* **22,** (No. 4), 33–52.

Gagnon, J. and Simon, W. (eds.). (1970). "The Sexual Scene", Aldine, Chicago.

Hargreaves, C. (1979). "Constructs of Sociality & Individuality" (P. Stringer and D. Bannister, eds.), Academic Press, London.

Hoggart, R. (1962). "The Uses of Literacy", Blackwell, Oxford.

Maher, B. (ed.). (1979). "Clinical Psychology and Personality: The Selected Papers of George Kelly", Wiley, New York.

Mair, J. M. M. (1976). *In* "Nebraska Symposium on Motivation" (A. Landfield, ed.), University Nebraska Press, Lincoln.

Schachter, S. and Singer, J. E. (1962). *Psychological Review,* **69,** 379–399.

11

Suicide, An Experience of Chaos or Fatalism: Perspectives from Personal Construct Theory*

Charles Stefan and Helene B. Linder

The purpose of this chapter is to provide a theoretical base and a set of procedures to employ in the initial clinical dealings with suicidal individuals. We begin by summarizing what we believe is a major theme in personal construct psychology (PCP). The complete range of human behavior has not yet been determined. There are countless, unimagined possibilities not yet envisioned, waiting to be expressed. Both individually and collectively, there is an opportunity to pioneer, creating new visions and new alternatives, alternatives to the present social order and its institutions, as well as alternatives for the individual to find new meanings and ways to communicate those meanings. This statement of the theme paraphrases Kelly's invitation to release oneself from boredom via the reconstructive life.

Culturally Provided Paths to Suicide

Yet there are those who become estranged from this opportunity to pioneer, seeing themselves and their environment as fully realized and determined. There are others who see the course of life events as entirely random and outside the range of personal control or influence. These views are expressed in the myth of Sisyphus, the eternal hopeless struggle against a predetermined universe, and the myth of Pandora's box in which eternal chaos threatens to overwhelm us. Both these myths endure in our culture. Indeed, many people who attempt to end their lives express a commitment to these beliefs of hopeless struggle or eternal chaos as the reason for their actions.

When one adopts the attitude of Sisyphus and concludes that all he or she can do is start and then start again at the bottom, to travel a well-worn path, only to fail and fail again, then the notion of ''why bother at all?'' becomes an insight to consider. There is, after all, nothing else to be done but to act out an established role in an unexciting and unsatisfying play. The person who approaches the events of life from this perspective attempts to end his or her life for what seems

*The authors are indebted to Judith M. Von who contributed to all phases of this chapter.

ISSUES AND APPROACHES
IN PERSONAL CONSTRUCT THEORY

183

good reasons. He or she is not in bad company as a thinker. Hillman (1976), arguing from analytic psychology, sees the act of suicide as sometimes necessary to free one's spirit from the pattern in which it is so utterly trapped. This same view posits, as the therapeutic goal, the engagement of the person in a symbolic death experience. In effect, the person bids farewell to those aspects of the self that are no longer seen as desirable. If, despite this therapeutic effort, he or she still requires organic death to satisfy his or her spiritual need for radical transformation, then Hillman (1976) views death by suicide as an unavoidable necessity, "a summons from God" (p. 94).

The psychoanalytic perspective features man perpetually involved in a balancing act, attempting to control the opposing instincts of his nature. Echoing Freud (1933), Litman and Tabachnick (1968, p. 25) identify these as "Eros (the life instinct) and the destructive instinct (the death instinct)." Menninger (1963) characterizes the most severe state of pathology, as the fifth order of dyscontrol,

> a rapid ascendency of the death instinct and perversion of life instinct. . . . When the virtually unquenchable spark of life flickers out in despair, when all hope, need and effort give way to futility, when the only relief seems to be the ending of all further struggle, . . . death by one's own hand often follows. (p. 265)

Such descriptors as futility, giving up, hopelessness, and despair dramatically echo the Sisyphus theme; why continue, when it is a foregone conclusion that nothing will change and there is no hope for control and no possible way to manipulate one's world.

The second view is held by those who perceive that their personal past–present–future results from totally random events—the contents of Pandora's box. Holders of this view conclude that there is little room for personal influence. To develop a strategy for living one's life in synchrony with naturally occurring events is considered useless. All one can do is adapt to circumstance and cope. Because it does not occur to them that they can direct their fate, they wander. Yet when confronted with the necessity of accounting for where they are, how they arrived there, and where they are going, they find themselves in a position analogous to being lost. It is as if they have wandered into a vast wilderness. Recognizing their lack of personal charts, they pin their hopes on anything and everything. Failing to secure a position, they look to suicide as a choice, to bring certainty into their lives and prevent a continuance of chaos. Surviving an attempt, they often are observed to place their fate entirely in the hands of others. Lacking personal conviction, they obediently look to others for direction and advice.

Cultural support for this view—that people are the victims of their circumstances—can be found in the expositions of sociologists and psychologists alike. One of the major contributions to suicidology was Durkheim's (1897) work, describing social conditions related to suicide. This view forced the focus on circumstances external to the individual. Ignored were the individual's own efforts to control or anticipate his or her circumstances.

The psychology of behaviorism takes a similar approach. Analogously, the person is placed inside a black box. One does not peer into the black box expecting to find answers or meaning. As Skinner (1953) has said, "Man can control his future even though his behavior is wholly determined. It is controlled by his environment" (p. 33). The environment is elevated to the causal force which drives the person. It follows that when all possible circumstances are completely cataloged and described, the behavior that ensues will be completely predictable.

What we have introduced is simply a description of two culturally endorsed approaches between which an individual may choose in order to derive meaning about himself and his world. Either choice can lead to entrapment. In one, there is the view that the world has evolved, unfolded, and is now statically suspended. All one can do is identify the limits of the system and sum it up. Nothing new is ever created and there are no new breakthroughs in the frontiers of understanding. Newness is simply juxtaposing parts, much as a child might rearrange a set of blocks. The individual has no means of controlling the events confronting him or her. Issues of anticipation and forecasting are irrelevant.

The other stance—the individual as victim—provides no means of forecasting or anticipation. The world is viewed in continuous flux, galloping off in whatever direction it fancies. People are either fortunate in their circumstances, or a casualty of their circumstances, or some random mix. In either case, should one's circumstances be viewed as utterly hopeless or deplorable, then one may decide that it is better to do anything, even seek self-destruction, rather than merely wait or wander.

THE KELLIAN VIEW OF SUICIDE

We have not described a novel idea here. These notions have been kicking around for centuries, calling to mind the myths of the ancient Greeks: Scylla, the rock of reality, and Charybdis, the whirlpool of chaos. Between these dangers all mortals must navigate, however impossible it may seem. To embrace either extreme would surely lead to despair, for control and anticipation are lacking. To commit oneself wholly to either psychological stance described previously is certain to ensnare any mortal. Kelly recognized these traps and foresaw the consequences that these psychological stances impose. Furthermore, by developing the psychology of personal constructs, he created a theoretical platform from which these positions may be observed and analyzed.

Representing his own theoretical point of view, Kelly (1961) was asked to join a panel of experts and respond to the case of "A.S.," a young man who had attempted suicide. Within his presentation, Kelly based his description of suicide on "two limiting conditions: realism and indeterminancy." *Realism* is described as that condition of personal construction wherein "the course of events is so obvious that there is no point in waiting around for the outcome" (p. 260). One therefore chooses to end his life rather than continue to bear witness to his own desperate and deplorable position in the world. *Indeterminancy* is described as the course of event becoming so unpredictable that "the only definite act left is to abandon the scene altogether" (p. 260). One can no longer make sense of his world and has no control except the decision to direct his final fate.

In choosing to label the positions as "limiting conditions," Kelly recognized them as the extreme ends of the individual's personal frontiers, beyond which there is futility and one is trapped. He characterized this, on the one hand, as "knowing everything worth knowing" and on the other hand as "knowing nothing worth knowing." To be in this position leads one to decide that suicide is the only "sensible thing to do." Suicide becomes an act which validates, gives meaning to, one's life. If, under these conditions, suicide is not considered, where indeed is the person left?

In the framework of PCP, life itself is viewed as the capacity to represent the environment, not merely the capacity to respond to it. It is from these grounds that we state that PCP is a theory of human life and meaning, which has much to say about the act of suicide. It follows that within personal construct psychology, the act of suicide has no independence or meaning outside the construct system of the individual.

As a behavior, suicide always occurs when it appears to be the best alternative among one's choices. One elaborates those choices for oneself in the way one construes circumstances and his or her relationship to them, as well as from what one has learned to anticipate as a result of past choices. When one construes his or her circumstances, he or she is not detached or uninvolved. Self-definition, that is, core constructs, are at stake. Therefore, if a person at either extreme does not choose death, he or she expects to be engulfed by ultimate intolerable chaos or doom. The act of self-destruction is subordinated to those constructs of the individual that give it meaning and that allow the person to anticipate beyond his or her immediate, intolerable state of affairs.

TRADITIONAL TREATMENT OF SUICIDAL INDIVIDUALS

Not only does culture provide us with root metaphors to view the world, to plot our behavior, and sometimes to speed us on the way toward personal limiting conditions; it also provides clinics and hospitals for treating individuals who become suicidally entrapped. Suicidal activity is a behavioral event that is public and considered deviant. As deviants, suicide attemptors choose or are encouraged to seek treatment. Frequently, they are involuntarily confined to be "cured" within social institutions.

Once hospitalized, the course of events experienced by the sucide attemptor is of major importance and concern. The concern is with the forms of intervention that occur. The traditional approach to the treatment of suicidal individuals in psychiatric settings is a direct extension of the "disease model." It does not allow the act of suicide to be interpreted as a reasonable act. Moskop (1979) points out that this tempts psychiatry "to view suicide as sufficient grounds for a diagnosis of mental illness" (p. 49). Kellians may interpret suicidal acts as rational, irrational, or even as something altogether different; the traditional disease model insists upon an either/or position.

Within the disease model, suicide is either an act that follows from a disordered, irrational state or it is not. It is generally viewed as an irrational act, and as symptomatic of some other much more important state—a psychosis or depression. Once viewed in this light, the actual issues that define and encompass the suicidal behavior are often overlooked; lost, simply because they are not addressed. Behaviors such as wristcutting and overdosing are regarded as symptoms or complications, evidence of a latent condition. Whatever personal significance the behavior or surrounding events have had for the individual tends to be disregarded. Treated as symptomatic, the behavior is not nearly as important as the condition it indicates. The suicidal behavior almost never should be taken at face value, simply because it is "only" symptomatic. The overriding preoccupation is, of course, to reach the goal of obtaining an accurate diagnosis and thereby to isolate the underlying pathology.

When the disease model is extended into the realm of suicidology, the root metaphors from which it flows should be understood. The disease model originates in the laboratories of the natural sciences. As a model, it provides the scientist practitioner (the clinician) with both a method and conceptions of self as clinician. Once employed, it has a resultant effect on the dyadic relationship between clinician and client. The posture provided for the clinician and the effect on the client needs to be examined in order to understand its limitations and applicability with regard to suicide.

The orthodox scientist in the physical laboratory deals with inanimate matter, while the scientist practitioner deals with animate subjects. The orthodox scientist in the biology laboratory deals with animate subjects but does not need to address the self-awareness of the subject. However, self-awareness of the individual is the focal issue for the clinician. The medical scientist also deals with a self-aware subject, but is primarily interested in the subject's awareness only in the sense that symptoms of diseased parts are communicated to the physician. As such, the self-aware individual is reduced to being a host for the pathology upon which the physician focuses. The clinician is hard-pressed to reduce the subject to the role of host. The clinician cannot ignore the communications that reflect the self-awareness of the individual.

The suicidal individual presents the clinician with a further complication, namely, the ability to self-reflect. His self-reflections regarding his self-definitions, his evaluation of his psychosocial context, and his overall judgments lead him to choose a repudiation of life. Within this context in which personal evaluations and definitions are the sine qua non, it is very difficult to begin to relate to the individual in any way analogous to the laboratory subjects of the orthodox physicist, biologist, physician.

The evident results and advances of the orthodox scientist make it a laudable role for the clinician to emulate. However, pushed to its extreme in clinical settings, the complementing psychosocial role expected of the client is one-sided cooperation. The client must conform to a role foreign to him. He must be passive, patient, and allow himself to be manipulated while the clinician is active, manipulating, and creative.

The clinician who expects the lopsided relationship to result in positive effects often resorts to covert treatment strategies in order to outwit and thereby contain the client in a passive role. The clinician hopes to minimize the client's power to distort the strategy dictated by his or her model. If the client is active and does not cooperate; either because he or she chooses not to or does not know how, the client's actions blur the roles. The client crosses into the realm the clinician reserves for her- or himself. If the clinician does not recognize the unreasonableness of the expectations regarding the proper role of the client, he or she as clinician begins to view the client's behavior critically and labels the client a manipulator, or attention seeker, and so forth.

This strict adherence to the medical model sets up a curious paradox. During their interventions, clinicians desire to maximize their own independent therapeutic activity, while at the same time minimizing the client's inclinations to be active in their own treatments. If the client insists on an active role he or she is pejoratively labeled. Yet the clinician must rely on the client to report that a "cure" has emerged. That is, the client at some point must spontaneously behave, think, and talk in a manner that signals a cure. When then, and by what means, can the clinician be certain that the cure is reliably and validly expressed? How does the clinician know that the client is not just manipulating or outwitting him or her? We believe that if one begins with the line of reasoning required by the medical model, one can never be certain and will always be skeptical of the suicidal client's genuineness.

The strict adherence to the methods of orthodox science leads one away from the client as an experiencing individual. The fact that the client is an expert on his or her own behavior is ignored. Ignored also is the fact that psychology as a science is not all-encompassing or finely grained enough to account for the total range of human experiences. In time, these limitations will probably be overcome. For the present, we must recognize that there are frontiers of science, areas where we have not as scientists explored. Once in those areas, it is not good enough to view the observed features as mere replications of the known, or to limit our efforts to fine tuning, which often is the essence of the diagnostic process. There are some personal dangers to the client. Consider the consequences of applying a diagnostic label. Misdirected goals for intervention dictated by the diagnostic label are often undertaken. By application of the label, one automatically extends the possibility for stereotyping the patient even further into the pattern. Furthermore, the label encourages the client to view all his or her reactions as symptoms of a diagnosed illness. The client comes to terms, not with his or her actual thoughts, feelings, or concerns, but with the concept of his or her "illness." For example, when individuals learn they have acquired a diagnostic label such as manic-depressive illness, both normal positive and normal negative feelings become the harbingers for loss of personal control. They must insulate themselves from their feelings and actions, and protect themselves from the anticipated cycles of mania and depression. They believe that if these conditions emerge, they may become suicidal. Furthermore, if the patients do report such thoughts of suicide, the thoughts are considered to stem from the clients' "condition" and are typically viewed as totally foreign to them. The resultant experience is one of possession, wherein the clients lack any personal control. Adherence to this model reifies the diagnosis, and in turn dictates a closed system of approach to the client and treatment; while the client's actions are seen as irrelevant and unrelated.

AN EXPANDED VIEW OF THE SCIENTIST PRACTITIONER

To the extent that the suicidal individual represents a new frontier for clinicians, we must proceed by keeping a focus on the individual. The clinician must accept cooperation as the method of the applied scientist. Cooperation must be sought from the beginning and maintained throughout the relationship. The basic task of psychology is to encourage, and to create an environment in which the client can communicate his or her self-reflections. Once communicated, the responsibility is on the clinician to attempt to understand them. Finally, the clinician must use the client's communications to determine where he or she and the client stand. The clinician must tune his or her experience of the client to the client's personal experience. By way of this approach, a role relationship occurs that constitutes reflexivity. From this relationship, maps of the client's territory encompassing the suicidal experience can be created as data for science. This approach exemplifies Bannister's (1970) view that "psychology is to be looked upon as a meta-discipline which overviews science."

When Kelly (1961) chose to describe the suicidal individual as a victim of a rigid adherence to a construction system characterized by realism or indeterminancy, he offered a bipolar diagnostic construct of personal experience leading to the crisis of suicide. One has but to briefly consider the implications of these two labels to recognize that he was describing the end results of personal strategies that lead to a point in which freedom to choose—even one more time—is effectively blocked. There are no alternatives except death. Issues of control, anticipation, or movement are irrelevant.

Although the role of scientist is esteemed by Kelly and Bannister, they recognized the inherent dangers in overcommittment to the philosophic systems that lead to realism-indeterminancy. Kelly (1955, 1970, 1977) took issue with the rigid underpinnings of a deterministic science. So, too, did Bannister (1970, 1977). At other times Kelly (1955, 1970) disavowed attempts to equate PCP with the philosophy of phenomenology.

The argument is that rigid adherence to either realism or indeterminacy can lead to entrapment. We are not arguing that as philosophical propositions, reliable personal evaluations and conclusions cannot be drawn, nor did Kelly attack the essential worth of other philosophies. As Bannister and Fransella (1982) put the argument:

> Kelly is not proposing personal construct theory as a contradiction of other psychological theories, but as an alternative to them—an alternative which does not deny the 'truths' of other theories, but which may provide more interesting, more inspiring, more useful and elaborate 'truths.' (p. 16)

We add that personal construct psychology provides a way out of the trap; namely, by legitimizing alternative reconstructions. In an unpublished manuscript, Kelly (1977, p. 11) described the act of construing as "transcending the obvious." The purpose of construing is not merely to avoid traps but to pioneer, and to seek adventure.

In order to apply this Kellian attitude of optimism to the field of suicidology, we offer three recurrent themes found in the writings of Kelly (1955) and of Bannister and Fransella (1982). First, there is a real world of people and events, and it exists independent of thought; second, this realm of the real is constantly evolving; third, individuals formulate their own interpretations of the world by replicating the world, and they are dependent on other people. In order to survive, individuals must arrive at some personal understanding of the world. They must construe it and keep their constructions abreast of change. More than this, to provide opportunities for personal freedom and control, individuals must be able to anticipate the direction the evolution will take.

This description of a human's task sounds like a large charge for one ordinary person. Yet, it is done by the individual, by his or her children, and by the family pet as well. The pet in anticipation of the swat it may get for lying on its owner's chair, slinks off when it hears the footsteps.

So, where are the dangers? Problems occur when we create our own personal traps. For instance, by ignoring the continual evolution and considering everything including ourselves as static and determined, we give up our power to influence events and lose the possibility for change. On the other hand, ignoring the rhythmical patterns of events around us and considering their occurrence to be random, we give up a sense of anticipation and find ourselves eventually in a chaotic world in which nothing seems to make sense.

In either instance, the individual creates for her- or himself the untenable context of limitation. A lack of ability to influence or to understand the world can hinder one's ability to live in it. The fact that traps of construction occur is certain and was recognized by Kelly (1955). From the point of view of PCP, personal movement, freedom, and control are insured to the individual who continuously engages in a reconstruing process. Effective reconstruction minimizes the possible traps by recognizing that the resultant construction is an articulated relationship involving the inner person together with the external events in his or her present context. The process, therefore, is ongoing and never complete.

Where reconstruction bogs down, a convenient focal point is found for discussing the crisis that leads to suicide as a choice. If we are successful in our construction of it, we should also be able to project conditions for therapy.

The Suicide Crisis Examined

A view of the suicide crisis can be had by considering Kelly's (1955) circumspection–preemption–control (CPC) cycle as a model that subsumes the everyday activities of an individual in applying his or her constructs to a specific situation and elaborating a course of action.

Considering the CPC cycle, suppose we observe an individual faced with a novel situation. Some event has occurred that he or she did not anticipate and must now make sense of it. Examples may include a death in the family, a promotion, a major shift in a relationship. At first, the person circumspects through his or her existing catalogue of constructs, seeking goodness of fit between the new situation and what he or she has previously experienced, selecting those constructs for consideration that promise relevance and utility in dealing with the new event, while excluding those that do not. After judging the relevance and irrelevance of the constructs to the novel event, the individual simplifies them under some convenient grouping and treats the new situation as if it were nothing more than the known past; that is, the person tentatively applies an existing construct to the new event he or she preempts.

As an aside, one of the authors was attempting to describe PCP to a colleague. After a few minutes of listening, the colleague exclaimed, "I've got it, it's just another gimmick." His statement, *"it's just another . . . "* is an example of preemption. Once preemption takes place, the control phase is entered. The issues considered relevant can now be put to the test.

The cycle begins with the individual dealing primarily with his or her personal construct system—his or her inner world. The individual then moves toward the control phase where one is face to face with the outer world of events, both physical and social. The theories (constructs) are tested against the outer world so that the individual may answer the question: "Was I right in viewing the situation as if it were nothing but what I preemptively figured it to be?'' By testing the question, the individual seeks evidence to support or not support his or her tentative view. This is validation. It is important to recognize that what gets validated is not the situation itself nor the individual her- or himself, but the construction of the situation created by the individual.

THE CHAOS EXPERIENCE EXPLAINED

If the construction is validated, the individual is satisfied for the moment that he or she is capable of functioning in the new situation. Suppose, however, that efforts to gain validation lead an individual to a mistaken view that it is *he* or *she* that assigns meaning and truth to the events around him. This contorted view sets the person up over the course of time for serious problems in reconstruction. The faulty premise, that the individual assigns truth, compels the person to ignore the details of events and to rely in a restricted fashion on the constructions and on her- or himself as a construer. When this occurs, one has ceased to engage in proper experimentation and has aborted the CPC cycle. If a series of events occurs that cannot be accounted for by one's range of constructs, she or he experiences invalidation. What are the choices? For awhile a person may resort to hostility, attempting to extort validation from others regarding his or her constructions. Eventually the person may resort to loosening his or her constructs, attempting to use them in new ways. If the loosening strategy is carried too far, it results in a sense of incomprehension and chaos; and nothing within one's construct system applies to or makes sense of the events one confronts. Indeed, this core construct of one's self as a construer is in jeopardy. "If I cannot make sense of the events surrounding me, what does this say about me?'' Repeated invalidation of self may be considered proof that one is impotent to employ or develop personally effective constructs. The resulting personal experience is defined as threat and guilt within PCP. As such these experiences are paralyzing. They involve recognition that one's entire view of self and events are in need of change. During such an intense crisis, an attempt at self-destruction may be made by the individual to prevent anticipated chaos. The suicidal–parasuicidal behavior occurring among diagnosed schizophrenics and often viewed as "impulsive,'' is an example of the chaos phenomenon.

THE FATALISM EXPERIENCE EXPLAINED

Next, suppose instead that the validation process led the individual to construe the novel event as if it were fully determined with inherent meaning, having nothing to do with him. The individual may see himself as accidentally witnessing the revelation of truth. This contorted view leads to different but serious problems in reconstruction. Operating from this basic stance, the individual construes her- or himself as a recipient upon whom the meaning of outer events is thrust. The person has effectively removed her- or himself from the validation process. The focus in this instance is on the events themselves, which are believed to contain complete meaning independent of the individual. Taken to extremes, the individual neither develops nor employs ways to control the events that he or she observes. In order to develop a more comprehensive base of movement and freedom, the primary strategy is to dilate one's field, that is, to regard more and more events to bring about and sustain meaning. The inherent difficulty, of course, is that there is not an infinite supply of events to consider. As this realization develops, the individual will often respond by interacting aggressively with the environment. This serves to further open the field, and may provide partial success. However, over time, there is increased awareness that aggression and dilation without personal interpretation will not work. The mounting evidence suggests that one is somehow cut off from opportunity. The dilation–aggression strategy comes to be viewed as ineffective and is increasingly devalued once the fallacy of having infinite choice is recognized. There is one other general strategy open to the "field determined" individual. If considering more and more events and facts does not lead to an ultimate understanding of the world around him, then closing off more and more bits of truth and meaning will. The individual can constrict the elements of his or her field in an effort to contain or find personal meaning. Should the person conclude that fate is predetermined and he or she is an unwitting victim of his or her circumstances, the ultimate constriction, suicide may occur. The cancer patient, the culturally alienated, the movie actors who lose their attractiveness, and the so-called rational suicides form examples of this group.

We describe two distinct paths to the suicidal crisis: one leads to the experience of chaos, the other to ultimate fatalism. We consider these to be intersecting paths rather than parallel. At the point of intersection lies the suicidal choice. The negative experiences blend. The knowledge that one does not know anything worth knowing is known with certainty while knowing everything worth knowing is put to a test.

SUICIDE GESTURERS AND RUMINATORS

The problems inherent in developing, maintaining, and employing a construct system have pitfalls other than those we describe involving control/validation. Our description thus far shows a much-biased individual moving methodically toward the suicidal crisis.

Others engage in suicidal behavior who exemplify problems with the circumspection phase of CPC. Problems occur if this phase is either foreshortened or prolonged. Foreshortening or abandoning the circumspection phase too soon results in hasty preemption and untimely and scattered testing, in which no real sorting out of the relevant issues can occur. This foreshortening of circumspection is, not surprisingly, termed "impulsivity" by Kelly (1955, p. 226). Prolonged circumspection was described by Kelly (1955, p. 516) as "an inability to make one's choice." This individual is indecisive. He delays sorting the relevant issues and therefore cannot put anything to the test. If such foreshortening or prolonging of circumspection becomes habitual, we observe behaviors that are traditionally known and diagnosed as "problems of personality." Self-destructive behaviors in this context are likely to be of the rumination or gesturing variety.

Ruminators of suicide are engaged in prolonged circumspection or intellectualization. They see life and their own future as predictably determined; they have telescoped their anticipations and predict a constricted future. When thoughts of suicide emerge as an alternative, they seem unable to make their choice. Being locked in circumspection, they are not able to control or anticipate the consequences of their demise. Kelly (1955, p. 488) illustrates the problem with prolonged circumspection in an example of "plans for suicide bogging down in the question who should inherit a prized gun collection." All too often, however, ruminators do act and choose suicide. This choice emerges when the ruminator employs the suicide as a test to bring into focus the consequences he or she is not able to predict. Indeed, the person is attempting to extort answers in a hostile manner.

Gesturers of suicide are prone to foreshortened circumspection leading to hasty preemption and control. Life's vicissitudes seen as continually portending crisis, gesturers are unable to incorporate elements of their psychosocial field. No matter what direction they look, their personal system is inadequate. When gestures of suicide are employed, it is to bring about resolution in the form of soliciting outside help. Suicide gestures, therefore, can initially be viewed as hostile acts intended to extort confirmatory evidence. However, escalation toward more serious attempts may occur if the individual is stymied by the results he or she has obtained. The person can engage in aggressive psychosocial interactions, attempting to gain answers for unthoughtout questions. The odds for gaining answers are not in his or her favor. The person has no concise verbal questions and may impulsively ask the question behaviorally, namely, to make a more serious attempt.

Both strategies—ruminating and gesturing—represent ineffective approaches because there is no balanced articulation between the outer world of events and the inner world of the construer. The resulting personal experience—perplexity in the face of novel situations—can overwhelm the individual and result in eventual serious attempts.

By using Kelly's notion that suicide involves issues of realism and indeterminancy, we attempt to describe how an individual may arrive at the self-destructive crisis. We argue that when the individual judges her- or himself to be the assigner of truth, problems occur leading to strategies of hostility and loosening. Suicide is then a choice undertaken to prevent total chaos of one's system. Likewise, when the individual believes he is merely a witness to truth that is determined by events, he or she develops strategies of aggression and constriction. Suicide is then a choice to prevent a fatalistic outcome.

Alternatives to the elaborative choice of suicide exist. The person expecting chaos may not choose suicide but may become psychotic, enter therapy, or go to a religious retreat. The person expecting rigid fatalism may also become psychotic, enter therapy, or seek geographical flight. Similarly, those with problems of circumspection may choose other alternatives.

THE SUICIDAL CHOICE

If alternatives to suicide exist, what is it that tips the choice in the direction of suicide? Here we must return to theory for an hypothesis.

We assume that the individual has woven suicide as an alternative into his or her personal construct system. We also assume that it logically occupies a position subordinate to a life and death construction, and, by definition, that it has anticipatory functions. In keeping with the choice corollary, suicide becomes the end of the construct chosen when it promises extension or definition of the personal system. The other end of the construct is ignored; it is entwined with expectations of chaos or fatalism.

The suicidal choice appears to occur at a penultimate point in personal crisis. The crisis—the sense of impending chaos or fatalism—is less of a look into the future than it is a self-reflexive evaluative review of the personal past. The evaluation reveals a history of contorted nonarticulated construction: core self constructs, those that specify one's identity and what one stood for, are in considerable danger of being disconfirmed during crises. While core constructions of self in the present have become arrested and useless, the awareness of bringing such rigid core construction up-to-date is an enormous task and may seem futile. This realization, we believe, constitutes the suicidal crisis. There is no retreat. While ahead of one individual is an emersion in chaos, ahead of the other is a constricted field of opportunity. To choose life is to choose utter senselessness, or complete boredom.

That PCP provides a useful view of suicide is not offered merely as an academic exercise. It is safe to say that there presently is no single dominant theory of suicide. We believe that PCP as a theoretical framework will stand the test of time and prove to be a useful model from which to deal clinically with the issues of suicide. Using PCP has the following advantages: (1) the suicidal individual is cast into the role of central focus; (2) the historical events leading to the suicidal choice are considered in terms of the individual's interpretations, and are not left behind as so much extraneous baggage; and (3) furthermore, the situation into which a survivor of an attempt is propelled is also considered. The surviving individual is viewed as a construer of his or her own attempt; and the individual is not left to wander on his or her own to gain meaning and perspective. Finally, by viewing the individuals in their own terms and in their situation, interventions can be tailored in their terms and on their grounds. The individual is not desensitized or taught problem solving or assertiveness skills on the off chance that they may be good for him. They may also be irrelevant or harmful if applied without consideration for the individual.

A CLINICAL APPLICATION OF THE CHAOS–FATALISM EXPERIENCE

A pilot test of these diagnostic constructs is to apply them a priori to known clinical examples.

Consider the suicidal–parasuicidal behavior associated with a negative reaction to hallucinogenic drugs as exemplifying the chaos experience. With the attendant unexpected changes in perception often associated with drug use, the individual's familiar and habitual confidence of being in control is dramatically shaken. The person often reports experiences of anxiety and threat, showing awareness that his or her constructs are imminently ineffective for prediction and personal control. The individual may even see that his or her very self-definitions are in need of change, which can lead to experiences of fear and guilt. In short, the individual finds himself in a situation for which nothing in the past has prepared him and which indeed may be personally overwhelming. Suicide emerges as an alternative to prevent further escalation of the experience and to put an end to the loss of personal control.

Another variant of the chaos theme may be seen in interpersonal situations such as a love affair. Consider the love relationship at the point in which one member decides it is to be broken off with finality. Our focus is upon the person left holding the bag. Very often the issue of control emerges, with the individual claiming inability to do or to know anything that might reverse his or her situation. This is a characteristic of anxiety. The awareness of being blocked from fulfillment of one's hoped for anticipations is communicated. When both not knowing anything effective to do plus anticipating the loss of unfulfilled possibilities are bound up in a relationship that once was a primary source of both validation and personal understanding, the resulting experience of being rejected may eventuate in suicidal behavior. As a social strategy designed to force a continuation of the relationship, perhaps in the hope of restoring it as well as to force the other to re-evaluate it, the individual engages in self-destruction to force the anticipated possibilities into existence. In short, the person believes he or she will gain control of both the situation and his or her personal system.

The second major context in which suicidal behavior emerges is the experience of fatalism. The "fatalistic" individual invariably predicts an outcome in which he or she is ineffective and unable to influence the situation. No matter what one does, one thinks one will lose.

The relatively high frequency of suicides of generals and physicians reported in the suicide literature may fit here. It has been argued that the availability of lethal means and the knowledge of their use increases their so-called potential for suicide, but this is an oversimplification. Lethal devices for suicide surround everyone and suicidal individuals use what is available.

Instead, we suggest that these professions have a mystique and an allure in our culture. It is a popular belief that whoever achieves that apex of success must surely have experienced a transformation of the self. This self-transformation is not viewed as a process to be personally developed by the individual, but is expected to occur as a simple acquisition from outside, much like one acquires measles. The individual arrives at that spot in which fame and honor are actually granted; yet an articulation between the acquired position and the self is not made. The person sees her- or himself as unchanged, still possessing rather ordinary and small constructions that signal his commonness. The person has not achieved the anticipated metamorphosis of self into a worthy or accomplished person. To continue to live in this dissonant fashion serves as evidence that the person has trespassed into territory where he or she does not belong or fit. What is more, once this point is reached, it is easy for the person to conclude that he or she cannot relive his past and make corrections. By choosing suicide, the person transforms the problem of the small self versus the great title into a demonstration of noble character. Thus, if the person cannot live with honor, he or she can die for honor.

A clinically analogous situation is observed in clients who are considered diagnostically depressed. Here the lofty goal sought by the client is being truly loved. The individual in fact may be loved; however, the anticipated transformation, coming from outside, that will turn the person into a content and fulfilled person is not experienced. The client has not engaged in the reconstruction process that allows one to consider one's self as qualified for being loved. Thus, the state of being discontent is used as evidence that one is not worthy of love. These clients are often referred to as "therapist burners." They earn this reputation by seeking from their therapists unqualified and unequivocal support and "love." They continually seek confirmation of their worth. A therapist may react by giving the message that the client is of course worthy but also needs to make changes. It is this message to change that invites these individuals to conclude that something is wrong with them and they must be unworthy. Evidence of this sort, gained through social experimentation combines with their basic fatalistic attitude and eventually leads the individual to the conclusion: "There is nothing I can do to change; I am what I am." For this individual, the alternative to suicide is to live a life that is always the same, with no power to influence the course of events. Suicide is viewed as a reaction to the confirmation of unworthiness.

To employ personal construct psychology as an aid to understanding the crisis of suicide is to look to the person for answers. He is the expert regarding himself, his circumstance, his conflicts. The artistry of psychology stemming from PCP is to allow the client to teach the clinician.

THE SUICIDE SURVIVOR

Using personal construct psychology as a guide, we propose a means of describing the contexts leading to the elaborative choice of suicide. Our focus now shifts to the other side of the suicidal choice, when there is a survivor. Suicidal behavior, like all behavior, is regarded in PCP as embodying a personal question. As such the act is viewed as anticipatory, because the individual expected a change to result. Where death was intended but survival results, the anticipated outcome did not occur, and the individual finds himself very much alive. In addition, he may find himself whisked off to a psychiatric hospital. It is this specific set of circumstances that we are addressing. The individual has engaged in a behavioral test, designed to either prevent complete chaos from overwhelming him or her or to terminate the fatalistic flow of events. The person has run his test and now has results from which to draw conclusions. In checking his or her personal hypothesis against these results, does the individual find he or she has confirmed or disconfirmed the original hypothesis?

The simplest course open to the person is to keep his or her hypothesis intact but to question the procedures. Here the person continues to regard suicide as a solution to ultimate chaos or ultimate realism, but the particular method employed, wristcutting, overdosing, and so forth, did not bring the anticipated results. He or she can, then, replace the method with another one. Some individuals go on to do this. Regarding their previous actions as mistakes of method, they escalate lethality in subsequent suicide attempts.

Something else may occur. The survivor may instead focus on his or her original anticipations. For whatever reason the predicted chaos or the ultimate fatalistic outcome did not take place, the survivor finds his or her hypothesis disconfirmed. For the person anticipating chaos, the suicidal behavior might have led to some unexpected result. The person may find himself once again supported in an understanding social network in the form of family or friends, who can offer alternatives, which may have been previously overlooked or ignored by him.

Similarly, the anticipated fatalism or ultimate realism hypothesis may not be confirmed. Here, the suicidal individuals spontaneously creates new constructions for themselves. The individuals may now view themselves as capable of exerting influence over their circumstances. One might say they have gained insight. This, too, may come about through an unanticipated reunion with others who offer alternative constructions of meaning. That these turnabouts take place, moving the previously suicidal individual out of the realm of future suicide, has been observed clinically and has been dubbed the "bonus life" (Shneidman, 1979, p. 152). This term has been used to describe the phenomenon when little or no clinical treatment occurs and the individual never repeats the suicidal behavior. It is, on the whole, rare and difficult to observe directly, because these individuals disappear from the view of hospital rolls.

It is more frequently the case that reconstruction does not take place in as short a period of time or as spontaneously as suggested previously. The bonus life phenomenon, while rare, is mentioned simply to point out that there are degrees of personal readiness to accept evidence of disconfirmation and to tolerate efforts of reconstruction. At the other extreme are individuals requiring the maximum amount of clinical intervention and a significant period of time to facilitate the reconstruction process.

Where suicidal behavior has led to a psychiatric hospitalization, there is still another important matter to consider. The individual not only has notions of suicidal behavior and life circumstances to deal with, but he or she now has the event of the hospitalization to consider as well. It is reasonable to assume that patients do form opinions about their hospitalizations throughout the length of their stays. In the very broadest terms, hospitalization can be evaluated as either a positive or a negative event. Miller and Goleman (1970) demonstrate that future suicide attempts can be predicted on the basis of evaluations and changes in attitudes toward the hospitalization. Their findings suggest that future attempts are most frequent with those who leave the hospital with a negative evaluation. The power of such a predictor is more enhanced when combined with an analysis of the case as representing either the chaos or the fatalism condition for suicide. We now turn to a discussion of each of the four types so generated:

Type I: Chaos was anticipated: hospitalization is viewed as likely to be positive. When this condition occurs, the individuals allow the experiences of hospitalization to impose an initial sense of order upon their personal construc- tions. They are often observed as treating the hospital as a personal haven or sanctuary. The experience is likely to be verbally characterized as something that is needed and as offering them an opportunity to re-evaluate. Staff are considered to be helpful, and the individuals can be observed making social contact with them. These social forays do not always go smoothly. If they do, the individuals are considered to be cooperative. If they do not, and if the social interactions go awry, the individuals are likely to be considered dependent or manipulative.

Because the individuals are in a transition state, that is, aware of the need for change in their construct system, the anxiety experienced in social contexts is likely to be diffused by strategies of personal atonement, that is, the individuals subsume the staff's generally held beliefs that suicidal behavior is unwarranted, short-sighted, and rather stupid. They frequently offer proof that they have benefitted from being hospitalized, spontaneously offering stereotypical state- ments such as "I have learned my lesson" or unsolicited promises such as "I will never do it again." Yet, these strategies do not signify that reconstruction has taken place.

Type II: Chaos was anticipated: hospitalization is viewed as likely to be negative. In this instance, the individuals may well focus on the hospitalization as providing further evidence that chaos is around the next corner. The hospitalization may raise the risk that their personal system will become disordered by addition of unfamiliar elements. Because they regard the hospitalization apprehensively, attempts to facilitate change are reacted to as threatening their already tenuous position. These individuals are not usually described as cooperative by staff. They often actively resist any therapeutic intervention. By resisting treatment efforts, the individuals avoid a major reconstruction job, something they currently feel incapable of achieving. They are often seen as actively withdrawing from social interactions, avoiding eye-contact, or, more extremely, refusing to get out of bed. This kind of behavior is sometimes mistakenly viewed as symptomatic of severe depression. What it accomplishes for the individuals, however, is to provide evidence, extorted by them, to validate their negative expectations. This hostile maneuvering has gained them confirming evidence that the hospital can do no good. The form and degree the hostility takes can vary. In a mild example, it can be expressed in the form of a repudiation of the staff: "You don't know what you're doing." In a severe example, the individual may express the firm belief that he or she is being made psychotic and anticipates never leaving the hospital. Here one hears "Let me alone. Don't waste your time, I'm going to be chronic." The individual often runs a gamut of such strategies, all to prevent the collapse of a system that obviously needs extensive revision. Mirrored in his or her behavior are the same hostile maneuverings that were seen prior to the attempt that was designed to prevent collapse. The focus now is the hospitalization itself, against which the individual rails in resistance.

Type III: Ultimate fatalism anticipated: hospitalization is viewed as likely to be positive. Here the individual finds himself in a new setting with a new set of circumstances to figure out. The hospitalization, in effect, offers this person an unsolicited dilation of his field. It is important to note that, while the staff may describe the hospital environment as highly structured, stress-free, and physically confining, the field is actually novel to the newly hospitalized individual. For the person to understand the novel field and thereby expand his or her system, he or she initiates assertive, aggressive action. To the degree that the individual can control and manipulate these new elements, the individual is removed from the sense of despair and hopelessness previously experienced. In the most ideal cases, the hospitalization is viewed by the individuals as an opportunity to demonstrate ability to handle the new environment. They may verbalize an appreciation that hospitalization offered them a chance to get back on their feet again while still asserting the rightfulness of their original fatalistic dilemma, continuing to regard their life situations with considerable cynicism exemplified by the theme "If you understand how dreadful life could be, you too would consider suicide." In such a case in which the individuals regard the hospitalization as an opportunity to assert themselves and exercise control, they may provoke difficulties with the staff. Their aggressiveness may be viewed negatively and regarded as defiance. However, the original and habitual strategy employed by these individuals looking to the outer world of events for the revelation of meaning, allows them to find temporary control in the hospital. Temporary control does not in itself guarantee that the reconstruction process of their basic fatalism has occurred.

A special concern arises where the individual seeks discharge by arguing "While I was suicidal in the past, I am not suicidal now. If things get as bad as they were before, it's my choice to consider suicide again." Even though the hospitalization itself may have been viewed as a positive experience, these individuals recognize that they are still no more prepared to deal with events outside the hospital than they were previously. Therefore they number suicide among their strategies. Inexperienced clinicians, when faced with these persuasive arguments must be alert to a tendency to begin treating the notion of suicide positively but preemptively themselves. Once suicide is viewed as "just an" existential act, a rational choice, or as a personal right, it becomes easy to develop the notion that suicide is something that ultimately cannot be prevented. For a clinician to adopt this point of view is not, in our eyes, advisable, therapeutic, or for that matter, life-oriented. What is missing in the argument, from our perspective, is an appreciation that the individuals' strategies and construction of the world have not altered, and that a reconstruction of the problems of their life can and must be pursued.

Type IV: Ultimate fatalism anticipated: hospitalization is viewed as likely to be negative. Represented are individuals who regard their hospitalization as proof that the worst has happened and nothing good can come of it. They see no reason for attempting to manipulate the new environment, since they expect only further confirmation that the cards are stacked against them. They do not take the initiative to either actively resist or assert. Submission to one's fate is their theme. In interactions with hospital staff, these individuals demonstrate an inability to develop or express a sense of personal futurity or progression, while they characterize their past life as punctuated with themes of disappointment. Hospital staff are likely to view them as complainers, and serious depression is the most frequent diagnosis applied. When therapeutic efforts are attempted, these individuals may show attitudes ranging from complacency to blank dejection, and passive resistance of a limited variety is often encountered by such arguments as "I tried that once, and it didn't work." These individuals frustrate therapeutic efforts, not because they actively refuse them, but because they do not permit therapeutic movement to occur; they will not experiment.

ASSESSMENT

In keeping with the traditional notion that diagnosis must precede treatment, we turn next to a consideration of assessment issues as they relate to the suicidal individual. A number of years ago, the authors of this article were engaged in a task of reviewing the literature and polling psychiatric hospitals to find the best set of tests, scales, and interview techniques to assess suicidal risk in suicidal patients. The problem was viewed as a practical and important one, but nevertheless as only the first step in dealing with the suicidal individual. It was pointed out to us in a very straightforward manner that if the solitary concern of the clinician is simply to determine whether the patient is thinking about committing suicide, one need only ask him (Farberow, personal communication, 1975). This approach agrees with Kelly's first principle: "If you don't know what's wrong with the patient, ask him, he may tell you." (1955, p. 323) However, the concerns of most clinicians go beyond a simple determination of whether or not the patient is currently expressing suicidal thoughts. A variety of traditional tools is available to the clinician, which can aid in obtaining diagnostic and descriptive information about the patient and his or her behaviors. Such tools include a clinical interview, the use of traditional psychological tests, and the use of specialized scales that focus on suicidal issues. We shall not argue either for or against any of these methods. We recognize that different clinicians have specific preferences and areas of expertise in applying assessment procedures. It is, however, crucial to appreciate the limitations of these methods. We must guard against the use of diagnostic dimensions that are limited or which say more about the clinician than the patient. Indeed Kelly (1955) has formulated a list of 10 specifications for a useful diagnostic construct. One need not eliminate from consideration such instruments as the MMPI, Rorschach, TAT, and so forth to achieve understanding of the patient. However, one must remain aware that these traditional tests are exceptionally limited when specific questions about suicide are at issue. Neuringer (1974) concludes a review of assessment procedures and tests on a pessimistic note, stating that "it is difficult to close this volume with a feeling that one has had the chronicle of an unalloyed scientific triumph." (p. 225)

There are, additionally, specialized scales relating specifically to suicide as an overt behavior, which can help the clinician form normative judgements about the patient. Such scales deal with issues of lethality, intent, and risk-rescue issues. In as much as they relate directly to the overt behaviors associated with suicide, they have demonstrated an improved level of content and predictive validity. They are, however, most useful in their contribution to clinical judgement, not in replacing it. These scales can provide the clinician with an increased opportunity to focus on relevant issues. Mischel (1968, p. 1) recommends simple self-assessment procedures rather than complicated tests: "Assessment is hindered by the failure to apply relevant principles about the conditions that produce, maintain, and modify social behavior."

We touch on assessment issues earlier in this chapter, when describing the problems with traditional treatment methods. With regard to assessment, Kelly

(1955) argues that the formation of a diagnosis is not simply a matter of forming a preemptive construction of the individual case, that is, establishing a category in which to place the person. To be sure, categorization plays a role in the clinician's understanding of the case, but is not regarded as an end in itself. The assessment procedure that Kelly described is a multifaceted outline of clinical issues that ultimately leads to the development of a plan for treatment.

Included as issues to consider are the normative formulations of the clinician regarding the deviant behavior. What does the behavior accomplish for the person and when does it occur? The social milieu of the person is to be assessed in terms of how tolerant the social context is in which the adjustment will occur? Most importantly, the client's point of view must be considered and evaluated.

A thorough assessment of the patient leads directly to treatment issues and may even overlap with treatment. To arrive, for example, at a complete psychological evaluation of the patient's construction system, Kelly (1955) acknowledged that the clinician might well have to conclude "a long period of comprehensive psychotherapy." (p. 801) Furthermore, for the hospitalized individual, many of the final issues of assessment may have to be resolved in the context of outpatient treatment.

To apply Kelly's diagnostic formulation to individuals who are hospitalized for suicidal behavior, we suggest focusing on the following: (1) How can the suicidal behavior be described? (2) How did the patient construe the suicidal behavior? What was he trying to accomplish? What does he make of it all now? (3) What psychological constructs can be employed to understand the case? (4) What is the effect of hospitalization?

We have proposed a set of construct dimensions stemming from PCP, by which we can begin to structure assessment of the suicidal individual. In addition to assessment procedures such as a mental status examination, standard tests, and special scales, we can also describe the suicidal behavior in terms of the chaos–fatalism dimension. In addition, we have proposed considering the attitudes regarding hospitalization itself as a predictive issue. To bring these proposed dimensions maximally into focus requires the clinician to establish a dialogue with the patient.

Dialogue is of crucial importance. It is necessary to first of all understand the patient's position before any subsequent therapeutic assistance is offered. The clinician must recognize and communicate that the patient is the expert about himself. The responsibility of the clinician is to create an atmosphere in which the individual is free to describe himself. Even if he has difficulty expressing himself in words or in actions, he must be the focus of concern and information must come from him. Once the clinician has developed this kind of rapport, he is in a good position to begin to apply his own psychological constructs to the case. Because the patient is the expert, the therapist's constructions must be checked out against the patient's viewpoints.

THERAPY

As a process, assessment is initiated in order to transfer both client and therapist into the realm of therapeutic intervention. Now, if all goes well, the client should be in a position in which he can use the therapist. The therapist is capable of understanding his point of view and the client recognizes that.

Before leaping directly into issues of therapy, three points concerning orientation of the clinician to client issues must be considered. First, as therapists, we must remember that we are dealing with an aware self-reflexive person who is developing his personal interpretations of events and experience. This is certain to include interpretations of assessment and treatment as well as of the therapist. The client is not merely waiting for treatment. The client is at a point in time and in a context wherein he has recently made an attempt to end his life. This is not an impersonal matter to be ignored. Represented is an individual's personal choice and it should not be separated from the individual as a mere symptom. Whether or not a therapist intervenes, the individual will engage in an ongoing process of anticipating his own future. He will construe the events of his past, his suicidal behavior, and will take up a posture from which to merge himself with his future. He will develop an adjustment. It is the nature of this adjustment, especially as it relates to his future, that can be affected by and is the target of therapy.

The second point of orientation for the therapist to consider is that when employing the diagnostic construct determinacy versus chaos, its use is to describe the progression an individual makes toward the suicidal crisis as well as the movement that takes him farther away from the crisis. As such, it describes the channel or conduit along which an individual moves, both toward and away from the crisis. Described, as well, are the internal experiences of the individual at given points nearer or farther from the crisis.

The final point offered to orient the therapist is that the nearer in time to the crisis that therapy is initiated—either pre or post—crucial issues of core construction are involved, that is, those constructs by which "the client maintains his identity and existence" (Kelly, 1955, p. 482). Likewise, the farther away in time from the crisis—either pre- or post-—that therapy is initiated, the more likely that problems of a peripheral nature will be encountered. This distance in time also changes the nature of the problem and the therapeutic intervention.

Because core constructs are constructions of self, they require the presence of others for validation and development. The closer in time after a suicidal crisis that the therapist enters the client's picture, the more influential he or she becomes in structuring the activities of self-definition, hypothesis building, and constructive alternativism. Despite the popular belief that one can only intervene after the individual "stabilizes" (whatever this means) we believe with Kelly (1961) that intervention is most effective when the therapist is involved with the stabilization process.

The client is very likely experiencing anxiety, fear, threat, and guilt. Self-destruction is engaged in to produce radical change. With survival, new evidence regarding the self now confronts the individual. Moreover, the individual has been projected into a new and novel context and his position in this new situation is uncertain. His efforts to position himself within the environment involve experiences of anxiety and threat. Furthermore, to the extent that his suicidal actions have disturbed his core role relationships, guilt is personally experienced. Guilt will certainly occur if both significant others and the individual interpret the suicide behavior as symbolizing the betrayal of the basic fabric that has linked them to one another. If this interpretation occurs, he becomes a pariah, and his position is precarious. Even this knotty situation, if left to resolve itself, may lead the client toward a position of adjustment. He may make his adjustment by casting about and discovering the roles provided by his culture for outcasts. He may then quickly move from an outcast position to a follower. For example, he may be reminded that suicide is stupid, wrong, or cowardly and enact a role that stresses self-deprecation, penitance, or weakness. If this enactment brings him into contact with others and produces role relationships that allow for mutual understanding and negotiation, there is nothing inherently wrong in this. The adoption of a culturally cast role becomes dangerous when it excludes further psychosocial experimentation, leads to preemptive constriction, and stultifies attempts at alternative reconstruction of one's system.

It is our belief that if alternative reconstruction of the issues surrounding the suicidal act does not occur, the client may well attempt suicide again. This is not an infrequent clinical observation. Reconstruction is often avoided because it involves coming face to face with the very experience from which he is trying to protect himself, that is, anxiety, threat, and guilt. The reconstructive life involves the task of creating an environment for personal growth with role relationships that insure and enhance self-growth. This can truly be a frightening experience. It implies that the individual takes personal responsibility, risks personal alienation, or provokes possible misunderstanding. Most important, it demands that he take charge of his past, present, and future—his spirit and life.

We have labeled the initial phase of therapy, in which the client is assisted in beginning the process of reconstruing the suicidal event, as *encoding*. To transfer from one system of communication (behavior) to another (words), the task of the therapist during encoding is to aid the individual in assessing what he was up to when he engaged in the attempt. The client is encouraged to do some thinking about his recent attempt and to put these thoughts into words. This cannot be a long, drawn-out affair, going on for several sessions. If the therapist dwells too long on past events, for example, he may be surprised to find the client solving the issue by preemptively assuming some role as has already been described. To the degree that the client casts himself in a "sick" or "helpless" role, he is unable to view himself as capable of influencing control or change. It is suggested that the therapist provide the client with the psychological role of "self-expert." By assuming this stance, he or she is not only respected for his unique status but also is kept engaged within the realm of core self-constructions. The client is offered an opportunity to experience his self-perceptions, and to consider them in cooperation with the therapist. To the extent that he engages in self-definition and its expansion, he or she will move inexorably but not precipitiously toward important role changes. At this stage, the therapist must seek to avoid hasty or preemptive self-definition by the client. The expert role aids in preventing such preemption by its very superordinate nature and position within a construct hierarchy.

Another feature of therapy at the encoding stage is the development of the proposition that suicidal behavior is multidetermined. When the client and the therapist are engaged in an analysis of why suicidal behavior occurs, the therapist may make a statement such as, "Suicide attempts are not uncommon occurrences if one considers it as an alternative that everyone has thought about, simply by virtue of having the word in their vocabulary." To avoid personal stress, such a discussion should be done at a relatively abstract level. The client is exposed to such notions as suicidal behavior as a means of control, a means of communicating, and a way of influencing the direction of one's life. It should also be stressed to the client that the suicidal event can be viewed as the individual's own sense of awareness of the need for transition. By keeping the level of dialogue fairly abstract, the client is given room and time to consider the ramifications of these notions as he or she applies them to her- or himself. The client is also provided with latitude to fit implied details and concrete issues into his or her own interpretation of his or her circumstance.

This phase of therapy is designed to allow the issue of suicide and the individual's suicide attempt to be lifted out of the personal context of the client and suspended in the space of therapy as a topic which can be talked about and discussed. During the process of therapy, the event itself can be and will be encoded within the client's construct system. The client's attempt will ideally be viewed as an event that had a personal meaning in the past but not as an event that has to be repeated. The client may come to see the attempt of suicide metaphorically as an action that brings the curtain down between acts of a play, rather than necessarily bringing down the final curtain. By the encoding procedure, the client is assisted in anchoring the suicidal experience. As in a tapestry, the client interweaves aspects of the experience, namely, the suicide and its effect on him- or herself and others. Finally, if the client is successful he or she orients toward a future that incorporates this information, enabling the client to choose life without dreading chaos or fatalism as being a necessary condition.

Although we have stressed the necessity of the encoding procedure to prevent future suicide attempts, and although we have pointed out the timeliness of such activity, it must be recognized that there are exceptions in which the encoding procedure must be delayed. In the case of either diagnostic extreme—for example, a severely depressed or an acutely psychotic individual—encoding must follow initial therapeutic efforts to engage the individual in structuring his or her experience or to assist the client in understanding the immediate situation in which he or she finds her- or himself. In either case, the therapist can be assured that encoding activities will eventually occur, even without therapeutic assistance, as soon as the individual begins to consider his or her context.

As we move further away, in time, from the actual suicidal experience, other therapeutic techniques can be entertained. We have found it useful to consider these techniques relative to the chaos–determinism construct.

For the person experiencing chaos, therapy centers on issues of getting the client to become more involved with the elements of his or her environment. Constriction may be necessary in order to focus on only a small section of his or her field, but the ultimate aid is to dilate and find meaning in the larger environment. A reliance on introspection and loosening techniques is avoided in the earlier stages. The focus instead might be on how to collect and use information from others and arrive at a consensus about an issue. Later in time, problem-solving strategies of a more structured nature may be employed.

For the fatalistically determined individual, the goal of therapy is to expand the construction system as a whole, and to admit new constructions that allow personal movement and control. This individual is encouraged to introspect for the purpose of loosening his or her rigid system. Eventually the gestalt techniques described by Daniels and Horowtiz (1976) designed to expand nuances of the self can be used or McFall's (1965) mystical monitor. In both, the familiar patterns of one's field are treated in a metaphorical fashion.

For both types of individuals, appropriate psychosocial experimentation is an important treatment strategy, although in one case the aim is to open up the field for exploration and in the other, to expand the individual's personal constructions. How the therapist goes about applying loosening and tightening procedures will not be covered here; the reader is referred to Kelly's and Bannister's works for further illumination.

The therapeutic issues and strategies we describe serve not only to engage the client in encoding his or her suicidal behavior but to encourage the client to make positive use of the therapist or of the hospital. The therapist acts to prevent a situation from developing in which the client views the effect of his or her hospitalization or treatment negatively. Such a judgment, by the time of discharge, has negative implications for continued suicidal risk. By initiating these therapeutic procedures, derived from an appreciation of personal construct psychology, we feel that the clinician can have maximum impact in directing a positive treatment outcome.

Perhaps it is wise in closing, to consider Kelly's view about the goals of psychotherapeutic treatment. We previously discuss the process of initiating treatment toward the goal of restoring the client to life's arena. As Kelly has said,

> The client needs enough structure to lay his wages, channel his aggressive efforts, and accept his losses. He needs to have a methodology for dealing with the world piecemeal instead of in catastrophic terms. He needs role relationships so he can sift out social outcomes and maintain himself as a distinct individual, related to but distinguishable from other persons. (1961, p. 277)

To accomplish these things, we use PCP as a theoretical base to develop a set of procedures for use in the initial dealings with suicidal persons. What was accomplished in a broader sense, however, goes far beyond the issues of immediately reducing suicidal risk. The procedures launch the person forward with a strategy for living his life. The ultimate objective of therapy then, as Kelly (1955) has said, is not to be viewed as "a terminal state of well-being but as a course of action to be embarked upon and continuously replotted throughout one's life." (p. 567)

In the course of preparing this chapter, we come to a remarkable conclusion, that through the treatment of suicidal individuals within the framework of personal construct psychology, one is engaging not in a morbid study of death but in a vibrant study of life itself.

References

Bannister, D. (1970). Science through a Looking Glass. *In* "Perspectives in Personal Construct Theory" (D. Bannister, ed.), Academic Press, New York and London, pp. 47–61.

Bannister, D. (1977). The Logic of Passion. *In* "New Perspectives in Personal Construct Theory" (D. Bannister, ed.), Academic Press, New York and London, pp. 21–37.

Bannister, D. and Fransella, F. (1982). "Inquiring Man", Krieger, Malabar, Florida.

Daniels, V. and Horowitz, L. J. (1976). "Being and Caring", San Franscisco Book Co., San Franscisco, California.

Durkheim, E. (1951). "Suicide" (J. A. Spaulding and G. Simpson, trans.), The Free Press, Glencoe, Illinois. (Original work published 1897)

Farberow, .(1975). Personal communication.

Freud, S. (1933). "New Introductory Lectures in Psychoanalysis" (J. Strachey, trans. and ed.), Norton, New York.

Hillman, J. (1976). "Suicide and the Soul", Spring, Zurich.

Kelly, G. A. (1955). "The Psychology of Personal Constructs", Vols. I and II, Norton, New York.

Kelly, G. A. (1961). Suicide: The Personal Construct Point of View. *In* "The Cry for Help" (N. L. Farberow and E. S. Schneidman, eds.), McGraw Hill, New York, pp. 255–280.

Kelly, G. A. (1970). A Brief Introduction to Personal Construct Theory. *In* "Perspectives in Personal Construct Theory" (D. Bannister, ed.), Academic Press, New York, pp. 1–29.

Kelly, G. A. (1977). The Psychology of the Unknown. *In* "New Perspectives in Personal Construct Psychology" (D. Bannister, ed.), Academic Press, New York, pp. 1–19.

Litman, R. E. and Tabachnick, N. A. (1968). Psychoanalytic Theories of Suicide. *In* "Suicidal Behavior" (H. L. Resnick, ed.), Little, Brown and Company, Boston, pp. 73–81.

Menninger, K. (1963). "The Vital Balance", Viking Press, New York.

McFall, R. M. (1982). Mystical Monitor. *In* "Inquiring Man" (D. Bannister and F. Fransella, eds.), Krieger, Malabar, Florida, pp. 184–186.

Miller, D. and Goleman, D. (1970). Predicting Post-Release Risk among Hospitalized Suicide Attemptors. *In* "Omega", Baywood Publishing Co., Inc., Farmingdale, N.Y., pp. 71–84.

Mischel, W. (1968). "Personality and Assessment", Wiley, New York.

Moskop, J. (1979). The Ethics of Suicide. *In* "Suicide Theory and Clinical Aspects" (L. Hankoff and B. Einsidler, eds.), PSG, Littleton, Massachusetts, pp. 49–57.

Neuringer, C. (1974) "Psychological Assessment of Suicidal Risk", Thomas, Springfield, Illinois.

Shneidman, E. S. (1979). Overview: Personality, Motivation and Behavior Theories. *In* "Suicide Theory and Clinical Aspects" (L. Hankoff and B. Einsidler, eds.), PSG, Littleton, Massachusetts, pp. 143–163.

Skinner, B. F. (1953). "Science and Human Behavior", MacMillan, New York and London.

UNIVERSITY OF SLURRY

B.Sc. Honours in Human Sciences

Part I Examination

PSYCHOLOGY OPTION: CONTEMPORARY ISSUES IN PSYCHOLOGY

0930 hrs.–1230 hrs. Wednesday, 31st June, 1984

MAJOR *and* JOINT *students answer* TWO *questions in 1½ hours.*

MINOR *students answer* FOUR *questions in 3 hours.*

Answer at least ONE *question from each section.*

Section A

1. How far can the central themes of Belsey's *Critical Practice* be transcribed into the framework of personal construct theory?
2. "... neither of these differences between the novelist and the scientist is very fundamental" (Kelly, 1964). Which differences; and why not? What is Kelly's psychology of "make-believe"?
3. Independently of its accuracy, evaluate the usefulness of Sechrest's "sociological" approach to personal constructs (sic) psychology. Contrast it with the main findings of Neimeyer's research.
4. How satisfactory is Moss's interpretation of *Hamlet* in terms of roles and constructs? Does personal construct theory appear to offer a fruitful basis for analysing the nature and origins of Shakespeare's "obsession"?
5. "Don Bannister's novels should *not* be interpreted in terms of personal construct theory". Indicate arguments from both literary and psychological theory for and against this proposition.
6. Briefly re-write "Epilogue: Don Juan (1960)" in terms of what you understand of Stringer (1985).

see next page

12

You Decide What Your Title Is To Be and [Read] Write to That Title†

Peter Stringer

The section which follows lies under erasure. It remains only as an archae-
ological trace of successive attempts to respond actively to the elusive title(s) of
this volume. At the last hour you are abandoned to write your own reflections on
Issues and *Approaches*.

Perspective: "The science of sight", "the art of delineating solid objects upon
a plane surface", "the proportion in which parts of a subject are viewed by the
mind", "a vista", "close inspection". Perhaps *this* perspective is "a picture or
figure constructed so as to produce some fantastic effect". Is it, though, a
perspective *in* personal construct theory, rather than *on, from, by, beyond?*

"One bit of news . . . is that we have decided to christen the book FURTHER
PERSPECTIVES IN PERSONAL CONSTRUCT THEORY [in place of *Perspectives in Personal Construct Theory*, volume 3]. On late reflection it seemed
odd to produce a book number 3 when initially there had never been numbers 1
and 2".

Yet it *would* have been interesting to have had a volume III without I and II.
The contradiction might have encouraged you to reverse normal expectations and
see this book as influencing the one of 14 years ago. Sequence, which produces a
linear constraint on reading, would have been denied. Volume 3 would have
owed no allegiance. You could have seen that *Perspectives* are a net, not a
sequence.

At least one does not have to search for a *new* perspective again. But a
"further perspective"? Clearly "close inspection" is no longer appropriate. The
editor is dissatisfied with our myopia to date. We are now to focus on the middle
distance. Should we expect in 1991 the *Farthest Horizons of Personal Construct
Theory?*

A 'newer perspective' would be somewhat easier to find. Should this volume
perhaps have been called *Newest Perspectives in Personal Construct Theory?* In

†This footnote nestles at the feet of the chapter. You are invited to respect its humility and take the
body first.

ISSUES AND APPROACHES
IN PERSONAL CONSTRUCT THEORY

211

that way we would have had the possibility of an endless series which gave no
titling problems. (The Dutch cleverly refer to contemporary history as *nieuwste
geschiedenis.*)

* * *

". . . the goal of literary work (of literature as work) is to make the reader no
longer a consumer, but a producer of the text".

(Hence the 'title' of this chapter.) That work does not lie in producing the text
as a writer, but in assembling potentialities. One way to liberate the reader, to
give the reader back her power and responsibility, is to stop trying to produce the
ultimate, inevitable, ordered persuasion.

The work in psychology is assembling psychological knowledge (theories,
concepts, methods; not 'facts') to help Everyman produce her own psychological
understanding and a more informed practice.

What is a 'text' in psychology, and who its reader? Not only a 'text'-book.
Data can be considered as 'text'. Pride in experimental design often gives them
the aura of poetry. Personal construct psychology is unusual in sometimes admit-
ting the subject to the data as a reader. Psychological 'literature', despite the
term, is generally destined for psychologists.

The focus of recent, productive literary theory on texts and readers has a
lesson for personal construct psychology. It needs to pay more attention to data
other than the grid or the clinical interview: conversations, speeches, newspaper
articles, novels, television plays. The purpose is not ethnographic; but to release
the implied subject(s).

*

> Once the Author is removed, the claim to decipher a text becomes quite futile. To give
> a text an Author is to impose a limit on that text, to furnish it with a final signified, to
> close the writing. . . . In the multiplicity of writing, everything is to be *disentangled,*
> nothing *deciphered;* the structure can be followed, "run" (like the threads of a stocking)
> at every point and at every level, but there is nothing beneath. . . . literature, (it would
> be better from now on to say *writing*), by refusing to assign a "secret", an ultimate
> meaning, to the text (and to the world as text), liberates what may be called an anti-
> theological activity, an activity that is truly revolutionary since to refuse to fix meaning
> is, in the end, to refuse God and his hypostases—reason, science, law.

The death of the Author frees us from authority; the text and the reader are
liberated. There is no longer a presence behind the text claiming responsibility
for its ultimate meaning, to whom we are answerable for our interpretations.

The Author produces texts which are realist, naturalising, persuasive. They
push unswervingly and relentlessly to an ordered conclusion, fulfilling the Author's intention, skillfully uncovering a truth which was previously hidden. In
the authorless text, no single truth-bearing message is privileged; it contains no

core-nugget of knowledge to be procured and banked. The authorless text is writable by the reader as she identifies the plurality of its meanings, new intelligibilities.

Kelly worked hard to suppress himself as an Author. Despite his good intentions, scholars labour to pin the psychology of personal constructs back to his biography, his bookshelf, his graduate seminars. A psychology appeared in 1955 in which authority was placed squarely in the hands of non-psychologists. Ask them what they mean, not what Kelly meant.

Constructive alternativism is a cunning in-built device of personal construct psychology to prevent its own texts being closed in a final definition. Seen reflexively, it turns reading into writing. Man-the-scientist cannot help but (re-)write *The Psychology of Personal Constructs* as she seeks to make sense of Man's attempts to make sense of the world.

Another Author is removed by personal construct psychology, the subject as Author, of her actions and herself. The Author no longer has privileged access to the texts which her construings constitute. The Author is no longer the constructor and seer of the mysterious self, with the authority to claim special powers for deciphering that self. At the same time tyrannical demands that another devote inordinate efforts, special insight, trained skills to decipher the self on the Author's behalf, to boost her self-esteem, are frustrated. The self in personal construct psychology is a text open to multiple readings. It takes its existence from the varied construings of others. Subjectivity is cast in language, which links it indefinitely to others.

* * *

It is difficult just to produce a text, to escape being an Author. A review of Bannister's *Burning Leaves* begins: "It isn't often that a prominent psychologist writes a psychological novel." Three novels in 4 years is not infrequent. Perhaps the other two were not psychological. They did not deal explicitly with madness. Most of the literature produced by prominent psychologists refuses to be categorised as 'novels'. I consistently fail to persuade students to read psychology as comical, historical, fantastic, tragic, or horrific. What is a 'non-psychological' novel?

Was *Burning Leaves* produced by a psychologist? Originally it made no such claims in its ephemeral margin, the dust jacket: "*The Author* Don Bannister lives in Yorkshire. He is the author of two other novels *Sam Chard* and *Long Day at Shiloh*". Why should that novel be chained to the editor of the book you are reading now? Admittedly he lets it be known here that he works in (or lives in ? or camps in? or uses as 'poste restante'?) a hospital, which may be a bin. But Yorkshire is of considerable size, and not only psychologists have psychological insight. The up-market paperback edition of *Burning Leaves* will not let the author alone, however. It insists on a full biographical sketch, and conceals the important message that *all* that was important originally for the author of the novel was that he lived in Yorkshire and this was number three. Not only must the Author die, but also all devices (blurbs, prefaces, reviews) which work to close our reading.

It is not often that an established novelist edits a psychological monograph.

Once the Author is pinned down, reading becomes difficult and quickly reveals its own contradictions: "Curiously, the protagonist's character is depicted primarily in behavioural terms. . . . extremely explicit and also curiously behavioural descriptions of several varieties of human coitus". Well, at least they are human! But what else would you expect from a prominent psychologist than 'behaviour'? It only becomes curious if you mistake him for a personal construct psychologist, who is assumed to have renounced the world of mere behaviour.

"Though the novel falls short of the historical resonance of Mann or Bellow, or of the allegorical pretensions of Sartre. . . ." Indeed it does, and of much else beside. Even so was Kelly rebuked for falling short of Merleau-Ponty, Husserl, Nietzsche, Sartre, and many others. One Author is banged about the head with Another, while the text fades away.

"For refraining from such heavy-handed editorializing, Bannister is to be congratulated". Has the reviewer in this concluding sentence replaced the Author by an Editor who assembles fragments of pre-existing texts? Unfortunately not. What Bannister refrains from in fact is making *authorial* pronouncements on the status of his hero's mentality. The reviewer cannot forget his 'alter ego' in the world of edited monographs. What he refrains from is commenting on "the protagonist's problematical consciousness of the traps of daily existence in post-secular society [which] comes jolly close to a statement of the relativity of madness". The novel does indeed grapple head-on, and in a far from jolly fashion, with the relativity of madness. Yet the reviewer, although pinning the Author down for a psychologist, will not face up to that. If a Psychologist writes a Novel, even if he is not as good as Mann & Co., at least he has to engage in the full Literary toil, with problematical consciousness in a post-secular society.

*

Not only the Author, but also the Editor, determines a review of *Perspectives in Personal Construct Theory*. It is their insistence on being present which leads the reviewer to certain contradictions. For us, their presence reveals presuppositions upon which he constructed his reading.

Perspectives has an editor, who is assumed like the Author to have had intentions, objectives. The work of a reviewer, as critic, seems to confer authority on these aims. He can see beneath the preface's careful refusal to state objectives, and has the 'critical insight' to detect objectives which are entirely absent from the preface, namely: "The book *is* . . . designed to demonstrate the relevance and viability of personal construct theory. The editor *believes* that the book comes to grips with basic issues in the field of psychology and psychiatry. Further, the editor *sees* the book as a way of encouraging much needed attention to an approach . . .'' (my emphases). This is *not* what the preface claims. A further contradiction arises in the review's final paragraph. In order for judgments on the value of the book to be made, quite new objectives are implied. Editorial goals are (re-)constructed in the reviewer's reading, in forms which are appropriate to the goals of the review itself. The difficult work of communicating a reading and an evaluation of the book in a few words is achieved with the reviewer's confidence that readers will share the presuppositions which he lays down about the roles of editor and critic.

An editor is not enough for the review. Behind an edited text there has to be an Ultimate Author; in this case, Kelly. The reviewer simultaneously introduces the possibility and defends himself against it, by suspecting a personality cult at work. The review is entitled "In praise of Kelly?". It claims that "here we have a book about George Kelly and construct theory", despite the fact that in answer to its own question "what does this collection of essays tell us about George Kelly and personal construct theory?", it concludes "not much"; and despite a failure to make any reference to the one essay in *Perspectives* which explicitly entitles itself an "appreciation" of Kelly the man. The 'praise' theme is loosely substantiated: "Some chapters . . . are wordy paeans to Kelly", "Salmon has nothing but praise for Kelly", and "Kelly is applauded". But the defensive rhetoric of the title's question is not intended to yield an answer.

The review may or may not be justified in implying the personality cult. What is significant is that it reproduces (or constructs) the cult, by itself treating the man as more important than the theory. The defensiveness is against its own unacknowledged reproduction of what it is criticising. Although the review (re-)reads the book's preface for evidence of intentions, it contradicts, as we have seen, the explicit claim there that *Perspectives* is about personal construct theory rather than about Kelly. The name 'Kelly' is used 27 times in the course of 1200 or so words—while in the preface it is mentioned twice in less than half the space. On seven occasions there are references to 'Kelly's theory/own work', where one might have found 'personal construct theory'. Once we even have "Kelly's personal construct theory". These unremarkable features of the way in which the review text is assembled are traces of the power which some assumptions about writing can exercise, and the influence which they can have upon reading.

* * *

A review, from the same source, of *New Perspectives in Personal Construct Theory,* is equally interesting for the light which it throws upon reading. A 'normal' view of scholarly, scientific reading would assume a detailed and objective attention to the text and an evaluation of its worth in relation to widely shared criteria of theoretical and empirical significance. This review, however, illustrates a quite different kind of interpretative practice, which in this case coexists with the more formal reading. The basis of the alternative construction lies in elements of a particular view of how science proceeds, and in a somewhat 'sociological' attention to its subject matter.

The central section of the review identifies two major controversies in personal construct psychology—the role of emotions, and the derivation of behaviour from constructs—and suggests that a "careful study" of *New Perspectives* will help to resolve them. Indications are given of what such a study might reveal. The conclusion that the book is a worthwhile "help in resolving these two major lacunae in our understanding of Kelly's theory" is consistent in form with a 'normal' view of scientific reading. Around this central section is wrapped the rest of the review, of approximately the same length. It deals with quite different points. The disjointedness of the text makes it particularly easy to identify the mechanisms at work in the more informal reading of the book.

It is a troubled reading. In the first sentence, Kelly's work is referred to as "rather stunning". Mitigations accumulate: "puzzling, to say the least", "puzzles or controversies", "perhaps (and most curiously)", "truly curious", "apparently . . . work seriously and productively", "mere disciples", "only the origin", "appear to be involved", "modest . . . trials". The form of these phrases insinuates an aura of doubt around personal construct theory. We can unravel four threads of unease which together make up the alternative interpretation of *New Perspectives*.

First, there is "the appeal of Kelly to English psychologists". What is noteworthy for this reading is not that Americans have ignored personal construct theory, but that a small set of psychologists from the United Kingdom should have paid it attention: "Perhaps (and most curiously) in England" there are disciples, who "apparently continue to work seriously and productively". The striking use of 'perhaps' and 'apparently' later receives an implicit gloss in the "truly curious" observation that none of the English proponents was Kelly's student.

The lack of students is a second cause for concern. What was missing in the United States was "a major department or training program known as a hotbed of personal construct theory . . . (a) band of ardent and proselytizing disciples". Not a minor department, mark; is has to be *known* as a *hotbed*.

The consequence was that Kelly's theory has remained incomplete. Kelly "left his theory untried in many ways . . . in the process of development and in the early phases of testing"; "his theory remained incomplete . . . was never widely engaged and challenged"; there are "major lacunae in our understanding". This was specifically because Kelly did not provide the true succession through his students: "Trials of personal construct theory . . . would probably have been much more frequent had Kelly survived and taught for a normal span''.

The argument ends with claims that the English proponents have aggravated the theory's incompleteness. They are a ''most tightly knit group''. Their conspiracy is to refuse to provide ''evidence . . . of any systematic testing of Kelly's theory or its implications''; they do not recognise ''the need to try the theory in the crucible of good science''. The reader feels ''disappointment, but not surprise'' about the virtual absence of empirical data, or at least data obtained in ''methodologically rigorous ways'', in *New Perspectives,* and sadness at the absence of the fiery crucible.

At face-value this reader's remarks might be treated as unproblematic sociological observation, commented on in the light of a received ideology of good scientific practice. However, a number of underlying contradictions reveal the strains under which the reading was constructed.

The role of students in good scientific practice is so important that, six lines after denying that any English proponent of Kelly's views was his student, the review claims that ''Bannister . . . did study with Kelly in the United States [i.e., not in England!] for a period of time''. It does so despite an explicit statement at the head of the review that Bannister had actually been Visiting Professor at Ohio State University (where Kelly then was). That was the limit of their contact in the United States. (While I am willing to treat any professor as a student, this appears to be a distinctly minority view!) The review does more or less recognise (''perhaps'') a band of disciples in the English proponents, but dubs them ''neo-Kellians'' and only allows them to be ''apparently'' working with serious and productive intent. True succession has to be denied, partly because they are English (the word is used four times in three successive sentences) and were not in direct contact with the master; but most importantly because they were ''inattentive to the advantages of informed interplay between empirical data and theory'' which a well-trained student would have used to test and develop the theory. (That inattention and the refusal to test the theory and its implications we find documented in such reviews as *A Manual for Repertory Grid Technique* or *Personal Construct Theory: Concepts and Applications.*)

But this line of argument is in turn negated by the review at several points. It indicates obliquely that Kelly lived to the age of 62, which is surely time enough to have exerted influence as a teacher. It recognises that ''Kelly himself never seemed to be very much impressed by data obtained through conventional research'', and the book is judged to be most suitable for fairly serious students of the theory, because of the familiarity with the work which is assumed. These points serve to contradict the dominant and somewhat complex claim that Kelly had no successors, apart from an alien and unsanctioned group of unrigorous and unsystematic scientists.

This reading (review) of *New Perspectives* does not have to be seen as mistaken or hostile, in error or misleading. It serves as an example of the difficulty of reading, and of the work necessary to construct a reading. It is not suggested that similar problems do not exist in the central, more formal section of the review. Very often formal and informal readings will be more closely interwoven than in the present example. Their fracture in this instance makes it a very convenient medium for drawing attention to and unravelling the possible alternative level of interpretation which more usually lies concealed in scientific commentaries and reviews.

* * *

Here are two different kinds of text, familiar but usually suppressed. First, the book proposal to a publisher, eventually to become the blurb. Like a preface, the blurb conspires to turn the reader into a consumer. And second, scientist's talk, which non-reflexively we have avoided taking seriously.

To defeat semantics, this trailer does not come last; else you may be too busy running for the next chapter to read it. The trailer draws, in this case, your attention to a film that has not yet been made, to a text that you may never have the opportunity to write. (A *Journal of Half-Baked Ideas* would have been a good institutionalised source of pre(-)texts like this one.)

*

> This volume extends the investigation of social scientific discourse by offering a number of analyses of semi-formal discussions which occurred in the course of a three-day workshop attended by twelve academic and clinical psychologists. The workshop discussed a range of theoretical issues in personal construct psychology. The present analyses are based on sections of a verbatim transcript of the discussions. Transcript selections are published in the book's appendix. . . .
>
> This volume brings together two fields: it contains not only discourse analytic treatments, from the standpoint of the social study of science; but also reflexive accounts of the same discussions in terms of personal construct theory itself. The reflexive nature of personal construct psychology makes it a suitable vehicle for carrying an analysis which contains three perspectives: that of the social study of science, of 'members' of a particular scientific group, and of 'critics' of the group. . . .
>
> Formerly, sociologists would look at broad categories of scientific activity (e.g., psychology, or social psychology). The preferred emphasis now is on sub-fields, networks of scientists, or particular limited controversies. This is precisely the emphasis which is represented in this volume: controversy over the status of the sub-field of personal construct psychology, as exemplified in talk between an informal but relatively well-established network of psychologists. The restriction in the topic of the talk which is analysed will make it possible for sociologists of science to make comparisons with other restricted and 'controversial' groups whom they have been studying for several years (biochemists working on proton transfer across cell walls, nineteenth century geologists studying the origin of the Earth).
>
> The study of sub-fields is advanced in this book by presenting an analysis from the three perspectives referred to above, including those of members and critics, participants

and non-participants. Each perspective has a specific and deliberate methodological contribution. The sociologists have elaborated their own methods within the sub-discipline of social studies of science, in many papers published by them in refereed journals and elsewhere. Personal construct psychology can provide its own method for analysis, being reflexive—and is for that reason perhaps uniquely interesting as a sub-field of psychology to choose for this study. The critics' perspective is one which comes from the normal practice of social psychological critique. It, too, is interesting in its own right, because the concept of 'normal practice' is so problematic. The book's conclusion contains a commentary on the three perspectives. It draws attention to some of the different readings produced by the contributors and suggests further, alternative readings.

In summary, this volume has four principal components:

(i)   a record of some informal social scientific discourse;

(ii)   examples of and commentary on three types of analysis which may be done on such records;

(iii) original material, of a kind hitherto unrecorded, contributing to the development of personal construct psychology;

(iv) critical comment on this material from the standpoints both of the social study of science and of personal construct psychology.

*

The workshop texts have already been taken seriously, by two potential contributors to the aforementioned project.

(1) The transcripts . . . make fascinating reading. Thinking this might be because I was a participant, I tried them out on a small group of four people with whom I meet up periodically. They were not at the workshop but are very knowledgable about personal construct theory. We each took on specific characters and enacted the transcriptions. Everyone became totally engrossed in the debates and it all came to life.

(2) A second kind of reading appeared when personal construct psychologists discussed a transcript of a previous personal construct workshop. Two extracts . . . were pre-circulated to participants at a second workshop who were asked to describe and evaluate its contents. This latter discussion was itself transcribed and forms a second set of analytic materials. In both these cases we can see how this group of scientists construct their versions of others' discourse.

*

Two random fragments of workshop discussion.

Anneke: Yes, I think mine was how to get out of the playpen. Sort of (inaudible) . . .

Fred: Can I ask a rather different kind of question? Um, which relates to development, but at a rather more abstract level, which is: what is it about personal construct psychology that has made people say, persuaded people, that it doesn't have anything to do with development?

Frances: Sorry, who is it persuading?

Fred: Well it . .

Peter Stringer

Frances: I haven't heard that said.

Fred: Well you see it repeated over and over again (Noddy: Umm.) in . . .

Abel: I think they are getting the angle wrong though. They are saying that nothing's been done, they are not saying nothing can be done.

Frances: That's right, that's right.

Fred: Yes . . .

Frances: Kelly never discussed it (inaudible).

Abel: Kelly never discussed it but he never said he *couldn't* or that it couldn't be done.

Frances: Not at least (inaudible).

Tracey: Some people do interpret it that way. That if, if Kelly didn't devote a section (Frances (laughs): I see) of his writings to this then it is irrelevant (laughs) to the theory.

Bob: Is that all the textbooks that are saying that then?

Abel: That's where I have got it from.

*

Noddy: The group has a kind of understanding that you are going to have to *kill* the experiment if you opt out because even if you opt out somehow you have done something that is part of the experiment, you know, that is you have said something about yourself. You know it is kind of like the question of freedoms and constrictions.
(pause)

Bob: When you say that the group has an understanding I am not sure that, he was saying that the reason he didn't want to do it was for purely personal reasons, he didn't want to tighten. In other words a personal construct theory analysis of why you didn't do it. I would say that we have to say more than that we have to look at the whole role structure of the group, the way it is beginning to develop and the fact that that was a piece of process that went on which was bidding for leadership of the group and saying "I am going to structure the next half hour".

Frances: But I don't like being rejected like that.
(Noddy: We don't like . . . Annie (laughs)) And I have a personal . . .

Annie: And I don't like role theory. (some laughter)

Bob: Yes, well I don't want to use the word "role" but that was the one . . .
(several people talk at once)

Tracey: I feel like a crab and I don't want to be a crustacean. (Laughter)

Noddy: You know in a way, is part of what we are talking about this notion of an ideal Kelly group, what would it be like? One of the things must be that whether you are in the group at a given point or not was entirely optional. That is that group members are, that is one understanding between some groups, like committees or encounter groups for instance, is that all members are present all the time,

(Annie: Yes, um)

Noddy: I don't mean just physically present but are *psychologically* present. Would a construct theory group, in fact have a kind of understanding or common constructs that there is no reason why all members should be psychologically present all the time, so . . . ?

Tracey: We are all free to construe the situation however we choose.[1]

* * *

"Kelly's theory was *expressly* cognitive . . .".

"Kelly . . . devised the Role Repertoire Test".

"Perhaps you *aren't* cut out, then, to be a cognitive theorist. But you can still use the insights of the Kellys and the Hebbs, you know. You *don't* have to buy into the whole thing—but understand it, sort through it, extract *what's* useful to you. Every story has its own truth".

*

Textbooks are unconcealed assemblages of anterior texts, channels by which students can economically approach those other texts. They are a reading of texts, but demonstrate despite themselves the inevitability of the re-writing which reading evokes. The absence of the "faithful translation", which perhaps students expect, is quite clear in the textbook treatment of personal construct theory. One again suspects Kelly of deliberately having removed the firing-pin before he handed over his grenade.

There are no grounds for indignation at misinterpretation; rewriting is necessarily at stake. For example, the frequent and unfortunate typification of Kelly's work as a cognitive theory takes extreme forms in personality textbooks. But it can be understood as a response to the acute problem of simplifying, ordering, and making memorable a rich complexity of theories for non-psychology majors who find this an attractive subsidiary subject. At the same time it creates its own internal problems.

*

A not atypical and by no means exhaustive personality textbook separately categorises each of eight theorists as an exemplar of one of eight approaches (psychoanalytic, psychosocial, and so on) and compares them in terms of eight

---

[1]*Cast, in order of appearance:* Anneke—Marica Rytovaara; Fred—Peter Stringer; Frances—Fay Fransella; Abel—Nigel Beail; Tracey—Spence McWilliams; Bob—Harry Procter; Noddy—Don Bannister; Annie—Laurie Thomas.

bipolar "basic assumptions" or "issues" (e.g. freedom–determinism, holism–elementalism, proactivity–reactivity). In the light of recent developments in other areas of psychology the wish to be able to fill a 'cognitive' category is understandable. To label Kelly as "the first personologist to emphasise the cognitive or knowing aspects of human existence as the dominant feature of personality" achieves this goal. Granted, it allows a commentary on constructive alternativism, Man-the-scientist, and reflexivity which produces few surprises. But the overriding attempt to differentiate Kelly exclusively and quintessentially on the chosen "issues" leads to the apparent contradiction of identifying Kelly with very strong forms of two of them, rationality and subjectivity. The strains imposed by this classificatory approach to personality theory are revealed in the lame and self-defeating penultimate sentence on Kelly: "Kelly's personal construct theory is applicable to behavioral domains far beyond that traditionally defined as cognitive".

*

Explicit and familiar criticisms of personal construct theory can also be seen as the product of particular pedagogic devices. Another textbook which adopts the categorising approach—using Rogers and Kelly to exemplify phenomenological strategies, alongside the psychoanalytic, dispositional, and behavioral—makes a particular play of characterising theories in terms of their "liabilities". Those attributed to construct theory include its inattention to emotions and its failure to explain development; it is simplistic, especially in the shadowy data of a rep test—if not 'romantically naïve'; there is an undue emphasis on self-report and linguistic data; and it tends toward description rather than explanation (especially, it seems, in the fundamental postulate!).

What is interesting in this case is not that these liabilities may be received critique or based on a superficial and unwarranted reading of the theory, but rather the way in which the authors simultaneously justify excessive criticism and discount their responsibility for it in the interest of a superordinate goal.

> In these liabilities chapters we have adopted the stance of presenting arguments that a harsh critic would make, in order to highlight the weaknesses of each strategy, and thus to complement the positive light in which it was originally presented. The liabilities chapters are not intended to be complete critiques or even-handed evaluations of the strategies; rather they are presented to illustrate the limitations and problems each strategy faces when it is applied to the full scope of personality. We believe that this approach will afford readers an opportunity to evaluate the merits and limitations of the strategy, thereby providing an optimal introduction to the scientific study of personality.

Just how this opportunity can be grasped when the limitations are presented through harsh, incomplete, and biased arguments is not made clear. Nor do the authors do anything to allay a suspicion that the positive light to be complemented is equally open to objections. The persuasive function of "full scope of personality'' and ''scientific study of personality'' in the preceding material is particularly worth pondering. This example shows rather clearly what may be involved in the re-writing with which students are presented. The 'innocent reading' conception of what the textbook offers needs to be re-thought.

*

Another, exceptionally interesting case is one in which the textbook takes an unusually detailed look at one of Kelly's papers, ''The threat of aggression''. He had proposed

> three key notions that must be lifted from the context of stimulus–response psychology and recast. . . . They are *threat, aggression* and *hostility*. Threat, for the man himself, is the experience of being on the brink of a major shift in his core construct system. Aggression, for the man himself, is one's own initiative, not what that initiative may lead another to do or feel . . . hostility is the extortion of confirming evidence to present to oneself when there seems too much at stake to undertake the personal changes that natural evidence requires.

The concept of aggression is a central theme in the textbook. But curiously, Kellian aggression is ''to make the events or the behavior of other people conform to the existing cognitive structure or rules. This choice may be considered *aggressive*''; ''such action is aggressive because it distorts events to protect the person's heavy investment in the construction of reality''; ''to force another person to comply with our preconceived expectations is an aggressive act but a frequent one among humans''. So complete is the avoidance of Kelly's crucial distinction between hostility and aggression as independent concepts that the account concludes: ''The aggressive man or institution is the eventual victim of his own extortion. As Kelly (1965) notes: 'With the adoption of hostility (as opposed to the humanistic choice) he (man) surrenders his capacity' ''. The textbook consistently contrasts aggression with humanistic accomplishment, whereas Kelly's purpose is precisely to draw attention to the audacity which is a feature of both aggression and humanism.

This re-writing is bizarre, until one sees its place in the textbook's monumental effort to give structure to a vast array of material ranging right across psychology (personality = psychology). In a 4×3×4 design, it discusses three levels of conceptualisation for each of four viewpoints (biological, experimental, social, psychometric) in their several treatment of the topics dependency, aggression, sexuality and competence. The discussion referred to is embedded in the cell which deals with the experimental approach to higher (cognitive) processes in relation to aggression; that is, at the heart of the stimulus–response prison from which Kelly was trying to liberate the concept! The topics were clearly selected for their particular interest to students. In such a context the challenge to reconstrue aggression as a positive, adventurous, and non-destructive tendency is too great. For the textbook, issues such as race riots, poverty, and war can only be confronted by "the nonaggressive pursuit of a better world". For Kelly, however, it was hostility not aggression which "substitutes extortion for disconfirmation, disengages itself from the world and abandons the future of mankind". The textbook extorts its own confirming evidence, because too much is at stake to undertake the change required of its 4×3×4 construct system.

* * *

"I cannot see that the kind of statements that Freudian ego psychologists make about personality differ very strikingly, if at all, from either naive or sophisticated statements about personality made by non-Freudians".

This is not so strikingly different from what Kelly found in "The autobiography of a theory". It is the final sentence of an essay "Psychology and Literature" by a professor of English and Comparative Literature; an essay which is one of the few in its field to come out from the other side of psychoanalysis.

How does he read psychology? How indeed does he make anything of psychology at all, when he includes in a parsimonious bibliography *Human Behavior: An Inventory of Scientific Findings, Handbook of General Psychology,* and *The Conceptual Framework of Psychology?*

Despite such solid stuff he survives, with the standpoint of a reflexive social psychologist. "Since any individual knows about himself in the same way that he knows about others, and since he generates instructions for himself in the same way that he generates instructions for others, he is most usefully regarded as a social dyad, that is, as a small group". An anticipation of Mair's "Community of Self"? Man as the "generator of instructions" suggests an intriguing model. It is introduced in the context of a discussion of creativity. Man is not a computer programmer, nor a sergeant major, nor a litigant; but an active teacher, a productive imparter of knowledge. If Everyman is a scientist, she not only gathers knowledge, she also informs herself and others with it. It is this act of instruction, and being instructed, which can create the basis for social relationships.

The English professor is critical of psychology. He finds problems in its lack of solid, verified propositions. Sophisticated statistical analyses swell the flow of the residual. The experimenter refuses to acknowledge her inevitable function of social control. There is no large-scale theory and probably never can be if we persist with controlled laboratory experiments and mini-theories. If psychology attends to literature, it simply gets into a mess.

An example is its treatment of 'creativity': "a word with multiple meanings in literary rhetoric is taken over into the rhetoric of psychology without having been subjected to semantic analysis". That is, psychologists are simple-minded when they set out to explain phenomena subsumed by such a concept. It may be legitimate that their operationalisations are limited; but what is not forgivable is that they are based on a superficial acceptance of a convenient component of the concept, independently of its complexity and its historical and cultural context. There are scores of examples—aggression, conformity, leadership, and so on. In the case of terms like 'creativity' or 'aggression' Kelly showed how a general theory of psychology enabled you to cut right through the thicket: you derive a theoretical definition of the term which may be startlingly unlike that in other rhetorics, and pursue the implications of the difference.

This argument might be asking for a psychology of personal constructs, as it explains how literary criticism can find so little in psychology to help it. "By building up from basic units of behavior, psychology will never construct a theory of human behavior which literature can use. It must begin with a level of explanatory regress that deals with what it calls higher cognitive activity, including its own. And that means it must begin with language, which is not the instrument of higher cognitive activity but is higher cognitive behavior itself". It is certainly calling for a reflexive psychology and opposing accumulative fragmentalism. One of the pitfalls of personal construct psychology has been the necessity to begin with language; as a result, sometimes forgetting the significance of the pre-verbal (though it is precisely that, defined by language), and that constructs are behavior.

*

What is the goal?

> Literary criticism ought to be able to find in psychology explanatory propositions for its justifications and interpretations; it ought to be able to find exemplifications for such propositions both in psychological experimentation and in literature; and it ought to be able from a knowledge of psychology to generate innovative explanations which will reveal hitherto unobserved aspects of literature and its origins in the individuals who produce it. And psychology ought to be able to use the theoretical explanations of literary criticism as directions for innovating scientific investigation; it ought to be able to find exemplifications for its explanatory propositions in literature as well as psychological experimentation; and it ought to be able to generate theory with the aid of the theoretical propositions of criticism. Psychologist and literary critic, then, each ought to be able to incorporate into his own rhetoric segments of the other's, both to generate and control high-level explanatory regress, or theory, and to generate and control specific investigations into categories or units of study in their respective fields. This kind of disciplinary interaction ought to be happening, but except for a very limited number of studies in both fields, it is not.

The omitted beginning of this passage, "Thus it can, I believe, be reasonably said that . . ." and the subsequent reincantation of "ought" raises suspicions. Interdisciplinarity is under discussion, an exercise *between* disciplines. But it is expressed as work by each discipline *on* or *from* the other, an independent reciprocal exploitation. If a field of study knows about itself in the same way that it knows other fields and generates instructions for each equally, then disciplinary interaction has the potential to be conversational, a simultaneous and co-ordinated movement forward. The essence of what occurs in such interaction must be located in the space between the parties.

It is unlikely that it is theoretical weakness which prevents fruitful interaction between psychology and the study of literature. What is required and lacking is modesty and courage: to acknowledge the creation of a relation which transcends individual identity, to relinquish some measure of control, and to risk possibly fundamental changes in one's construct system at the "instruction" of another's. Disciplines, which can be considered as large-scale construct systems, are as proud and anxious as people when confronted with change.

It is, then, not a question of the psychology *of* literature, or literature *for* psychology, nor even psychology *and* literature; anymore than we could accept a 'John of Janet', 'Janet for John', or the precedence in 'John and Janet'. Couples might follow the example of religious converts who take an independent name to celebrate their freedom and express their new relation. Disciplines which do not do this will drift towards asymmetry, colonisation. What I look for is literature $\rightleftharpoons$ psychology; but I have no name for it.

***

Footnote

"Footnotes to the text should be used only if they are essential. They should be indicated in the text by superscript asterisks, daggers or letters".

A footnote is an integral part of a text; it cannot "be indicated in the text" as something apart. I chose a dagger to excise this footnote, preferring it not to be essential, not to be read; unless you choose to write it or to suspend belief, your capacity to be persuaded. As an 'explanation' of this chapter, the footnote will contradict it.

*

Texts play an important part in personal construct psychology, perhaps an unusually significant part. The visible remnants of Kelly's own work are an invitation to reconsider the forms and institutions of psychological writing. At death his bibliography listed three papers in major journals, seven contributions to edited volumes, and a monograph of 1218 pages. Nine of the 15 previously unpublished papers which have since appeared have no attribution, not even as lectures. Kelly did not rush into print. Many of his writings can best be referred to as 'essays', in several senses of the word. A number of contributions to the *Perspectives* volumes continue this example. And Bannister's novels may be read, though not without invoking some very difficult theoretical issues, as a radical extension in the same spirit.

The nature of Kelly's legacy has encouraged a much richer bookshelf than most other psychologies or theories of psychology. Apart from books on therapy, personal relationships, person perception, for example, we are drawn into the folds of architectural design, stockmarket transactions, classrooms, the birth of a first child, management training, South African politics. The comprehensive character of personal construct psychology is partially reproduced in the range of topics considered within its framework, and in a corresponding variety of styles and forms of written expression. The texts to which the work attends (what we normally call 'data') are also much more varied than the alleged preoccupation with repertory grids would suggest.

To say "partially reproduced" is to call up the many possibilities which have not yet been explored, not so much of subject-matter, as of experiments in communication. Talking, for example, not only in such contexts as therapy and training, but about *and within* personal construct psychology (reflexively), is an integral feature of it. There is scope for taking talk more seriously; in itself that is, not as though it was questionnaire responses or words which might as well be written on and read from the printed page.

This chapter attempts to set you on the road to ask more questions about just a few of the more obvious texts which you regularly face as a social scientist—textbooks, examination papers, reviews, blurbs, citations. The questions are not peculiar, however, to social science, nor to personal construct psychology. They can be extended to all forms of discourse. But personal construct psychology, in particular, should be attentive to its texts and how they construe.

*

Reviews, for example. Do we take them seriously in psychology? At least we might think about them more. What are our expectations of them? How do we read them? What are their variations? What role do they serve? Are there differences from reviews of other literature? They form one kind of commentary on personal construct psychology. Because construct psychology is not splintered or splintering, we may assemble these reviews as a single text for examination. In the terms of this chapter, their least desirable characteristic is their tyranny, their closure of texts. At their best they offer a rare access to the leisurely examination of the reading practices of a selected set of people.

A few reviewers may be a large part of the audience for this chapter—though their thorough perusal of what they review is by no means guaranteed! Their reactions may be the only ones we ever hear in any detail. This chapter is a challenge to them. Is it a perspective in/on/from/by/beyond personal construct theory? Its subject is reading, on the margins of personal construct psychology. It falls between personal construct psychology and the theoretical treatment of texts, confronting neither directly. It defines its goals by avoiding them, in order to leave the chapter to be written by the reader. It is inward-looking, reflexive.

Reviewers have with suspect consistency awarded black marks because construct psychology books are judged to be "for serious students of Kelly", to demand unforgivingly "familiarity with the literature". This chapter is for people who are sufficiently serious to be able to transcend their curiosity over or commitment to his theory.

What is behind the insistent rebuke that construct psychologists write for one another, expect their audience to know something of the subject? This would be a curious criticism of most psychological monographs. At the other end of the spectrum, could we, as professional psychologists, adequately read a textbook without prior familiarity? The remarks could be construed in various ways as hostile. Or are they a part of the mystification of psychology—only initiates can really understand it? Perhaps personal construct psychology leads people to expect that its writings should be transparent, instantly and exceptionally intelligible—even to the *Contemporary Psychology* reviewer who disarmingly confessed that he was looking forward to his task because he had never read anything of construct psychology before. It is more likely, however, that you do not really have to know much about the system at all—beyond, say, what you can find in *Inquiring Man*—in order to confront these books. You have to be prepared to write rather than read. Once again construct psychology flouts psychology's mystifying precepts.

This chapter certainly requires familiarity with literature—perhaps with an introduction to critical literary theory, Don Bannister's novels, reviews in *Contemporary Psychology,* representative personality textbooks, Potter *et al.* In order to write this chapter as a reader, you need to spend some time doing research in the library. No text exists by itself. It is incomplete, fragmentary, to be written. That character is concealed if the reader is persuaded that he has already the resources to make sense of it. It would be more helpful to the active reader–writer to provide only a list of quotations, references, a bibliography. Or to suppress references, as Kelly did; whose example we have tried to follow here. To confront a quotation without knowing its source can be a disorienting experience.

Sources of Quotations (In Order of Appearance)

Examination paper: Kelly (1964), p. 151; Stringer (no reference).
Perspective: Onion (1944), pp. 1479–80; Bannister (letter to an "author").
Death of the Author: Barthes (1974), p. 4; (1968), p. 147.
Burning Leaves: Rippere (1982).
Reviews of Perspectives: Thoresen (1972); Sechrest (1979).
Book proposal: Potter and Stringer (1980); Various (1980).
Textbooks: Geiwitz and Moursund (1979), pp. 315, 316, 319; Hjelle and Ziegler

(1976), pp. 211, 246; Liebert and Spiegler (1978), p. 23; Kelly (1965), pp. 200–201; Wiggins *et al.* (1971), pp. 257, 258, 258, 260; Kelly (1965), p. 201.

Psychology and Literature: Peckham (1976), pp. 67, 51, 51–52, 64, 55.

Footnote: Academic Press (undated).

*

The work of this chapter then, as of all chapters, is to be done by the reader. We have withheld much direct reference to construct psychology in itself, in an attempt to incite the reader to (re-)write the chapter. The chapter tries to point to what might be a perspective in personal construct theory, for those who are willing to climb to the vista-point in preference to staying at home in comfort to look at my transparencies. (I am collecting a quite useful set, which one day I may be lazy enough to publish).

It would be possible to explain this chapter in more personal terms, and through its connections to Stringer 1977, 1984, 1990. But the Author, who has been a guest, or ghost, is in dissolution. If you need an Author, you may for the time being make direct contact. (Is that why they put our addresses in the front of these books?).

The title should long since have become clear; though probably not that it is an obscure and tactless in-joke. It is taken from a note (22 October 1982) from the Editor, originally written entirely in capital letters, reproduced here in full: ''You will shortly be receiving your personal contract from Academic Press and this will give your chapter a title. Please ignore the title shown in the contract—it was made up by me as a matter of convenience [sic] for the publishers. You decide what your title is to be and write to that title''. The Editor made up this chapter's title to the inconvenience of the passive reader. He successively changed the book's title for the inconvenience of an over-active writer.

Bibliography

Academic Press (undated). Notes for editors of and contributors to a multiauthored volume. Academic Press, London.

Adams-Webber, J. R. (1979). ''Personal Construct Theory: Concepts and Applications'', Wiley, Chichester.

Bannister, D. (ed.). (1970). ''Perspectives in Personal Construct Theory'', Academic Press, London.

Bannister, D. (ed.). (1977). ''New Perspectives in Personal Construct Theory'', Academic Press, London.

Bannister, D. (1979). ''Sam Chard'', Routledge and Kegan Paul, London.

Bannister, D. (1981). ''Long Day at Shiloh'', Routledge and Kegan Paul, London.

Bannister, D. (1982). ''Burning Leaves'', Routledge and Kegan Paul, London (Paperback edition, 1983, Picador, London).

Bannister, D. (1983). Letter to an ''author''.

Bannister, D. and Fransella, F. (1971). "Inquiring Man: The Theory of Personal Constructs", Penguin, Harmondsworth.

Barthes, R. (1968). The Death of the Author. *In* "Image-Music-Text" (R. Barthes, 1977), Fontana, London.

Barthes, R. (1974). "S/Z", Hill and Wang, New York.

Belsey, C. (1980). "Critical Practice", Methuen, London.

Berelson, B. and Steiner, G. A. (1964). "Human Behavior: An Inventory of Scientific Findings", Harcourt, Brace and World, New York.

Brunswik, E. (1952). "The Conceptual Framework of Psychology", Chicago, University of Chicago Press.

Fransella, F. and Bannister, D. (1977). "A Manual for Repertory Grid Technique", Academic Press, London.

Geiwitz, J. and Moursund, J. (1979). "Approaches to Personality: An Introduction to People", Brooks/Cole, Monterey, California.

Good, J. J. (1962). "The Scientist Speculates: An Anthology of Partly-Baked Ideas", Heinemann, London.

Hjelle, L. A. and Ziegler, D. J. (1976). "Personality Theories: Basic Assumptions, Research, and Applications", McGraw-Hill, New York.

Kelly, G. A. (1955). "The Psychology of Personal Constructs", Norton, New York.

Kelly, G. (1960). Epilogue: Don Juan. *In* "Clinical Psychology and Personality: The Selected Papers of George Kelly" (B. Maher, ed., 1969), Wiley, New York.

Kelly, G. (1963). The autobiography of a theory. *In* "Clinical Psychology and Personality: The Selected Papers of George Kelly" (B. Maher, ed., 1969), Wiley, New York.

Kelly, G. (1964). The language of hypothesis: man's psychological instrument. *Journal of Individual Psychology*, **20**, 137–152.

Kelly, G. A. (1965). The threat of aggression. *Journal of Humanistic Psychology*, **5**, 195–201.

Kelly, G. A. (1982). 'Les Gens de Lettres': An Introduction. *In* "Essays in the sociology of perception" (M. Douglas, ed.), Routledge and Kegan Paul, London.

Liebert, R. M. and Spiegler, M. D. (1978). "Personality: Strategies and Issues", Dorsey, Homewood, Illinois.

Mair, J. M. M. (1977). The community of self. *In* "New Perspectives in Personal Construct Theory" (D. Bannister, ed.), Academic Press, London.

Moss, A. E. St. G. (1974a). Hamlet and role-construct theory. *British Journal of Medical Psychology*, **47**, 253–264.

Moss, A. E. St. G. (1974b). Shakespeare and role-construct therapy. *British Journal of Medical Psychology*, **47**, 235–252.

Neimeyer, R. A. (1983). The Development of Personal Construct Psychology: A Sociohistorical Analysis. *In* "Applications of Personal Construct Theory" (J. R. Adams-Webber and J. Mancuso, eds.), Academic Press, New York.

Onions, C. T. (ed.). (1944). "The Shorter Oxford English Dictionary on Historical Principles", Clarendon Press, Oxford.

Peckham, M. (1976). Psychology and literature. *In* "Literary Criticism and Psychology" (J. P. Strelka, ed.), Pennsylvania State University Press, University Park.

Potter, J. and Stringer, P. (1980). "The Construction of Social Scientific Talk", Book proposal.

Potter, J., Stringer, P., and Wetherell, M. (1984). "Social Texts and Context: Literature and Social Psychology", Routledge and Kegan Paul, London.

Rippere, V. (1982). Review of Don Bannister's "Burning Leaves". *Bulletin of British Psychology Society*, **35**, 428–429.

Sechrest, L. (1977). Personal Constructs Theory. *In* "Current Personality Theories" (R. J. Corsini, ed.), Peacock, Itasca, Illinois.

Sechrest, L. (1979). A passion for theory. *Contemporary Psychology,* **24,** 19–20.

Stringer, P. (1977). Participating in Personal Construct Theory. *In* "New Perspectives in Personal Construct Theory" (D. Bannister, ed.), Academic Press, London.

Stringer, P. (1984). *In* "Social Texts and Context: Literature and Social Psychology" (J. Potter, P. Stringer, and M. Wetherell), Routledge and Kegan Paul, London.

Stringer, P. (1985). You Decide What Your Title Is To Be and [Read] Write to That Title. *In* "Issues and Approaches in Personal Construct Theory" (D. Bannister, ed.), Academic Press, London.

Stringer, P. (1990). Personal communication.

Thoresen, E. (1972). In praise of Kelly? *Contemporary Psychology,* **17,** 121–122.

Various (1980, March 24–27). Transcript of workshop on personal construct theory. Lorton Vale, Cumbria.

Wiggins, J. S., Renner, K. E., Clore, G. L. and Rose, R. J. (1971). "The Psychology of Personality", Addison-Wesley, Reading, Massachusetts.

Wolman, B. B. (ed.). (1973). "Handbook of General Psychology", Prentice-Hall, Englewood Cliffs, New Jersey.

13

Nothing More Theoretical than Good Practise: Teaching for Self-Organised Learning

Laurie F. Thomas

How Are Gifted Teachers Made?

This chapter sets out to refute the idea that "gifted" teachers are born, not made. It is argued that teachers are made, but that we are not yet fully conversant with the process of construction. It is also suggested that what is true of teachers is also true of therapists, trainers, tutors, consultants, counsellors, and coaches. The primary task of all these practitioners is to enable others to learn. The best of them aim to do this in the fullest and most complete sense of the verb *to learn*. But to deny that coaches of Olympic champions are born with unique gifts is not to suggest that someone has taught them or trained them into all they know. There are other possibilities.

Many top coaches have learnt how to coach by first having learned how to learn. Learning is very different from being taught. Most significant learning is self-organised. It may happen in the presence of a teacher, trainer, or therapist and it may relate to how they are thinking, feeling, and acting at the time, but it is not directly caused by what they do. Thus the first step towards understanding how good teachers are made is to recognise that in part, but crucially, they make themselves. They were not born with the specific seeds of good teaching in them, any more or any less than the rest of the human race. But, by happenstance, design, or perseverance they have become—in personal construct psychology terms—good personal scientists taking responsibility for creating their own personal knowing. Here we will use the term "personal myth" to designate the personally relevant and viable meanings that are the personal knowing that results from personal science. The term myth is meant to carry all its positive, negative, allegorical, and transcendental implications.

James (1977), Rogers (1969), and Menuhin (1977) each appear to have been outstanding enablers of others' learning. How did they achieve this? They achieved it through a tacit understanding (Polanyi, 1958) of how to conduct a learning conversation. Rogers spent a significant proportion of his professional life in attempting to make his version of this tacit understanding explicit, to himself and then publicly. This effort after awareness enabled him to develop his personal science steadily throughout his life (Rogers, 1969). James and Menuhin seem equally to have achieved some considerable understanding of themselves and their own methods. But being severally a rugby specialist and a musician rather than professional psychologists, they have used their awareness of their own development to illuminate their understanding of how to enable learning in others. They did this without going on to develop their methods into theories of learning. One has however founded a school for musicians and the other became the doyen of rugby coaches of his day.

It is suggested that the processes by which these three outstanding teachers, and indeed all other gifted teachers, achieve their results might usefully be designated "learning conversation". Minimally, a learning conversation enables the client to learn more effectively and more completely. At best it enables the learner to achieve self-organisation by becoming capable of sustaining such conversation with and for himself or herself. This migration of the conversation from without to within carries with it a change in effectiveness that appears as a qualitative leap. The internal conversation does not cease in the absence of the external mentor, so its effect can extend far beyond the scope of any external conversation.

The first move in the making of a good teacher was identified in their acceptance of responsibility for their own learning. Whilst most of us are forced, by default, to accept this responsibility in some areas of our learning, it is less usual for us to do so when being taught. Most outstanding performers do, however, report having done just this in the area of their achievements, for example, Trueman (1978) and Freud (1937). The second, (necessary but not sufficient) move towards the making of a good teacher is now seen as their acquiring the ability to sustain a learning conversation with and within themselves. Each of these steps probably, in turn, takes them beyond 90% of their peers, already separating them out as "one in a hundred" before we begin to consider the quality of the products of their learning or the quality of their internal conversation. Now for the next quantum change.

Most of those who become self-organised learners continue to value the *products* of learning (e.g., achievements and performance) high above their increased insight into their own *processes*. This emphasis is perhaps best illustrated in tennis in which coaching is a second best occupation for ex-champions, but many of the outstanding coaches may never have been champions. It is only those self-organised learners who remain vulnerable enough to maintain an awareness of their own development who are able to conduct sustained and effective learning conversations with others. This probably disposes of another 90% of our already fairly exclusive group of potentially good teachers taking us into the "one in a thousand" class. Thus, whilst gifted teachers are made, they do not make themselves very often.

At this point we come to what is probably the greatest obstacle in our quest to understand how good therapists, trainers, tutors, consultants, counsellors, and coaches are constructed. The problem is that they all behave differently, they all give different explanations of how they achieve their results, and they all describe different developmental experiences as significantly influencing them. What is worse, many of their disciples, the Rogerians, the Fred-Truemans, and the Freudians who appear to behave in roughly the same way as their masters, who expound their masters' theories, and who identify a meeting with (or reading of) the master as a crucial developmental influence on them, do not begin to achieve anything like the master's results.

How are these obvious observations to be explained? Let us continue the personal construct psychology paradigm. The "originals" operate as personal scientists construing and validating their own personal views, theories, or myths about their own, and then other peoples, processes of learning. They develop their own personal myths about

1. individual capacity and talent,
2. optimal conditions for learning,
3. what constitutes good performance in their chosen field,
4. what constitutes a proper approach to learning–teaching, and
5. how to enable those they select for learning to learn.

The differences between their myths in each of these five areas are vast. But the myths "work" for the range of people, situations, and purposes for which their originator developed them. What good teachers have in common is more difficult to discern. It is here suggested that what they share is a tacit recognition that the learning process must be self-constructed and that the teaching–learning process must therefore be truly conversational.

Only by learners being freed to exercise whatever weak and vulnerable capacity for personal science they possess will they eventually develop a strong and healthy capability to create and validate effective personal myths of their own. Only a truly *conversational process* simultaneously allows the learner the real freedom to say and mean whatever he or she thinks or feels, whilst protecting, supporting, and guiding him or her into ever more valid "personal science". Learners' views, theories, and personal myths must be the robust and thoroughly tested outcomes of their own personally evaluated experience. This experience may (indeed should) include being exposed to the best of public knowledge, but their use of this knowledge, their idiosyncratic analogies, selection, re-organisation, rejection, and re-construction of it will have subtly transformed it and made it personal. Even when the resulting personal myth appears identical to the public version, the active process of self-organised learning will have made it their own. The skilled learning conversationalist has recognised that the primary object of learning is the construction of these personal myths via an increasingly more valid, personally scientific process.

This brings us to the critical distinction between a "gifted teacher" and a "successful instructor". The successful instructor is concerned with the "correctness" of the knowledge that is transmitted and received. The gifted teacher is concerned with the quality of the personal knowing and adequacy of the personal validation that is achieved. Good teachers may challenge and criticise the learner's 'personal myths' but in the last analysis they value the ability to construct, develop and test out personally relevant and viable meanings (constructions of experience) above the specific content of any particular meaning that is currently held.

The paradox is that many good teachers have not made this conversational process explicit either to themselves or to others. They have a feel for it but they have not identified it as the central essence of what they do. Indeed, they often ascribe their success to the particular personal myths about their specialism, about people, and about the teaching methods that they have constructed, found, and/or made to work for them. These are as varied as the teachers, therapists, tutors, trainers, coaches, counsellors, and consultants who espouse them. Each personal myth will work in some less or more viable way for the individual who constructed it. But it will almost inevitably restrict the range of people that the teacher is able to work with, the area and extent of personal meaning that they can tolerate in another, and the capacity for growth that they believe the other capable of generating. Thus, most gifted teachers are only gifted for certain people, in certain topic areas, for certain periods in their development; and to reverse our earlier "one in a thousand" rhetoric it is also likely that everybody has the capacity to be a good therapist, trainer, tutor, consultant, counsellor, or coach for at least one other person, on some particular topic for some small but crucial period during their development.

In developing their own personal myths (i.e., mix of metaphor, analogy, and observation and combination of prejudice, understanding, and self-validating hypotheses) the good teacher does not differ from the rest of the human race. Where they differ is in recognising that this ability to generate personal myths *is* the process of learning. Those who believe that learning is a process of unquestioningly acquiring already-established public knowledge will never make good teachers.

The Personal Myths of Psychologists

The second theme of this paper is an attempt to add a little to our view of psychology as a joint enterprise by a community of humans concerned with and for other humans. Let us take the topic of chemistry as an analogy to illuminate our concerns. What was the state of pre-chemistry prior to the emergence of the atomic theory of matter and Mendeléyev's table of elements? The alchemists and apothocaries saw naturally occuring substances such as frogs' legs, lime, slugs, saltpeter, and the eyes of toads as the components out of which they could construct their practises. Only when attention shifted to what came to be recognised as more fundamental and universal entities such as elements, atomic structures, and valences did the practise of chemistry begin to cohere. As chemistry moved away from the idiosyncratic myths of the magicians and alchemists towards the more meticulously validated and therefore more easily shared representations of the chemists, one person's practise began to be systematically informed and influenced by another's.

Magicians and alchemists were almost certainly thought to be born, not made, and the trials and tribulations of a long apprenticeship was considered to be a necessary condition for achieving the state of grace which was a prerequisite for being allowed to practise. Ritual and rote learning also played their part. (Whilst the author has no intention of seriously comparing contemporary psychology with the state of alchemy prior to the emergence of chemistry as we know it, the analogy may help us to sort out one or two ideas.) Each magician and alchemist of any note seems to have developed a system, style, and domain of their own that had little logical or coherent relationship with its predecessors, or with its successors. The personal myths that informed their practise seem to have been culled from experience, formulated and validated in applications. Apprentices, acolytes, disciples, and fellow travellers took these personal myths and treated them as gradually more authoritative dogma. They usually developed their own practises in forms that were increasingly validating of the master's myths.

It would be invidious within this analogy to name names, whether of magicians or psychologists, but the reader may experience very little difficulty in perceiving the history of psychology (until how recently?) as a record of heroic attempts to construct and validate personal myths about human nature that were validated by the disciples. Each heroic myth appears to have had only a slender connection with what came before and not to have informed those formulated later. There often were and are many competing myths available at any one time. Another aspect of the analogy is that the alchemists and magicians could not always guarantee that their spells and potions would work and had, what are to us, quite bizarre ideas about the properties of matter and the influences upon it to explain their failures. The intermittent working of their methods might be thought to be due to the composition of their personal myths. These contained assumptions that do map, but only very patchily, onto the rather more viable chemical myths that came later.

Another more positive part of the analogy is that in pursuing their dreams, the magicians and alchemists had invented many of the tools that helped to launch the new science of chemistry. Finally with hindsight, chemical historians can identify many of the ideas that were later re-invented or re-discovered as lying dormant in the writings of the earlier workers. The problem was to discover the paradigm that allowed the chemical scientist to sort the relevant and viable from the merely plausible, elegant, or misleadingly impressive. As embryo soothsayer, I would like to suggest that psychology now contains a number of ideas analogous to those that launched chemistry or that with hindsight we see could have launched chemistry as a coherent body of knowledge.

One such idea is that meaning is personally constructed and always contains in indivisible form what psychology has often separated and called perception, thought, feeling, and action. Kelly's invention of construct systems is one exposition of this idea. His idea of "personal science" is a powerful embodiment of the humanistic psychological paradigm.

A second related idea is that the evidence of psychology comes in two forms that are differently available to participants in the quest for psychological explanation. These are "behaviour" which is available as evidence to the external observer of the psychological phenomena; and "experience" which is directly available only to the subject of the psychological phenomena. Psychological explanation requires its own theory of relativity in which the psychological perspective of the explainer is an essential component of the explanation (Bannister, 1977).

A third idea is that "cause and effect" or "system relationships" in the sense pertaining within the paradigm of the physical sciences (Butterfield, 1949) can never be an adequate means for explaining how one human being influences another. The construction, reconstruction, exchange, and negotiation of psychological processes between human individuals requires some "different" concept of relatedness. The process of conversation could be analysed, resynthesised, and progressively refined into such a concept. The idea of personal science requires amending or supplementing into a fully "conversational science" paradigm.

A fourth idea follows from the second. Psychological relativity applies not only to the subjects of psychological investigation but also to the investigators. This usefully blurs the distinction between psychologists and people.

A fifth idea which in many ways transcends all the others whilst deriving most directly from numbers three and four is that the whole nature and intentionality of psychological investigation will change. Psychology will generate a participant conversational method of investigation in which the psychologist is both conductor and technical assistant. The conductor will articulate the conversation, and the technical assistants will provide special tools and procedures for facilitating those parts of the conversation that cannot proceed unaided.

The Author's Personal Myths

The construction of personal meaning is central to the understanding of human beings and to human beings understanding themselves. Meaning always exists in context and therefore nothing has personal meaning except in its personally significant similarities and differences to other things.

The idea of bipolarity can be a useful means of expressing meaning (especially its submerged aspects). But this does not mean that a hierarchical structure of bipolar constructs is the only, or even the most, convenient and useful form in which to elicit and represent personal meaning. For example, the role of perception as a dynamic feedback loop in purposive activity is not easily represented in bipolar terms but it is central to all understanding of human activity. This is most easily appreciated in work with the sensorily handicapped.

The inclusion of such representations of internal process into personal meaning require new concepts of time structure. Various cybernetic models offer ideas about how meaning might be given such dynamic forms of representation. When meaning is no longer expressed as elements aligned on bipolar constructs, the repertory grid is no longer an adequate or even feasible means of representation. New techniques are required which, whilst preserving the essential "elicitation" process by which a person reveals the forms in which they construct experience, may capture personal meaning in whatever forms the individual feels best represent it. These techniques need to be such that their representations of personal meaning can be mapped one onto another to articulate the process of conversation.

The idea that personal meaning can be operational (e.g., riding a bicycle) but properly non-verbal implies that it exists in many different forms. An effective conversational technology would embody forms for representing and exchanging personal meanings that are compatible with the forms in which they exist within us.

A Personal Reconstruction of Kelly's Theory

A person may, perhaps, best be viewed as a system. Each new system has properties that cannot be deduced from its parts and how they relate one to the other (Lorenz, 1977). The system properties emerge and are retrospectively "explained" by changing the meaning attributed to each part (sub-system) and to the consequences of their dynamic interaction. The whole *is* greater than the sum of the parts.

THE FUNDAMENTAL POSTULATE AND INSPECTING RAZOR BLADES

Let us give meaning to the system properties of a person by reference to the fundamental postulate.

A PERSON'S PROCESSES ARE PSYCHOLOGICALLY CHANNELLED BY THE WAYS IN WHICH HE OR SHE ANTICIPATES EVENTS.

Here the person is an inspector at the end of a razor blade production line. He samples the products, rejecting some and accepting others. When asked why he has just rejected a blade, he has to look at it again before saying that it has a "second grind fault".

> This man's job is:
> a. to alert previous manufacturing operations if they begin to go out of control
> b. [to] prevent items going further if they will disrupt subsequent operations, and
> c. [to] prevent faults from getting to the customer.
>
> (Thomas, 1962, p. 15)

During a conversational "perceptual grid" elicitation, he decides to use 17 different types of fault as elements. Twelve of them are named by reference to an operation in the manufacturing process feeding to the inspection bench, four by reference to their consequences for subsequent operations, and one in terms of possible customer reaction.

The fundamental postulate reveals that the inspector's processes (i.e., perceptions of faults) are psychologically channelled (i.e., differentiated, elaborated, and named) by the ways. in which he anticipates events (i.e., anticipates the consequences for him of finding particular types of fault) (Thomas, 1965). As the grid elicitation proceeded, this became clear. All his constructs were expressed in operational terms, for example, difficult to identify, frequently occur, cause friction between inspection and production departments.

The inspector experienced considerable difficulty when asked to concentrate on constructs that were expressed in direct sensory terms (e.g., visual, tactile). Indeed it was only by referring directly to a set of physical examples of the faults that he was gradually able to "ladder" down to the datum of sensory experience. A complete perceptual grid (Thomas, 1975, p. 27) contains three levels of construct:

1. inferential (i.e., for personal anticipation)
2. interpretive (i.e., universal descriptive terms)
3. sensory (i.e., direct sensory evidence).

By separating these out, and then analysing how construing at one level related to construing at another, the inspector was enabled to become more thoroughly aware of his own perceptual processes. His inability to name the fault when challenged immediately after rejecting a sample of blades is now illuminated. He was inspecting blades, not to name the fault, but to offer control information to the production staff. His psychological processes were channelled accordingly. There are other examples that illustrate this perceptual channelling:

1. managers' perceptions of two-person (person–management) events recorded on videotape
2. students' views of mathematics examination questions

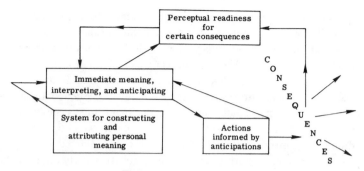

Figure 1. Purposive activity.

3. a "blender's" classification of "raw" whiskies
4. magistrates perceptions of an accused person's court room behaviour.

One part of a systems analysis of such experiences of the fundamental postulate in action might be indicated by Figure 1.

A "whole job" grid exploring how managers perceived their subordinates revealed the structure of that part of their construct system involved in conducting an appraisal interview. Their grids were structured very differently from the items on the appraisal form. Detailed interviews began to reveal some of the mechanisms by which they built a model for anticipating the behaviour of each subordinate. This mechanism might be outlined as in Figure 2. The manager, the student, the inspector, the blender, and the magistrate have all acquired some experience (*experience corollary*) of the tasks expected of them. But each magis-

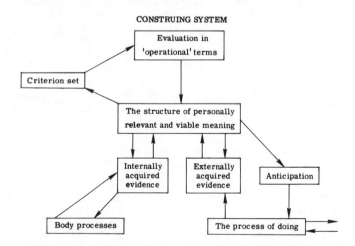

Figure 2. The mechanism of internal review: a construing system.

trate (etc.) construes replications of events differently (construction and individuality corollaries). Exploration of the magistrate example used the Raiffa
method for identifying the weightings given to individual constructs in arriving at
a decision (McKnight, 1977; Thomas and Harri-Augstein, 1985).

Using "court sentences" as elements (e.g., unconditional discharge, £20.00
fine, probation, 3 months' imprisonment) each magistrate elicited a grid. When
"talked down" into a particular court case, the magistrate systematically assigned weightings to each construct. The court cases were then themselves
construed and categorised. Notional sentences were also passed. The weighted
grids predicted the sentences for each case with embarrassingly high reliability.
The categories of cases mapped one to one onto the different patterns of weightings assigned. "Similar" court cases produced similar patterns of weightings
and thus a "consistency" to the individual sentencing behaviour. But a different
cluster of "cases" carried a different set of construct weightings and a different
pattern of sentencing behaviour. Thus the meaning attributed to an "offence"
makes the apparent inconsistency of a magistrate understandable through his or
her personal myth. In a similar study using mathematical examination papers
(Chapman, 1975) showed that not only was the tackling of examination questions predictable on an individual basis, but the basis of prediction (the grid and
the weightings) offered a powerful diagnostic and counselling tool.

Such studies throw light on the mechanisms of what is sometimes called
attention (dynamic set, the drive mechanism of anticipation), and they also begin
to reveal some of the structure of the processes by which the enduring meanings
of the individual are being constructed. This might be represented as in Figure 3.
Feelings influence, and are indeed part of, the anticipation of events. The control
of heart rate, temperature, and adrenalin release as well as psychosomatic influences upon health are equally a part of the internally orientated doing process, as
is the production of feelings (e.g., you give me a pain in the neck). My deeply

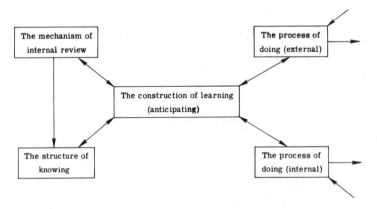

Figure 3. The person as construer.

felt personal elaborations of the fundamental postulate led me back to the gaps in my personal construct psychology grid.

DIRECTIONALITY AND THE JOE BAILEY EXERCISE

In "Behaviour is an Experiment", Kelly (1970) acknowledges behaviour as the test bed of construing. Behaviourism was such a predominant theme in the psychology of his time that the corollaries are, in reaction perhaps, deliberately lacking in reference to the outward appearance of any action. In emphasising the person as prior, and the constructing of experience as its central "subject matter", personal construct psychology, by implication, depreciates the usefulness of another's report of the person's behaviour. This counterbalances the behavioural psychologists' propensity to explain behaviour without further recourse to the behaver. But in anticipating, the person inevitably acts and this, coupled with the related state of perceptual readiness, maintains a process of doing (i.e., of action).

The Behaviour Corollary
ANTICIPATING EVENTS PRODUCES BEHAVIOUR FOR INTERVENING (I.E., AVOIDING, CONTROLLING, OR OBSERVING THEM). THE STRUCTURE OF BEHAVIOUR DEPENDS UPON THE PATTERN OF THE CONSTRUCTIONS OF EXPERIENCE OF EVENTS CONSTRUED AS RELATED.

The "Joe Bailey" exercise is well known in industrial training. It is a programmed "management" problem. A man is taking days off, and becoming unpunctual. The reader is concisely briefed and then offered four choices of action. Decision leads to additional briefing and more structured choices. Each move is recorded and the exercise proceeds until one of five end points (e.g., sacking him, sending him to personnel) is reached. Chell (1978) has used this exercise for some time. He began to add a repertory grid exercise to it. He listed all the choices at all the decision points. When the participants had completed their paths through the problem, each also completed a repertory grid using the choices as elements and eliciting their own constructs. The grids were FOCUSed and used to talk each individual back through their decision-making behaviour. The results were highly illuminating showing clear relationships between the thoughts and feelings of the individual and the anticipatory nature of the behaviour. Records of reading behaviour have also been used (Harri-Augstein, 1979; Harri-Augstein, Smith and Thomas, 1982; Harri-Augstein and Thomas, 1982) to talk people back through the micro-structure of behaviour into a reconstruction of the experience of reading. Such studies have, for me, indicated that personal construct psychology requires some formal acknowledgement of the *structure of behaviour* in addition to the construction of experience. Together these lead to additional corollaries.

Directionality Corollary

THE PATTERN OF PERCEPTUAL SELECTIVITY INHERENT IN THE CONSTRUCTION OF EXPERIENCE OF AN EVENT GUIDES BEHAVIOUR DURING THE EVENT. THE "CYBERNETIC" LOOP GENERATES DIRECTIONALITY IN BOTH BEHAVIOUR AND EXPERIENCE.

A Range and Time-Span Sub-Corollary to the
Directionality Corollary

DIRECTIONALITY WILL ENCOMPASS A CERTAIN RANGE OF EVENTS AND WILL EXHIBIT CERTAIN COHERENCE OVER TIME. THIS RANGE AND TIME-SPAN ARE FUNCTIONS RELATING THE EVENTS THEMSELVES TO THE CONSTRUCTIONS OF EXPERIENCE OF THEIR REPLICATIONS.

AWARENESS: REFLECTING UPON ONE'S OWN PROCESSES OF
CONSTRUING

A system (a person) exhibits and experiences directionalities that are certainly not to be inferred directly from the sum of the parts. Freud invented the unconscious to cope with such system properties. Many users of the repertory grid appear to equate the constructions of experience with consciousness. Since the client offers the constructs, the practitioners assume that he or she must have been aware of the construing. The elicitation of the grid is itself a constructive activity. What emerges is often new. Reflection upon its contents by the client often, indeed usually, provides new insights. It reveals the structure of an individual's systems for attributing meaning to events, that is, the structure of knowing. But what is it that becomes conscious. It is the content of the knowing and some aspects of its structure. Our inspector learned about his own perceptual processes by being forced to systematically identify the sensory evidence from which he drew his conclusions. The perceptual activity was rehearsed in the presence of a commentary arising from his own constructions of experience. He developed an awareness of his own processes. Similarly the Joe Bailey managers were conversationally encouraged into greater awareness of their own decision-making processes.

Six first-year social science students failed a "mock" statistics examination. To enable them to reflect on their thoughts and feelings about statistics, they all did conversational grids, three used computer-aided conversations (Thomas, 1978), and three used a hand grid sorter. They each identified 8 or 10 personally significant statistical concepts as elements, for example, "risk", "chance", "probability", "standard deviation". They reported that the experience had released their feelings about the subject and enabled them to begin to learn and think about it logically. Three weeks later they all passed the statistics examination. Four of them scored more than 65% and were in the top half of their year.

Awareness Corollary

TO THE EXTENT THAT A PERSON CONSTRUES HIS OR HER OWN CONSTRUCTIONS OF EXPERIENCE, HE OR SHE ACQUIRES CONSCIOUSNESS. TO THE EXTENT THAT A PERSON CONSTRUES HIS OR HER OWN PROCESSES OF CONSTRUCTION HE OR SHE ACQUIRES MORE COMPLETE AWARENESS OF HIM- OR HERSELF AS A PERSON.

INTENTIONALITY: THE AWARENESS OF DIRECTIONALITY

Within the confines of this chapter, examples of the practicality of personal construct psychology have been restricted. Each has been elaborated only sufficiently to illustrate a point. The whiskey blender was introduced merely to exercise the imagination and no mention was made of his construct pole ''green stick''. This referred to his use of branches from a particular bush in the distillery grounds. When freshly broken, these emit an odour which he uses to calibrate one dimension of his sense of smell.

A recurring problem experienced by many (if not all) people is that they often decide to do one thing and end up either not doing it or doing something else (Laing, 1970). The converse is also experienced. Having decided not to do something, the person ends up doing it after all. Being able to express an intention is not equivalent to achieving it. The process of achieving recognised purposes involves one of two strategies: the passive or the active. Passively one becomes reconciled with the directionalities inherent in one's construction of experience, acknowledges them, and thereby achieves intentionality by learning to anticipate the outcome of the directionalities over which one has no control. This is called acknowledging your own limitations and learning to live with them or learning to make the most of yourself. The whiskey blender is revered for his skill, which he has acquired during 40 years with the same firm. Whilst knowing about the green stick and using it to maintain his judgement during blending, he is totally unable and disinclined to construe his own processes of construction. Only by so doing could he hope to pass on his skills rapidly and efficiently to another.

The nature of this passive intentionality is only revealed if or when an attempt is made to interfere with the directionality on which it is based. Active intentionality is achieved when awareness extends into the process out of which the constructions of experience arise. This enables the person to systematically review how they are constructing their experience and to intervene in the construction process. They are thus able (when they have learned to modulate their interventions) to control their own directionalities achieving true intentionality.

Intentionality Corollary

A PERSON ACHIEVES INTENTIONALITY BY AWARENESS OF HIS OR HER DIRECTIONALITIES. THIS MAY REMAIN PASSIVE MERELY

ANTICIPATING DIRECTIONALITIES OUTSIDE HIS OR HER CONTROL.
ACTIVE INTENTIONALITY REQUIRES SUFFICIENT AWARENESS OF
THE PROCESS OF CONSTRUCTION TO INTERVENE AND CONTROL
THE DIRECTIONALITIES GENERATED BY IT.

Finally let me reveal some of my own disagreements with personal construct theory. I do not believe that meaning is constructed only from bi-polar constructs. Whilst logically everything can be seen to evolve from a raw basis of similarity and difference, psychologically I do not rest easy with this restriction. The Fuzzy set theory of Zadeh (1971) and the network descriptions of Pask (1975) offer other very enlightening forms with which to mould meaning.

Also, the choice corollary is either wrong or I do not fully appreciate it. People do not always operate to maximally elaborate their systems. For me there are at least three positions on the bi-polar construct "choice–no choice". Construing systems (people) can fall into radically different modes of operation. *They can become habituated.* In this state not only do their constructions of experience rigidify but their anticipations and actions, based on these constructions, ensure that they remain in an environment that offers no challenge. This leads to either static or dynamic "ultra-stability".

Or the system can operate optimally, but not necessarily as personal scientist. The internal process for evaluating the construction of meaning (Figure 2) can recount its "criterion set" from three different sources.

1. the outside world including other people as objects (e.g., as personal scientist).
2. the inside world (e.g., Rogers's fully functioning person uses his or her own organism as the ultimate test of fitness—e.g., as personal artist)
3. other people as a community of meaning (e.g., the law of the land—e.g., as personal politician).

Personality is largely a function of the mix of these referents in the personal criterion set. Ultra-stability and optimal operating define two very different modes of functioning.

Finally *the construing system may operate creatively* (Kelly, 1977). The "process of doing" may link back onto the constructive process itself providing a positive feedback that generates the phasic system of provisionality and decisiveness, of loosening and tightenings, of looking out and looking in, which seems to indicate the functioning of creativity. Any adequate conversational theory/technology of psychology should be capable of generating movement between these modes of operation.

Expanding the Paradigm

Another role of psychology will, for some time, be that of natural historian. The natural history function will be to collect, describe, and taxonomically classify examples of human function as they contribute to the enhancement of the human condition as seen from different meta-perspectives. The conversational technology will develop to enhance the quality of human intercourse: intra-personally, inter-personally, in small groups, between small groups, and between what we now call institutions.

In various studies of human learning in its natural habitats, the areas of investigation explored by the author have been concerned with a rather different mix of human endeavours and conditions than the mainly clinical issues that formed the main thrust of Kelly's work, (although his early academic studies, his wartime activities, his comments on teaching post-graduates, and his own practical skills show him to have had and used a wide base of experience out of which to formulate his psychology). Work in schools, colleges, universities, prisons, industrial, and commercial training departments, and a wide variety of "learning on the job" projects, (in which I have been as concerned to enable learning as I have been to study it), gradually pushed me towards a paradigm of psychological work that is very similar to Kelly's. This paradigm is implicit in the first half of the chapter. It differs from personal construct psychology in the following ways:

1. Being no longer oppressed by an all pervasive behaviourism, it does not discount the systematic evidence provided by records of behaviour.
2. It acknowledges biological and physical endowments without believing that any existing public myth about talent, personality, intelligence, and so forth gets anywhere near categorising endowment in forms that are useful for enabling change, growth, and learning.
3. Ideas about the exchange, sharing, and negotiation of personal meanings and ideas about social self-validation (and therefore about ultra-stable systems of public meaning) offer opportunities for the paradigm to be extended more solidly into the field of social psychology and sociology.

Kelly made a major breakthrough in his invention of the repertory grid, but a full paradigm of the psychological enterprise calls for a fully developed symbiotic methodology.

Another way of presenting this view of the psychology of the future is as follows:

1. There will develop a series of complimentary, supplementary, competing, and/or mutually exclusive paradigms of the psychological enterprise. These will constitute a pattern of meta-psychologies which are content-free and in fact embody alternative knowings and expectations (i.e., hopes, fears, plans, plots, and fantasies) about the past, present, and future of the human race in its various contexts. The comparative study of such meta-psychologies will illuminate and thus transform philosophy and religion. Perhaps a less psycho-centric way of expressing this would be to say that philosophy and religion already perform this function and psychology will be illuminated and informed by them. Either way there will be a conversation.

2. Each meta-psychology will have the potential differentially to facilitate and inhibit certain future developments of the human condition. They will therefore constitute a more powerful political and ethical reality than we have previously had to face.

3. Each meta-psychology will generate its own resources of ideas and methods including a library of personal myths. Each new participant will use these as nutrient to their own development. Literature and all other art forms will form a part of this library.

The reader may now discern a second reason for the title of this chapter. The imminent threat of the development of some powerful psychological practises not only implies the existence of some rather effective theories but it also imposes the need for a meta-conversation that will preserve the freedom of choice of both psychologists and all their potential clients. Readers of this book will recognise that Kelly is one major source of such ideas. But the most encouraging aspect of the prospects for psychology is that similar ideas have appeared and are appearing in many unexpected and expected places.

The final theme of this chapter is therefore an attempt by the author to place himself within one meta-psychology and to reflect upon his own personal myths as developed in 30 years work on human learning in its natural habitats. Kelly's personal myth already stands powerfully and centrally within this meta-psychological position. As Kelly's myth is more coherent, better presented, and more widely known than that of the author it has been taken as a template against which the author's myths can be defined by their differences.

On Construing Personal Construct Psychology

In the belief that the psychologist should be his or her own prime laboratory, I have sought signposts from personal construct psychology which have positions within my own personal myths. Using the fundamental postulate and the corollaries as elements for a grid, the following constructs emerged:

C1. Relates to how people differ	versus	Treats people's similarities as constructions of personal meaning
C2. Is static and concerned with the structure of the system of personal meaning	versus	Introduces the concept of time and relates to the process of constructing meaning
C3. Clarifies relationships between meanings	versus	Defines the nature of meaning

C4. Requires bi-polarity	versus	Bi-polarity unnecessary for the main myth to be viable
C5. Only logical	versus	Psycho-logical
C6. Concerned with only one person	versus	Admits of more than one person
C7. Implies only one mode for constructing meaning	versus	Requires a meta-level of meaning construction
C8. Acceptable to me	versus	Questionable
C9. Has added significantly to my understanding of psychology	versus	Already contained in psychology
C10. Treats person as object	versus	Treats person as subject

Having elicited these constructs I completed the grid, FOCUSed it (Thomas, 1975, 1978) using two-way cluster analysis and REFLECTed upon the pattern that emerged. The results worried me for a variety of reasons, some of which will emerge. Having worried, I sat back and began to seriously consider why, for me, Kelly's myth has been so useful and why I find personal construct theory so practical.

Cogniscent of established repertory grid techniques, I have, nevertheless, along with other fellow seekers (Radley, 1977; Mair, 1976; and Harri-Augstein, 1978) reinvented, selected, discarded, used, distorted, and developed "tools" to serve my own particular purposes. Some years ago, reflecting on this activity of psychological toolmaking, I listed some 63 tools of the psychologists' trade. These varied from client-centered therapy to the Skinner box, from the ta-chistoscope to interpretation of dreams and from Raven's matrices to the eye movement camera. The preferred poles of the clusters of constructs that emerged from this "tools grid" serve as criteria for my evaluation of the theoretical coherence of "good practise". Comparing the constructs from my postulate and corollary grid against this criterion set immediately led back to my view of the theory. Much of what I value was missing. What else should I have included as elements to make the sample more representative of personal construct psychology, as I understand it? Repertory grid, hostility, personal scientist, reflexivity, behaviour as experiment—the sample rapidly expanded and the balance of ideas completely changed. I merged my two sets of constructs and attempted to complete a new (complimentality) grid (Thomas, 1979) by assigning every element in this new sample of items of my experience in personal construct psychology to each construct. After FOCUSing this new grid, I was able to identity some of what had been missing from the postulate and corollaries. By "SPACE"ing the FOCUSed grid, I was also able to identify gaps which were still not yet filled by any of my elements. During the elicitation process I found that some elements represented more than one "item", and I therefore ended up, for example, with repertory grid A, repertory grid B, repertory grid C and repertory grid D. For reasons of space and clarity, I have not included any evidence from these grids. Their purpose was served in my reflections.

In examining my view of the implications of personal construct psychology for social psychology (Thomas, 1979), I have already elaborated suggestions for "missing corollaries". These relate to "self-awareness", "social awareness", and "complimentality". Preparation for this present chapter has again raised my doubts about the propriety of such an exercise. The "acceptable to me" versus "questionable" and the "has added to my understanding" versus "already contained . . ." constructs helped to clarify this issue. Personal construct psychology embodies a paradigm for psychological activity. "Bi-polarity necessary" versus "Bi-polarity unnecessary" indicates a part of the theory that seems too specific to stand at the meta-theoretical level. Thus my simple complimentality grid had already helped to clarify one issue. For me, there are two types of gap in personal construct psychology. One is missing corollaries which would expand the paradigm to more nearly fit that within which I feel comfortable. The other gap concerns those personally useful and specific elaborations that I have found necessary to include in those personal myths that enable me to teach and study human learning.

References

Bannister, D. (1977). Preface to "New Perspectives in Personal Construct Theory". (D. Bannister, ed.), Academic Press, London.

Butterfield, H. (1949). "The Origins of Modern Science, 1300–1800", Bell, London.

Chapman, L. (1975). "Investigations into a Mathematical Command system", Doctoral dissertation, Centre for the Study of Human Learning, Brunel University, Uxbridge, Middx.

Chell, N. (1978). "Conversational Repertory Grid Procedures for developing Man-Management Skills and for Course Evaluation" (In conjunction with E. S. Harri-Augstein and L. F. Thomas), Centre for the Study of Human Learning Publication, Brunel University, Uxbridge, London.

Freud, S. (1937). "The Ego and The Mechanism of Defense", Hogarth, London.

Freud, S. (1925). The Unconscious. *In* "Collected Papers", Vol. 14, Hogarth, London, pp. 84–97). (Original work published 1915).

Harri-Augestein, E. S. (1978). Reflecting on Structures of Meaning: A Process of Learning to Learn. *In* "Personal Construct Psychology, 1977" (F. Fransella, ed.), Academic Press, London.

Harri-Augstein, E. S. (1979). "The Change Grid. A Conversational Heuristic", Paper presented at Third International Congress on Personal Construct Psychology, Utrecht,

Centre for the Study of Human Learning Publication, Brunel University, Uxbridge, London.

Harri-Augstein, E. S., Smith, M., and Thomas, L. F. (1982). "Reading to Learn", Methuen, London.

Harri-Augstein, E. S. and Thomas, L. F. (1974). Learning-to-Learn, The Personal Construction and Exchange of Meaning. *In* "Adult Learning" (M. Howe, ed.), Wiley, Chichester, London.

Harri-Augstein, E. S. and Thomas, L. F. (1982). Learning Conversations: Reflective Technology for Learning-to-Learn. *In* Quarterly Source Book, *"Helping People Learn How to Learn"*, Jassey-Bass.

James, C. (1977). "Lions Down Under", Rugby Football Books, London.

Kelly, G. A, (1970). Behaviour is an Experiment. *In* "Perspectives in Personal Construct Theory" (D. Bannister, ed.), Academic Press, London.

Kelly, G. A. (1977). The Psychology of the Unknown. *In* "New Perspectives in Personal Construct Theory" (D. Bannister, ed.), Academic Press, London.

Laing, R. D. (1970). "Knots", Penguin Books, Harmondsworth.

Lorenz, K. (1977). "Behind the Mirror", Methuen, London.

Mair, M. (1976). Metaphors of Living. *In* "Nebraska Symposium on Motivation 1976" (A. W. Landfield, ed.), University of Nebraska Press, Lincoln.

McKnight, C. (1977). "Purposive Preferences For Multi-Attributed Alternatives", Doctoral dissertation, Centre for the Study of Human Learning, Brunel University, Uxbridge, London.

Menuhin, Y. (1977). "Unfinished Journey", Futura, London.

Pask, G. (1975). "The Cybernetics of Human Learning and Performance", Hutchinson Education, London.

Polanyi, M. (1958). "Personal Knowledge", Routledge and Kegan Paul, London.

Radley, A. (1977). Living on the Horizon. *In* "New Perspectives in Personal Construct Theory" (D. Bannister, ed.), Academic Press, London.

Rogers, C. R. (1969). "Freedom to Learn", Charles E. Merrill, Columbus, Ohio.

Thomas, L. F. (1962). "The Perceptual Organisation of Industrial Inspectors", Paper presented at Ergonomics Conference, Centre for the Study of Human Learning Publication, Brunel University, Uxbridge, London.

Thomas, L. F. (1965). "The Control of Quality", Thomas and Hudson, London.

Thomas, L. F. (1975). "Perception. A special case of Construing", A Centre for the Study of Human Learning Publication, Brunel University, Uxbridge, London.

Thomas, L. F. (1978). A Personal Construct Approach to Learning in Education, Training and Therapy. *In* "Personal Construct Psychology 1977" (F. Fransella, ed.), Academic Press, London.

Thomas, L. F. (1979). Construct, Reflect and Converse. The Conversational Reconstruction of Social Realities. *In* "Constructs of Sociality and Individuality" (P. Stringer and D. Bannister, eds.), Academic Press, London.

Thomas, L. F. and Harri-Augstein, E. S. (1985). "Self-Organised Learning and the Repertory Grid", Routledge and Kegan Paul, London.

Trueman, F. (1978). "The Thoughts of Trueman Now" MacDonald and Jane, London.

Zadeh, L. A. (1971). Towards a Theory of Fuzzy Sets. *In* "Aspects of Network and System Theory" (R. E. Kalman and N. Declares, eds.), Holt, Rinehart and Winston, New York.

14

Personal Construct Psychology and Contemporary Philosophy: An Examination of Alignments

W. G. Warren

While the contemporary relationships between psychology and philosophy have been somewhat confused by developments in each discipline, Kelly was sufficiently sensitive to these relationships to raise the question "philosophy or psychology?" in connection with the theory of personal constructs formulated in the period up to 1950. In response to this question, Kelly indicated that the conventional conceptions of philosophy and psychology were in themselves questionable and that his endeavour was inclusive of both these fields: "As a philosophy it is rooted in the psychological observation of man. As a psychology it is concerned with the philosophical outlooks of individual man" (1955, p. 16).

Kelly (1955) went on to relate the psychology of personal constructs to then-existing philosophical "systems" in the following manner:

1. Epistemologically the theory was indicated to be within the subcategory of *gnosiology*—the analysis of concepts used in formal and informal thinking about the world.[1] Further, it was *positivist* in the sense of the more abstract features of Comte's system (these features not specified); and it was *empirical* in relying on pragmatic logic, at the same time as it contained a measure of rationalism. Finally, it was *anti-realist* if realism was conceived as holding that man was always a victim of his circumstances.

2. Metaphysically, personal construct theory accepted a form of monism, *substantival monism,* which in simplest terms holds that the apparent diversity of substance is really a manifestation of the same substance in different forms; at the

---

[1]This term, from the Greek *gnosis,* meaning "knowledge" (though in a full or qualitative sense), is usually taken as synonymous with *epistemology,* rather than a subcategory of the latter. In fact, Kelly's own definition of gnosiology comes very close to what modern sources give as a definition of epistemology, (compare Kelly's [1955] comment at page 42, for example, with the entry under epistemology in Bullock and Stallybrass [1977]). Kelly does place his definition in parentheses and the source would appear to be Baldwin (1901/1960), which is now somewhat out of date. Ogden and Richards's work, in particular their *The Meaning of Meaning* (1923/1945), has significant affinities with Kelly's psychology and a biographical account might more clearly display other influences in the 20-year development of this psychology.

ISSUES AND APPROACHES
IN PERSONAL CONSTRUCT THEORY
253

same time, now following James, it was *neutral monism* in that the ultimate "stuff" of the world was individual, fleeting experiences that were neither mental nor material, but which in different manifestations comprised both minds and material things. *Free-will* and *determinism* Kelly considered "relatively unimportant"; but he does point out that within the system of constructs employed by an individual, there are sub- and super-ordinate constructs and that the sub- are "determined" by the super- (p. 20).

3. Finally, Kelly considered *phenomenology,* chiefly under the heading "Design Specifications for a Theory of Personality" and in the context of a discussion about individuality and individual differences. He then concludes this first, introductory chapter: "we believe it is possible to combine certain features of the neophenomenological approaches with more conventional methodology" (1955, p. 42). These *neo*-phenomenological approaches, in turn, were the extension of the phenomenological approach into psychology in field theory, in gestalt psychology, in self-concept theory and its variants, and in non-directive psychotherapeutic approaches like that of Rogers (1951). The "more conventional methodology" was less clear but appears to be simply "observational", and in view of later comments, "normative".

The discussion of these complex issues was, defensibly perhaps, quite brief and casual in Kelly's introduction. In addition, it takes some effort to unravel a number of points. For example, just what is meant by "the abstract features of Comte's system" (p. 17) that are accepted?; how can one, or in what terms can one, be both rationalist and empiricist?; and can realism be so summarily dismissed, and is it properly characterised as having the view that "man is always the victim of his circumstances"? (p. 17).

The present chapter addresses in the next section the manner in which personal construct theory might be related more satisfactorily to the traditional positions or to the issues Kelly himself raises. Then, in the third section, the present situation in the more central of these positions and issues is examined and related to personal construct theory, including a reference to a recent development in psychology itself, radical psychology. The aim is to examine in general terms the alignment between personal construct psychology and relevant contemporary philosophy.

It might be noted that the present approach bypasses an equally relevant consideration of Kelly's more specific formulation of a philosophy in his *constructive alternativism.* That consideration would hinge on the internal coherence and consistency of constructive alternativism and its adequacy as an epistemological, and perhaps ontological, theory. However, the present interest is more related to the manner in which the psychology aligns or fails to align with developments beyond it, so to speak; and the evaluation of constructive alternativism as a philosophy is left as a future task.

Under the discussion of epistemology Kelly (1955) refers to several positions that can be here taken in turn: *empiricism, rationalism, realism, positivism,* and *pragmatism.*

In simplest terms, empiricism takes the view that all knowledge comes from "experience"; rationalism, that at least some knowledge is independent of experience. Different empiricists give different accounts of the "how" and the "what" of knowledge, and, equally, different rationalists give different accounts of the "how" and "what" of that knowledge that is experience-free. Thus the familiar historical pattern runs something like Plato to Aristotle than a re-emergence in Descartes, a rejection of Descartes by Locke, and developments of empiricism from Locke to Berkeley to Hume. In turn, Kant attempts a synthesis of the two positions, to be found ultimately with more of a rationalist position; and Peirce, in a similar attempt, leans to empiricism in developing pragmatism.

At first sight, then, Kelly's allegiance is equally to positions that are themselves antagonistic; but taken in this historical development that leads to Kant and Peirce, that allegiance is more defensible.

Kant's synthesis was to argue that knowledge came from sense impressions but that these were pre-ordered by the mind in terms of certain categories: chiefly, for him, space, time, and causality. On the other hand, Peirce suggests that while the mind does operate on, rather than passively receive, sense impressions, a significant limitation on this operation was certain "requirements" of the impressions, or the data of the world themselves—thus, the "it works" characterisation of pragmatism referring to the coherence of an hypothesis about the world with observations of a situation or event. Knowledge in this position is tentative, with the notion of *certainty* replaced by that of *acceptable* belief.

Kelly's "pragmatic logic" refers to Peirce's *abduction* or *retroduction* (usually contrasted with induction and deduction) which is expressed: "a surprising fact C is observed; if A were true then C would be a matter of course, therefore there is reason to believe that A is true". In turn, when a new fact C' is observed that is incompatible with A, a new hypothesis A' is framed to explain both C and C', and so on. Clearly, this type of logic is quite compatible with personal construct theory in that constructs themselves serve as hypotheses or predictions about the world, and the change and variability of hypotheses is analogous to the idea of "construing replications" (construction corollary), and related to the choice and experience corollaries.

Finally, realism and positivism. Kelly rejects realism in so far as it takes a fatalistic view of humankind's predicament; but such a view of realism focusses an older meaning concerned with the relation of individuals to universals, and only in the most extreme form is realism characterised the way Kelly characterises it. Epistemologically, and more usually, realism accepts that reality exists independently of our apprehension of it, and this position, sometimes called naive or commonsense realism, Kelly, and indeed most of us, explicitly accepts.

In relation to positivism, Kelly defends what he calls the abstract features of

Comte's system and notes that it is the emphasis on "the constructs through which the world is scanned" that suggests the link to positivism. Positivism in psychology, again in most straightforward terms, is the position that takes the view that the enterprise of studying "behaving man" (see Koch, 1973, pp. 636–652)[2] can employ the same principles and methods as enterprises that study physical and natural phenomena. Finding its classic expression in Comte's work, the notion takes pride of place in his three-phase developmental hierarchy of human enquiry: theological (explanation in terms of supernatural events or intervention), metaphysical (explanation by invention of abstractions) and positive (explanation by cause–effect). However, Kelly appears to be in favour of the looser meaning of positivism that simply rejects metaphysical speculation and insists on an observational method in science—putting his positivism very much closer to his empiricism.

In relation, finally, to metaphysics, not a lot need be said. Kelly's own development ran through a period that saw the rise of logical positivism on the one hand, and on the other, the impact of German idealism on American philosophy. In the first case was a significant rejection of metaphysics as vacuous and meaningless; in the second, the insistence on non-material substance as the basic "stuff" of the world. Kelly seems to have been removed from logical positivism (though the significance of language that this position was to champion would have been applauded) and thus not caught up in the demise of this position when it was hoisted on its own petard: if the truth of a proposition lies in its manner of verification, then what is the verification procedure for this statement itself? Again, in accepting a form of idealism by opting for James' notion of the priority of the mental, he remained within an older tradition that at that time, at least, was defensible. In both cases, however, it seems unnecessary to come down too strongly in support of either position, or in fact to address the metaphysical questions at all, unless these are worked out in full. And it is not clear that personal construct theory would be incompatible with a materialist theory that might suggest that the construct-forming activity we observe as "mental" is nothing more than, for example, an epi-phenomenon of brain. Personal construct theory in fact would seem to be compatible with a number of incompatible metaphysics, and Kelly's indication of the alignment with substantival neutral monism might be explained by reference to social–historical forces in the United States during the period of the development of the theory, or equally by a link to phenomenology given James's own consistency here.

What is evidenced, and usefully so, in the foregoing material is that philosophical issues were addressed in an attempt to reconcile a new approach in psychology with them. Sadly, (because it limits horizons) contemporary psychology has in the main lost sight of the importance of these issues.

[2]Koch's phrase to contrast the more limited and limiting "human' behaviour".

Perhaps the most significant single development in philosophy since the mid-1950s has been in epistemology, in particular through philosophy of science. Developments in epistemology, in turn, have affected many of the "philosophies of . . .", especially philosophy of education, philosophy of economics, and philosophy of language.

Two general, related lines of development can in fact be discerned in philosophy of science (including philosophy of social science). On one hand has been a concern to examine science internally, to reconsider old notions that science was explanation, prediction, and control, and to analyse different models, indeed to accept that models play a very significant role in the activity of science as such. The second line of development attacked the *a*social and *a*political pretensions of science and argued, most forcefully by Feyerabend (1975), that science was significantly a *social* activity. More accurately this second line argues that what was accepted as scientific and thus as *knowledge* was significantly influenced, if not determined, by "extra-scientific" forces, and, moreover, such forces determined that *only* science would provide knowledge.

Feyerabend in fact stands in both lines of development in arguing that as a matter of fact science does not proceed by a "method", "the scientific method", but rather proceeds in a haphazard, fortuitous manner; and in any case this is a desirable thing:

> Science is an essentially anarchistic enterprise: theoretical anarchism is more likely to encourage progress than its law-and-order alternative . . . This is shown both by an examination of historical episodes and by an abstract analysis of the relation between idea and action. The only principle that does not inhibit progress is: anything goes. (1975, p. 10).

What is in fact represented in these two general lines of development is a significant attack on the dominance of positivism in science, positivism now more precisely defined in terms of two central notions: the idea that science has its basis in the certainty of its observations, and the idea that one can *deduce* from these observations. In psychology, moreover, positivism means that the human must be seen as "continuous" with the non-human, and it finds its expression in behaviourism, information-processing theory, cybernetics, and more—generally in empirical and experimental methodology that makes inferential judgements in disregard of the problems of induction, and resorts to reductions.

The next step in these developments is in process of its own development at this time and a strong claim is made by realism. Bhaskar (1975) in England and Hooker (1974, 1975) in North America have both made strong cases for a realist position in science, a position that comes down relatively more strongly on the role of the activity of science qua science. By contrast, Marxist epistemologies give relatively greater significance to the social dimension and the way in which power elites structure the world such that knowledge is really "desirable" or "acceptable" knowledge. A forceful statement of this last position, including an indication of how it occurs through schooling, is given by Harris (1979) the title of whose book carries the message here: *Education and Knowledge: The Structured Misrepresentation of Reality.*

What these developments indicate is that a wave of criticism has swept over the area of epistemology, and it has come significantly from the philosophers of science and the philosophers of society. It has occurred in epistemology because this was the area that had assumed centre stage for philosophy; the scene had been set, certain forces and unexamined assumptions had outlawed metaphysics and raised science, as conceived by positivism, to pride of place. In psychology, equally, the hope of a scientific psychology was replaced by the fact of a scientific psychology and variety in approaches to examining human behaving was substituted by a single "acceptable" approach.

Now, in relation to personal construct psychology, it is suggested that unlike other psychologies and because of the relative *remove* from the empiricism, pragmatism, and positivism Kelly sought to show a link with, the theory not only "weathers" these developments but is strengthened by them. Only in the sense that, methodologically, Kelly proceeds on the basis of observation is there a need to refer to empiricism; only in so far as he accepts the hypothetical nature of our knowledge claims is there the link to pragmatism; and only in so far as there is the methodological aspect contained in the use of observation and recording is there a link to positivism. In fact there are serious breaches with positivism in according the individual a central role in giving *meaning* to the world. Again, in terms of Kelly's empiricism, there is no attempt to go beyond the data of the individual and that complex and idiosyncratic structure of meaning with which the individual confronts the world: there is, that is to say, no attempt to develop an epistemology as such. And his pragmatism is, as he himself indicates, only the pragmatic logic that, while it might lead to a problematic relativism, remains in the psychological domain at least a valuable model of the way in which individuals deal with the data of the world.

Thus, while Kelly appears to be concerned to show the "bona fides" of his theory by aligning it with then contemporary notions in philosophy and psychology, it is as well that he does this in a relatively casual manner. Thus he is not burdened with these notions when they are brought under close scrutiny and shown to contain unexamined assumptions and questionable premises.

Perhaps a brief but more direct statement of the central premises of the more important notions here, positivism and empiricism, is finally appropriate.

At least three empiricisms can be noted: a positivistic empiricism, empiricism "proper", and a Popperean empiricism; a sketch of the first two will suffice to indicate present contentions. This sketch is taken from Hooker (1974, 1975) who appears to be the first to tease out in explicit terms both the philosophy and metaphilosphy of the three. Further, Hooker goes on to state a realist position, with which personal construct theory appears quite compatible.

A first observation is that, as an approach to the world, positivism is a form, a more austere form, of empiricism. Hooker (1975) calls positivism "logical empiricism" (p. 178), and in stating the philosophy of positivism finds it almost co-extensive with empiricism (as he similarly finds Popper's position). The basic doctrines are spelled out in full address: *a theory of rationality* (the goal of rational man is to acquire knowledge, understood as certain truth in the case of positivism, as "justified true belief" in the case of empiricism); *a philosophy of language* (which restricts meaningful language to that which is descriptive of sensory experience); *an epistemology* (analytic–synthetic distinctions with the significance resting only with the synthetic and this based in sensory experience); *a theory of science* (maximising truth, or empirical knowledge); and, important-ly, *a psychological theory of man* (man is a sensory reception chamber plus a deductive logic machine).

While each of these empiricisms is internally coherent and plausible, apart from any "poverty" in the view of man (which "poverty" would have to be justified in some normative grounds), significant critical questions arise. There is, for example, need to account for the origin of each position in its own terms: to account for positivist and empiricist premises and theories in terms of positiv-ist or empiricist theory itself. These positions, it might be said, are non-reflexive, do not and do not have the theoretical equipment to look back on themselves. In addition, in psychology, there is the need to account for a range of well-known feelings and mental states, even the concept of will, that do not fit neatly, into sensory experience language. In simple terms, against the reductionism of em-piricism might be asserted the notion of *emergent* properties at levels of interac-tion between, say individual and individual, and individual and natural world. These are obviously complex questions and take us into philosophy of science as a critical activity, but what these questions do, through a very wide literature or the two strands previously noted, is to cast significant doubt on the adequacy of empiricist–positivist accounts of knowledge including the functioning of the human person in this process.

Clearly, personal construct theory does not embrace in more than a superficial way the detailed positions that positivism and empiricism represent; the theory thereby avoids the thrusts of the critical literature. By contrast, in fact, Kelly's position provides a psychology that might form part of a realist position being developed against positivism in that here the individual is accorded a creative, active role in ascribing *a* meaning to the sensory–non-sensory inputs. And in the commonality and sociality corollaries, perhaps also in the experience corollary, is provided the basis for avoiding relativism and accounting for intersubjective agreement. Again, the choice of theories of explanation, choice of theory repre-senting a meta-philosophical principle in a realist position, is potentially explica-ble in terms of the same corollaries. And, personal construct theory is also not at variance with that strand of reaction to positivism that emphasises the social

dimension of knowledge (significantly the Marxist reaction): the theory emphasises the way we operate with constructs and the role of reality in their formulation and operation, it does not consider this or that *origin* of constructs—whether
their origin is in child-rearing practices or pressures of class, sex, or race is not
central to this theory. In fact Louis Althusser, when he writes epistemology,
emphasises that the ultimate locus of hegemony is in a *cognitive structure*
transmitted by a system, and this is accommodated by a notion of a shared
construct system (sociality corollary).

At this point it is appropriate to raise the question of phenomenology. Kelly
(1963) noted in his introduction to the republication of the early chapters of his
work that it was necessary to address some "philosophical assumptions without
which the notion of personal constructs would be little more than another outcropping of nineteenth-century phenomenology" (p. xi). It is not apparent why
being an outcropping of phenomenology, even another one, would represent a
reproachable position; and it is now apparent that stating links to other philosophical positions was not sufficient to downgrade the relationship with phenomenology, nor indeed were those links themselves direct or deep. In fact and
clearly, there is a great deal more in the link between personal construct theory
and phenomenology, and therein lies some of the strength and endurance of this
theory. In so far as personal construct psychology is more than another out-
growth of phenomenology, this lies in its elaborate, precise, complex, and thor-
ough-going nature as a psychology rather than in its concomitant acceptance of
the traditional philosophical positions.

Now phenomenology itself is quite a complex position with, moreover, its
own developmental aspects. Again, it has a sense in psychology, particularly in
psychology of perception, as well as a philosophical meaning. Spiegelberg
(1960), one of the ablest commentators, notes different senses of the term, (a
wide, a broad, and a strict sense), some uses that are not strictly phenomenological at all ("pseudo-phenomenologies" as in Kant, Mach, Plank, perhaps Hegel),
and indicates the "essential features" of the phenomenological method as a
"protest against the reductionism of positivism", and a method of investigation
of particular phenomena, of general essences, of relationships between phenomena, and of interpretation of meanings of phenomena (pp. 7–20, 655–698).
Throughout, phenomenology is seen to be opposed to explanatory hypotheses,
and generally it is an attempt to enrich the world of our experiences by bringing
out previously neglected aspects of that experience. Spiegelberg discusses the
previous general features of the phenomenological method in detail, defending it
in particular against charges of subjectivity (at least "mere" subjectivity as the
term "subjective" is itself not entirely clear):

> Husserl's phenomenology of subjectivity involves the attempt to discover the essential—
> i.e. the objective or absolute—structures in what otherwise would be merely subjective
> phenomena. Even more important is the fact that phenomenology in this sense is disin-
> terested in the whole question of whether or not reports of such "introspection" are

faithful accounts of one individual's actual experience at the time, whether, for instance, the particular introspectionist is or was really in doubt or in love or merely believed that he was. (1960, p. 666)

Given these observations, Kelly's own elaborated comments on phenomenology are of interest. First, he accurately locates phenomenology, in its general psychological sense, in the work of the gestalt and field theorists, in Allport and Rogers, and here makes the observation noted previously: "We believe it is possible to combine certain features of the neophenomenological approaches with more conventional methodology" (1955, p. 42). Then, in a curious paragraph he indicates in relation to "the meaning of experience" that

> so far our approach to personal constructs has been almost phenomenological or descriptive. Yet our theoretical position is not strictly phenomenological, for we recognise that personal constructs locked up in privacy cannot be made the subject of a book designed for public consumption. . . . All this means that we cannot consider the psychology of personal constructs a phenomenological theory, if that means ignoring the personal construction of the psychologist who does the observing. (1955, pp. 173–174).

Later, Kelly notes that in going beyond a person's (patient's) viewpoint, the person's way of seeing the world, one might

> turn to an analysis of the validators against which his new constructs would have to be checked . . . then to the hypothetical constructs which might be proposed as alternatives to the ones he is now dependent upon, and finally, to the means by which the therapist might seek to make the new constructs available to him. Particularly in these last two steps, we should be supervening in the case with an approach which goes beyond that of classical phenomenology. (1955, p. 359)

One might note here that there appears to be a shift in relation to phenomenology from psychologist acting as psychologist to psychologist acting as therapist; and this is not so much an extension of phenomenology as an extension of the role psychologist. Finally, Kelly provides the most explicit statement of his divergence from phenomenology:

> If we construe only bits of behaviour we tend to limit ourselves to normative thinking. If we concern ourselves solely with the client's personal constructs we limit ourselves to phenomenological thinking. Instead, the psychology of personal constructs is a system in which the normative is superimposed upon the phenomenological. We attempt to use the phenomenologist's approach to arrive at personalised constructs which have a wide range of meaning for the given individual; then we attempt to piece together this high-level type data with what we know about other persons. (1955, p. 455)

From this indication of how Kelly sees phenomenology, it is possible to compare and contrast the type of statement of phenomenology made by one of the most reliable commentators on it, with Kelly's own construal. And what this comparison indicates is that Kelly is much closer to a position indicated by Spiegelberg as a more adequate statement of what phenomenology is, than his own construal would suggest. What appears to happen is that qua psychologist, that is, interested in *understanding,* there is no inconsistency between personal construct psychology and phenomenology; and qua *therapist* equally, while phenomenology makes no specific statement in this regard, personal construct-oriented work does not run counter to any of the ideas of the method. In fact in having regard to the therapist's own construing, the therapeutic aspect of personal construct theory comes as close as an intervention process can to the phenomenological method. In short, phenomenology as a method of enquiry is well exemplified in personal construct psychology; personal construct psychology when it extends to normatively based interventions (as all interventions must be) is tangential to phenomenology but not inconsistent with it.

The conclusion at this point, then, has to remain merely suggestive. Whether personal construct theory is more phenomenological than Kelly thought has to depend on which phenomenology one takes as a bench mark. On the other hand, it is not clear what Kelly, (and indeed Rogers [1956] in reviewing the book), means by the addition of the *normative* aspect, at least *qua psychologist* conceived as interested in understanding, as compared with psychologist as therapist. One reason for the difficulties here may well be that Kelly was explicitly writing from the perspective of therapy, and this perspective was central to the formulation of the theory. Thus shifts from the position of psychologist to therapist, and back again, may lead to the claim to be "more than" phenomenology (whatever this might mean in view of the complexity of this position) in one position, but a necessary rejection of the claim in another.

Finally, it is interesting to note the way in which psychology has been significantly challenged from "within". This challenge has found expression as radical psychology, a movement aimed at changing the basic orientation of the discipline and focussing critically the way in which the person has been both *regarded* and *treated*. There are in fact two major and two minor tributaries to the radical psychology reaction: existentialism and Marxism as the major, feminism and considerations of race, the minor. In view of previous comments it is worth noting that existentialism is allied to phenomenology (its "social face" perhaps) while one of the lines of critical development in philosophy of science was significantly informed by Marxist principles.

Following existentialism, radical psychology insists that emphasis be placed on the individual as an active, responsible creator rather than a passive receptor at the mercy of external forces. The treatment of this individual, accordingly, rejects the notion of one person defining for another that other's condition, position, and situation; rewarding insights and manipulating change. Rather, "any interpretation the therapist wishes to offer the patient should be proposed in the course of a long common adventure in interiority and not *come* to him anonymously, like stone tablets" (Charlesworth, 1975).[3]

---

[3]This expression comes from Charlesworth in a section where the impact of existentialism on psychiatry is being discussed (p. 43).

The Marxist tributary provides radical psychology with a social position. Here, the significance of social pressures and forces is emphasised, these being chiefly those of social class. Interestingly, one of the criticisms of Marxism is that it lacks "a psychology", such that the support drawn by radical psychology is tenuous. Marx's notion of economic base significantly influencing features of individual mental life does, however, provide the beginning of a psychology and allows radical psychology to draw attention to the *a*political pretensions of psychology as an enterprise or activity.

These two influences, however, do not exhaust the attack on scientific psychology. Considerations of race and sex have also been influential in the formation of a reaction. These manifest in the "old chestnut" about race and intelligence, ostensibly a purely psychological consideration but seen to have very significant social overtones and underpinnings. And in the way psychology defines the female: traditional psychology and psychiatry have respectively defined, and then sought to repair as necessary, certain fixed modes of sexual differentiation, "proving" inherent female inferiority, and theorising as to women's instinctual incapacity to handle analytic thought and to women's weakness and dependency.

These four tributaries merge as that reaction to psychology, a *radical,* that is to say *fundamental,* reaction that is radical psychology. From the foregoing comments and from considerations of personal construct psychology itself, it is clear that this last position escapes this critical reaction. Kelly's (1955) model of humankind as "man the scientist–psychologist", his admission that values are implicit and inescapable in psychological method and theory, and the acceptance of the importance of liberating the person (including the psychologist himself) from restrictive constructs of his or her and the world is quite consistent with the re-orientation demanded by radical psychology.

Conclusion

In the early part of this century numerous influences played across psychology developing in the United States and elsewhere. While positivism–empiricism was to win out, it now appears that the philosophers of science and the philosophers of society combine to mount a serious attack on the claims of these approaches, their dominance, and their social and political consequences and underpinnings. It appears that the psychology of personal constructs does not in anything but superficial terms conform to the austere positivism, nor to the relatively passive empiricism. Kelly's rejection of realism appears also too hasty. In fact a realism that is framed in terms of there being a world of material things existing independently of our apprehension of it, but to which in apprehending we accord meaning, is quite consistent with personal construct theory. Pragmatic logic accepted by Kelly is also not inconsistent with phenomenology nor with Marxist epistemologies. In the last case, Marxists would reject the pragmatists' reliance on "the experiment" and their relative poverty when it came to dealing with competing theories, and their social dimensions. But the logic, or better the methodological aspect, appears unexceptional to a Marxist context. This leaves rationalism unaccounted for, and here too, on the one hand, the reference to rationalism is casual, while on the other, a simple meaning of according some "power to the mind" in framing knowledge offends no significant developments since the 1950s.

Finally, in neither regarding nor treating the individual in the way reacted to by radical psychology, personal construct theory avoids this reaction. Indeed, it provides a viable psychology that can accommodate both major and minor strands of this reaction.

Personal construct psychology might well emerge in the climate obtaining in at least two major dimensions of philosophy (of science and of society) to a central position. In as far as it does this, moreover, it will do so in line with the renewed interest in phenomenology in psychology (and education). And whatever the objections to phenomenology bought by Marxist epistemologies (essentially matters of degree), personal construct psychology would appear to be not incompatible with these epistemologies. In fact, to the significant extent that Marxism lacks a psychology, personal construct psychology might well be a basis of such: though this proposal might not sit too well with proponents, nor the originator, of the theory. Personal construct theory, then, aligns in a more satisfactory way with contemporary developments in philosophy than it did with positions apparent at the time of its origination.

References

Baldwin, J. M. (ed.). (1901/1960). "Dictionary of Psychology and Philosophy, Peter Smith, Gloucester, Mass.

Bhaskar, R. (1975). "A Realist Theory of Science", Leeds Books Ltd., Leeds.

Bullock, A. and Stallybrass, O. (eds.). (1977). "The Fontana Dictionary of Modern Thought", Collins, London.

Charlesworth, M. (1975). "The Extentialists and Jean-Paul Sartre", A. B. C., Sydney, Australia.

Feyerabend, P. (1975). "Against Method", New Left Books, London.

Harris, K. (1979). "Education and Knowledge: The Structured Misrepresentation of Reality", Routledge and Kegan Paul, London.

Hooker, C. A. (1974). Systematic realism. *Synthese,* **26,** 409–497.

Hooker, C. A. (1975). Philosophy and meta-philosophy of science: Empiricism, Popperianism, and realism. *Synthese,* **32,** 177–231.

Kelly, G. A. (1955). "The Psychology of Personal Constructs, 2 Vols., Norton, New York.

Kelly, G. A. (1963). "A Theory of Personality", Norton, New York.

Koch, S. (1973). The image of man in encounter groups. *The American Scholar,* 636–652.

Ogden, C. K. and Richards, I. A. (1923/1945). ''The Meaning of Meaning: A study of the Influence of Language upon Thought and of the Science of Symbolism'', Routledge, London.

Rogers, C. R. (1951). Client-centred Therapy: Its Current Practice, Implications, and Theory'', Houghton, Boston.

Rogers, C. R. (1956). Intellectualised psychotherapy, *Contemporary Psychology*, 1(12), 357–358.

Spiegelberg, H. (1960). ''The Phenomenological Movement: An Historical Introduction'', Martinus Nijhoff, The Hague.

Author Index

Numbers in italics show the page on which complete references are cited.